M000290008

SOCIAL WORK RESEARCH SKILLS WORKBOOK

SOCIAL WORK RESEARCH SKILLS WORKBOOK

A STEP-BY-STEP GUIDE TO CONDUCTING AGENCY-BASED RESEARCH

Jacqueline Corcoran

Mary Secret

OXFORD
UNIVERSITY PRESS

OXFORD
UNIVERSITY PRESS

Oxford University Press is a department of the University of Oxford. It furthers the
University's objective of excellence in research, scholarship, and education by
publishing worldwide.

Oxford New York

Auckland Cape Town Dar es Salaam Hong Kong Karachi
Kuala Lumpur Madrid Melbourne Mexico City Nairobi
New Delhi Shanghai Taipei Toronto

With offices in

Argentina Austria Brazil Chile Czech Republic France Greece
Guatemala Hungary Italy Japan Poland Portugal Singapore
South Korea Switzerland Thailand Turkey Ukraine Vietnam

Oxford is a registered trademark of Oxford University Press in the UK and certain other countries.

Published in the United States of America by
Oxford University Press
198 Madison Avenue, New York, NY 10016

© Oxford University Press 2013

All rights reserved. No part of this publication may be reproduced, stored in a retrieval system, or transmitted,
in any form or by any means, without the prior permission in writing of Oxford University Press, or as expressly
permitted by law, by license, or under terms agreed with the appropriate reproduction rights organization.
Inquiries concerning reproduction outside the scope of the above should be sent to the Rights Department,
Oxford University Press, at the address above.

You must not circulate this work in any other form
and you must impose this same condition on any acquirer.

Library of Congress Cataloging-in-Publication Data
Corcoran, Jacqueline.
Social work research skills workbook : a step-by-step guide to conducting agency-based research / Jacqueline
Corcoran and Mary Secret.
      p. cm.
   Includes bibliographical references and index.
   ISBN 978-0-19-975351-2 (pbk. : alk. paper)   1. Social service—Research.   2. Social work education.
   I. Secret, Mary. II. Title.
   HV11.C71875 2013
   361.3072—dc23
   2012000445

This workbook is dedicated to the MSW social work
students at Virginia Commonwealth University
who persevered and met the challenge of
learning and appreciating the importance of
research for social work practice and thus
helped us to experience the rewards and joys of
teaching research.

ACKNOWLEDGMENTS

To all the students in Dr. Corcoran's Research in Clinical Practice class who contributed examples that considerably enlivened this workbook: Leila Abtahi, Nicole Anselona, Joanna Aragon, Melisa Atkeson, Keri Barrett, Hannah Berglund, Katie Boxer, Emily Britt, Emily Brown, Jeanne Cowan, Meghan Crowley, Megan Davis, Christina Devers, Traci DeMerchant, Joseph Eddy, Oriel Estrada, Donna Fengay, Gidget Fields, Courtney Fragala, Genevieve Frey, Karen Grane, Orielle Estrada, Ann Holmes, Kara Ireland, Jason Jacob, Angela James, Arya Karki, Kara Kojcsich, Penelope Konstas, Jacqueline Larkowich, Melissa Lee, Erica Makowski, Christine Malklewitz, Beth Martin, Donald McCauley, Wendy Meissler, Noelle Moreland, Michelle Pineda, Kate Costello, Zoe Rizzuto, Caitlin Ryan, Kerry Ryan, Jeanne Ryan, Poonam Singh, Jan Steele, Jason Spatz, Ann Talley, Mary VanWyngarden, Sarah Wilch-Spamer, Margaret Robinson, Kymberly Walker, Kristen Wheeler, Rachel Wilson, and Bianchinetta Suarez Valverde

The following students' research projects from Dr. Secret's Research in Clinical Practice course provided many of the examples used throughout this workbook.

Ryan Arey
Wendy G. Bowie
Erin Boyle
Amanda Browning
Michele Burtner
Carter, Jennifer
Jessica Davison
Lauren Dickey
Diane Forse
Melissa Foublasse
Khalilah Garrett
La'Quina Fulton-Garvin
Jayme Glover
Danielle Green
Regan M. Harker
Joanna Hopkins
Amy L. Herman
Meghan A. Hovanic
Alexa S. Hryciak
Katie Hughes
Connie Jones
Gabrielle Jordan-Cooley
Inna Katsev
Kristen Long
Cristina Lugo
Mariane Macedo
Connie Macaluso-Dickerson
Maggie A. Mann
Michelle Moore

Carolyn McCloud-Paterno
Allison G. Middleton
Carie Ott
Jada Overton
Linda Nicholson
Crystal N. Pintac
Bethany Pippin
Jennifer Plouffe
Michelle Reese
Carla Renner
Shelley Shipman
Katie Tanner
Libby Tofflemire
Jenny L. Warne
Celie Weaver
Michelle Wells
Haila White
Suzanne M. Wilberger
Karen Vassar
Liz Young

CONTENTS

1   Introduction and Overview   1
        With Nicole Lynn Lee

2   Research Fundamentals   10
        With Nicole Lynn Lee

3   Review of the Literature   31

4   Systematic Reviews   51

5   Ethics and Values Related to Research   68
        With Nicole Lynn Lee

6   Quantitative: Research Designs   94

7   Sampling   107

8   Measurement   117

9   Quantitative Data Analysis   138

10 Qualitative Research Methods and Data Analysis   157
        With Nicole Lynn Lee

11 Program and Practice Evaluative   175
        With Nicole Lynn Lee

12 Write-Up, Presentation, and Dissemination of Results   199

REFERENCES   213
INDEX   219

DETAILED CONTENTS

1	Introduction and Overview	1
	Workbook Format	1
	Beginning Thoughts about Learning Research	2
	Why So Much Research?	3
	Research Vocabulary	4
	Math Anxiety	5
	Gap Between Research Findings and Real-World Practice Settings	6
	Chapter Highlights	7
	Conclusion	8
2	Research Fundamentals	10
	The Big Picture	10
	Step One: Developing your Research Question	11
	Step Two: Making Decisions about Methods	20
	Step Three: Data Collection and Study Implementation	21
	Step Four: Data Processing and Analysis	24
	Step Five: Discussion and Application	26
	Involvement of Your Field Agency	26
	Establishing Principles for Research	28
	Conclusion	29
	Websites	30
3	Review of the Literature	31
	Introduction	31
	Definition and Purpose	31
	Why Conduct a Literature Review?	31
	Steps of the Literature Review	33
	Step One: Searching the Literature	33
	Step Two: Reading the Literature	38
	Step Three: Writing the Literature Review	44
	Conclusion	50
	Websites	50
4	Systematic Reviews	51
	How Are Systematic Reviews Different from Literature Reviews?	51
	Meta-Analysis	51
	How to Find Systematic Reviews	53
	Steps in a Systematic Review	57
	Conclusion	66
	Websites	67
5	Ethics and Values Related to Research	68
	Ethical Considerations in Social Work Research	68
	The IRB Application	76
	Is IRB Review Always Required?	78

	Conclusion	80
	Appendix 5.2	85
	Websites	93
6	Quantitative: Research Designs	94
	Surveys	94
	Creation of Surveys	95
	Intervention Research	97
	Single-System Designs	97
	Pre-Experimental Designs	99
	Experimental and Quasi-Experimental Designs	101
	Decision-Making for Intervention Research	102
	Threats to Internal Validity	104
	Conclusion	106
	Websites	106
7	Sampling	107
	Representative and Nonrepresentative Sampling	108
	Populations and Sampling Frames	108
	Sampling Methods	111
	Research Designs and Sampling: How They Work Together	113
	Sample Size	115
	Conclusion	115
	Websites	116
8	Measurement	117
	Operationalization: How to Measure Your Idea	117
	Using Standardized Measures	118
	Adapting and Creating Instruments	122
	Data Collection Instruments from Agency Records	124
	Levels of Measurement	125
	Assigning Values	129
	Independent Variable: Treatment Fidelity	133
	Conclusion	136
	Websites	137
9	Quantitative Data Analysis	138
	Where Do the Numbers Come From?	138
	How Many Variables?	141
	Univariate	141
	Bivariate Analysis	142
	Multivariate Analysis	152
	Conclusion	156
	Websites	156
10	Qualitative Research Methods and Data Analysis	157
	Understanding the Differences Between Qualitative and Quantitative Methods	157

Qualitative Research Designs   160
Note-taking and Recording   165
Qualitative Data Analysis   166
Putting it All Together   168
Ethics in Qualitative Studies   170
Conclusion   171
Websites   174

11   Program and Practice Evaluative   175
     Defining Evaluation   175
     Program-Specific Questions Answered by Evaluation Research   178
     Evaluation Research in Agency Settings   180
     Logic Models   181
     Evaluability Assessment   184
     Applying Research Methods to Formative or Process Evaluations   186
     Applying Research Methods to Cost–Benefit
        or Cost-Effectiveness Evaluations   187
     Applying Research Methods to Summative Program Evaluation Efforts   188
     Evaluation Research: Focus of Research Design   191
     Conclusion   195
     Websites   198

12   Write-Up, Presentation, and Dissemination of Results   199
     The Research Project Final Report   199
        The Results Section   200
        Discussion Section   204
     Agency Presentations   207
     Practice-Research Panel Discussions   207
     Presentations Requiring Institutional Review Board Approval   210
        Publishing in Academic Journals   210
     Advocate's Forum   211
     Conclusion   212
     Websites   212

REFERENCES   213
INDEX   219

SOCIAL WORK RESEARCH SKILLS WORKBOOK

INTRODUCTION AND OVERVIEW

Because of the preeminence of evidence-based practice in the social work profession, social work students are often required to demonstrate competency in research by designing and conducting research projects in practice settings. However, despite many good research texts, we have found that students in bachelors and masters social work programs often find it difficult to grasp and apply the material found in these texts to their own research projects. Even the best social work research methods texts do not always convey the information in a way that is helpful to students as they plan and carry out "real-world" research projects. Using a learner-centered approach, this workbook includes step-by-step guidelines, examples, exercises, and worksheets to help social work students apply research concepts and methods to the research projects that they are undertaking in practice settings.

This *Social Work Research Skills Workbook* is the result of many years, not so much of teaching research, but of learning from students how they come to understand and use basic research concepts and methods. Rather than duplicate information that is well covered in standard research textbooks, we summarize this detailed information in tables or other visual means and add specific examples from student research projects. In other words, we provide clear and brief explanations of basic research methodology and data analysis topics and will follow each concept with examples not only from published social work research but from actual student projects and our own research to help students increase the applicability of relevant research material to field practicum and classroom projects.

WORKBOOK FORMAT

The workbook is designed for social work students who are planning to conduct research projects as part of their social work educational experiences in either bachelor or masters programs. It is not a replacement for the standard text that you use in your research methods or statistics courses but, rather, is meant to be read in concert with, and supplementary to, the major social work research texts required in many bachelor of social work (BSW) and masters of social work (MSW) programs. Thus, the workbook presents chapters that parallel those found in many of these texts and that take you through the stages of the research process. The focus of the *Research Skills Workbook*, however, is on practical advice about what is important at each stage of the research process.

Each chapter includes an assortment of four basic learning tools—Summary Content, Agency-Based Research Examples, Test Your Skills Exercises, and Project Development Worksheets to help you think through and implement the stages of your research project in a social work practice setting, whether that setting is your field practicum or your place of employment. The Summary Content learning tool highlights information that is detailed in research texts and emphasizes its relevance for agency-based research. Agency-Based Research Examples illustrate the application of this information to research projects, often conducted by BSW and MSW social work students, in practice settings. Test Your Skills Exercises help you to identify the level of your understanding of applied research methods and analysis. Finally, the Project Development Worksheets provide the format for you to begin developing research skills customized for your own research project.

Much of this first chapter captures the beginning thoughts about learning research expressed by social work students we have taught in the last 15 years and elaborates on the rationale for studying research presented in many social work texts such as those by Engel and Schutt (2009) and Rubin and Babbie (2011). Perhaps most importantly in this chapter, we urge you, the social work student, to consider how research connects to your area of interest and invite you to begin thinking about possible projects in your agency or field placement.

We also use Chapter One as an opportunity to reiterate some of the more common research concepts and methods, such as independent and dependent variables, which you no doubt have encountered in your research texts and which will be more fully addressed in subsequent chapters of this workbook. You will notice that we review much of the basic research material within the context of the overall research process early in the workbook and then expand on this same material in later chapters. You will see the examples presented in earlier chapters incorporated into the exercises in later chapters. Consistent with the learner-centered approach, we believe that continual and repetitive reference to these primary research terms and procedures ensures that you are developing the foundation, or "schemata," to construct new insights and build new skills for use in your project. This is a nod to the many social work students who have assured us over the years that "Repetition is good and helps reinforce learning."

BEGINNING THOUGHTS ABOUT LEARNING RESEARCH

Most students tell us they understand the critical role that research plays in evaluating effective interventions and in identifying the reasons for, and consequences of, specific social problems like substance abuse or domestic violence. At the same time, students use words such as "intimidating," "hard," and "math" in reference to the actual research course and often express apprehension and fear as they approach the reality of taking such a course or conducting their own research project. These apprehensions can be categorized as follows: (1) concern that research courses distract from and replace needed practice courses in the social work curriculum; (2) unfamiliarity with the research vocabulary; (3) intimidation related to math and statistics; and (4) perceived distance and difference between research findings and real-world practice settings. Below we address each of these worries and suggest ways that you can work through them as you begin to plan for your research project.

WHY SO MUCH RESEARCH?

Students tend to have difficulty understanding why research courses comprise such a large part of the social work curriculum. Direct practice students in particular, eager to learn skills and interventions, often lament the amount of the curriculum devoted to research courses. Because experienced instructors are aware of student skepticism about the value of research, the introductions to social work research texts dutifully and appropriately outline the need for you to develop sound and scientific reasoning about the social world (Engel & Schutt, 2009), to use evidence-based knowledge to solve practice problems (Rubin & Babbie, 2011), and to engage in meaningful practice–research collaborations (Monette, Sullivan, & DeJong, 2011).

But let's put all this into terms with which you are more familiar and in which you are perhaps more interested. You have probably heard the summons, from instructors in other social work courses and from reading the literature, for social workers to be "change agents." The particular skill set you choose to employ in a particular setting or with a certain client is intended to bring about some change in client behavior, values, and knowledge or in the policies and procedures of larger social systems. *You* are the person who makes something happen or who is responsible for something that happens. Therefore, in this sense and in "research language," you, the social worker, can be considered the "independent variable." By independent variable, we mean that the way your behavior varies (what you choose to say or do or how you relate to clients, either at the macro-, meso-, or microlevels) brings about the intended change. The change, also referred to as client outcome, is the dependent variable.

The following examples help you to connect research with the social work activities that some of our students have studied in practice settings. Try to identify the independent and dependent variable in each of the projects.

Example 1.1.

INDEPENDENT AND DEPENDENT VARIABLES IN STUDENT RESEARCH PROJECTS

Project 1: Kelsey completed her internship at an in-home counseling agency whose client population was primarily Latino and African-American. The agency was interested in knowing whether diversity training could increase cultural competency of the support staff in the agency. Kelsey conducted a two-day intensive diversity training and measured cultural competency of the staff before and after the training.

Project 2: Jacob was placed in a homeless shelter that provided a variety of services, including group and individual counseling, job training, financial counseling, and substance abuse counseling. Jacob noticed that some of the services were better attended than others and wanted to find out which of the services the clients found most helpful. He developed a research project to interview a small sample of shelter clients to find out which services were associated with higher levels of satisfaction.

Project 3: Lillie was placed in a day treatment program for children with developmental delays. Lillie noticed that many of her clients had difficulty interacting with others so she implemented a social skills group. After being in the placement for a few months, Lillie noticed that there were some children who seemed to learn the skills better than others. She also noticed that these children had family members who were very active at the program. For instance, the family members volunteered in the individual classrooms and met regularly with the program officials. Lillie wondered

---

if family engagement impacted how well children did in the program. Lillie developed a Parental Engagement Survey and mailed it to each child's primary caregiver. Her goal was to understand if family engagement was related to children's success in the program.

Project 4: LaTonya, interested in children, was placed in an elementary school. Children designated as having "special needs" participated in a variety of extra services. The school administered a survey to parents to assess whether they felt services were making a difference in their children's lives. Specifically, the 30-item survey sought to determine whether participation in extra services decreased children's negative behaviors, increased self-esteem, and improved academic success. Parents read the items and then identified how much they agreed or disagreed with statements.

Explanations: The training in Project 1 is the independent variable that is expected to cause some change in the cultural competency (the dependent variable) of the staff. In Project 2, the independent variable is the type of service provided by the shelter, and the dependent variable is satisfaction with the service. In Project 3, family engagement is the independent variable, and children's success in the program is the dependent variable. Finally, in Project 4, the extra services provided to children were the independent variables, and self-esteem, academic performance, and behavior were the dependent variables.

Hopefully these examples have helped you realize that, more often than not, learning research is much like learning how to pinpoint and clarify what social workers do (the independent variable) and whether there is any change in client outcomes (the dependent variable) as a result of social work actions. If, at certain points along the way of your research journey, you become lost in a myriad of terms and methodologies, we urge you to return to this very basic idea that social work research is really about documenting that what social workers do matters.

RESEARCH VOCABULARY

The mention of the terms *independent variable* and *dependent variable* brings to mind another apprehension: the research vocabulary. Students sometimes compare learning research to learning a foreign language. Although many of the terms, such as *design*, *variation*, and *reliability*, have meaning in everyday conversation, students often draw a blank when confronted with these same terms in a research context. It is also true that the meanings of some terms change, depending on the text and the instructor, and this heightens the challenge of distinguishing which definition applies in which circumstance.

Our students have suggested that referring to the dictionary definition of the terms and considering the terms in everyday usage helps them apply these terms in the research context. As an example, consider the term *research design*. The dictionary definition reminds you that "design" is both a noun and a verb. As a verb, to "design" a research study means to identify the steps or procedures that you will use to answer your research question. As a noun, a research design is often used interchangeably with the term *method*, meaning the overall plan of collecting the data or the way an investigator conducts a study.

Following is an example of a tool to help you begin to master and use the research vocabulary. The first column in the box contains terms associated with research, the second column is the dictionary definition, and the third column is an example of how the term can be applied to a particular research project. Think about the student research projects in Example 1.1 as you study Example 1.2 below. In Project 1, Kelsey will be "measuring" cultural competency. In Project 2, Jacob will be using a small "sample," and Lillie will be "surveying" primary caregivers by mail in Project 3.

Example 1.2.

APPLICATION OF RESEARCH VOCABULARY

RESEARCH TERM	DICTIONARY DEFINITION	APPLICATION IN RESEARCH CONTEXT
Measurement	• A standard used for determining the dimensions, area, volume, or weight of something. • Something used to determine a quantity (e.g., a ruler, or a small container that holds a known volume).	Project 1: Kelsey used the California Brief Multicultural Competence Scale (Gamst et al., 2004) that measures cultural competency by asking respondents 21 questions about their multicultural attitudes/beliefs, knowledge, and skills.
Sample	• To use a technique to select members of a population about whom you will collect data (information). • A group of cases drawn from a population about which you will collect data (information).	Project 2: Jacob arrived at the shelter and saw clients waiting for services. He asked 10 persons to participate in his study (Convenience or Availability Sampling). The sample is 10 persons who are currently receiving services from the homeless shelter.
Survey	• A research method where a researcher gathers data (information) from a group of respondents in a short period of time and then analyzes responses. • An actual measurement tool that collects information.	Project 3: Lilli used a mailed survey to collect data on family engagement in the program. The Family Engagement Survey is an agency-created tool that asks family members to identify how involved they are with their child's program.

Because instant recall of many research terms is improbable for those just beginning the study of research, we encourage you to use the above example as a template to develop a terminology worksheet for your own project and add to it as you learn new terms. Think of it as a "terminology cheat sheet," and refer to it routinely as you read your research texts or complete your research assignments.

MATH ANXIETY

The third challenge that many students confront as they approach their social work research courses is the fear of statistics or anything remotely connected to numbers. Students often wrongfully assume that research is primarily about statistics and math. They can carry with them into social work research class earlier school struggles with math or the negative experiences of undergraduate statistics courses that consisted of memorizing seemingly meaningless formulas and symbols. We do not intend to minimize the challenges inherent in grasping statistical terms and data analysis, but one way to begin thinking about numbers that you come across in statistical analysis is to remember that they represent the people and situations you are trying to learn about. In most instances, any number in a statistical analysis can be traced back to characteristics of the person, such as age, race, or marital status, as well as reports from that person about how he/she behaves, feels, or thinks. Frequently the numbers are assigned by the researcher to identify (measure) these characteristics and/or behaviors of the people in the study. To reiterate, there is nothing mysterious or magical about the source or the meaning of the numbers. They are assigned by the researcher to symbolize or represent something about the people in the study.

Let's focus on Jacob's project at the homeless shelter as an example of how numbers can be assigned in a study and then used for statistical analysis. If one of the clients in the shelter is a male, then the student-researcher (Jacob) assigns "1" for male gender; if a female, then the researcher assigns a "2" for female gender; if that client indicates that he/she is very satisfied with the counseling services, then the researcher assigns a "5" for "very satisfied" with counseling; if another client is not at all satisfied, then the researcher assigns a "1" for "not at all satisfied." When the data are collected from the entire sample of respondents in the shelter, Jacob will perform data analysis by using the assigned numbers in statistical calculations (done by the computer) to convey how many males were very satisfied with counseling and how many females were very satisfied with counseling. In statistical terms, the data analysis reveals whether or not there is a relationship between gender and satisfaction with counseling.

GAP BETWEEN RESEARCH FINDINGS AND REAL-WORLD PRACTICE SETTINGS

A fourth student concern about research courses stems from the seeming remoteness of research as presented in the literature (texts and articles) compared to what social workers experience in practice settings, in "the real world." Despite the thoughtful discussion and conclusion sections in research articles, it is often difficult for practitioners to establish meaningful connections between complicated statistical findings about large groups of people, even those of interest to our profession, and the day-to-day challenges confronting clients who interact with practitioners in service organizations.

On the other hand, researchers—especially those with a singular investment in methodological rigor—can become frustrated when research goals are superseded by client need or agency feasibility issues, as so often happens in practice settings. Fortunately the gulf between social work practice and research has begun to narrow, bridged by the commitment of both researchers and practitioners to evidence-based practice, defined as the use of research to understand what works for clients.

We hope to bridge some of the gaps between research and practice by encouraging you to acknowledge the difference between "**ideal versus real**" research in the following workbook chapters. In other words, we will talk about the "ideal," or gold standard, of methodological and statistical rigor, but we will also discuss the "real"— that is, standards or steps that are acceptable to take in community agency research and evaluation projects. In Example 1.3, social work student Amber's research project in an afterschool art program illustrates the difference between "ideal and real" in a practice setting.

The emphasis of this workbook on student research that is undertaken in community agencies is another way to bridge the gap between research and practice. In this workbook, you will read about research studies like Amber's that apply to the clients that seek services at social work field placements and employment settings. Research implemented in community agencies provides opportunities for students to put research concepts into practice while broadening their knowledge about client populations. Students, even those who feel initially apprehensive, can use this workbook to demystify and enrich their experience with their research project experience.

Example 1.3.

UNDERSTANDING "REAL" VERSUS "IDEAL" IN STUDENT RESEARCH PROJECTS

Amber wanted to know whether participation in an afterschool art program increased children's levels of hope. She administered the Children's Hope Scale (Snyder et al., 1997) to the children at two different times, once before the children began the program and then when they completed the program.

Real Versus Ideal: If we evaluated Amber's design based on the "ideal" standards, then we would note several methodological issues, the most apparent being the lack of a true experimental design to evaluate "cause" and "effect." Simply put, to determine whether an intervention "causes" changes in participants, we need a true experimental design, one in which participants are randomly assigned to either an treatment/intervention group or a control\comparison group. Thus, Amber's design makes it difficult to see whether the intervention or some other factor influenced the children's levels of hope.

That said, it is important to acknowledge that we can also evaluate Amber's design based on the "real" world standards. Amber had to conduct a study that could be implemented within the agency's current structure and was consistent with the agency's policies and procedures. Amber also had to think about the "real" limitations that these considerations provided. Amber's project reflected her knowledge of the agency's functioning, strengths, and limitations. She knew that randomly assigning children to one of two groups was not practical or consistent with the agency's mission. In summary, Amber was aware of the "ideal" methodology but had to make adjustments based on the "real" functioning of the agency.

CHAPTER HIGHLIGHTS

We begin Chapter Two by providing a detailed overview of the research process from start to finish, introducing you to the types of decisions that you will need to make at each stage of the process and incorporating many basic research concepts and activities that will be developed in more depth in later chapters. This chapter will not only help you to adequately identify the research problem, formulate and refine the research question, and consider the theories related to your topic but will provide useful guidance about initiating research in agency-based settings and interacting with the agency staff where you hope to carry out your research project.

Chapter Three guides the beginning of your research project by outlining the steps for a generic literature review, including identifying and using relevant databases and by providing detailed examples and worksheets for both conducting and writing the literature review for your project. An important focus in this chapter is learning how to integrate various, individual articles into a scholarly presentation of the literature review. Chapter Four introduces you to meta-analysis and formal systematic reviews of the literature. These research activities are not often covered in standard research texts, but knowing how to locate and understand systematic reviews is invaluable for gathering and organizing vast amounts of literature in your area of interest. They can provide a "jump start" for your own literature review.

In Chapter Five, we discuss the ethics involved with doing social work research. After reviewing the primary ethical guidelines that you must consider when conducting social work research and sharing the tools to support your implementation of these guidelines, we ask you to study the standard Institutional review Board (IRB) criteria and procedures and to decide on the extent of IRB involvement needed for your particular project. As you may recall from your research methods texts, IRBs are committees constituted by Universities or other organizations to protect the rights of of human subjects in research activities.

The next four chapters focus on the methodological aspects of mainly quantitative approaches. In these chapters you will find learning tools and discussions about the range of designs for answering your research question (Chapter Six, Quantitative Research Designs); options for selecting participants for your project (Chapter Seven, Sampling); considerations about how you collect your data (Chapter Eight, Measurement); and the menu and instructions for statistical tests from which you decide how to analyze your data (Chapter Nine, Data Analysis). In Chapters Seven and Eight, we discuss both quantitative and qualitative approaches to sampling and measurement, respectively, and then in Chapter 10, we have a standalone chapter on Qualitative Methods and Analysis. We debated how best to present material on qualitative approaches so as not to diminish the contributions of qualitative research. Although we could have added qualitative material in each of the above methods chapters, we thought that such add-ons might dilute the richness and purpose of qualitative techniques. Rather, we decided to first alert you to the qualitative compliment of quantitative methods in Chapters Six through Nine and to elaborate on the benefits and strategic use of qualitative approaches in this standalone chapter.

In Chapter Eleven (Evaluative Research), we have a similar standalone chapter. Because evaluation research encompasses all aspects of the research process and all types of methodologies, we thought it important to develop a standalone chapter to help you: (1) match the basic research terms presented in standard methods texts with similar terms specific to program evaluation; (2) introduce you to program evaluation logic models that organize the essential elements of research discussed in earlier chapters into a structure suitable for program evaluation; and (3) reiterate the centrality of human service organizations and program services as the target of social work research.

We conclude the workbook with Chapter Twelve (Write-Up and Dissemination) by concentrating on the full report and how to present your findings to student colleagues, your agencies, and possibly more broadly.

CONCLUSION

We began this chapter by identifying the reasons for this workbook and informing you of the tools (Summary Content, Agency-Based Research Examples, Test Your Skills Exercises, and Project Development Worksheets) that are provided to help you implement your student research project within the "real-world" of social work practice. Each chapter of this workbook focuses on specific concepts while providing tools to deepen your understanding, integrate theoretical knowledge and practice, and reduce some of the anxiety held regarding research.

The emphasis of this workbook is on student research that is undertaken in community agencies. Why community agencies? As mentioned in this chapter, this is another way to bridge the gap between research and practice. In this workbook, you will read about research studies that apply to the clients who seek services at social work field placement and employment settings—studies that we hope will be helpful to you as you plan and carry out your own projects within the requirements of your course.

Chapter Two will provide an overview of the research process. As you read it, please think about all of the steps as an integrated whole. Additionally, you may want to think about any potential barriers that you may encounter at each phase of the research process. Identifying potential barriers will be an important step in developing strategies to reduce the impact of these barriers, and this workbook can help you as you move through that process.

In conclusion, as you will see in Chapter Two and throughout this entire workbook, research implemented in community agencies provides wonderful opportunities for students to put research concepts into practice while broadening their knowledge about client populations. Students, even those who feel initially apprehensive, can use this workbook to demystify and enrich their experience with their research project experience.

RESEARCH FUNDAMENTALS

THE BIG PICTURE

Social work students often remark that learning research is like putting together a jigsaw puzzle—many different pieces have to be fitted together to get to the finished product. Without question, the finished product is easier to achieve when you have a picture image of how the final product should look and you can lay out all the separate pieces of the puzzle at the beginning. Think of the following figure of the Research Process at a Glance modified from research text authors Rubin and Babbie (2011, p. 112), as the picture image or layout or plan for your research project.

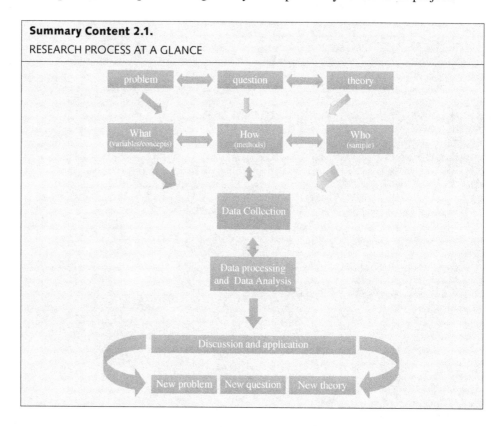

Summary Content 2.1.
RESEARCH PROCESS AT A GLANCE

The first line of the Research at a Glance graphic (Summary Content 2.1) is noted as "Problem, Question, Theory" and concerns formulating and refining the research question. Think of this as Step One in the research process. The second line, Step Two, refers to decisions that you will make about the measurement, design, and sampling methodology needed to answer the research question. Both Step One and Step Two are heavily dependent on your review of the literature. One of the most important things to remember about the research process is that it is not something that you can develop or implement without 1) an extensive reference to the literature, and 2) a good understanding of the agency setting where you will be doing the study. You will refer to, and cite, the scholarly literature as you finalize your research question and as you decide what measures, designs, and samples to use. Step Three is data collection, what some think of as the actual implementation of the research project. This step greatly depends on what your agency will or will not allow in terms of research activity. Step Four is the data processing and analysis. Although this step follows Step Three in quantitative research, qualitative research often requires the data collection and the data analysis activities to occur in a back-and-forth sequence. Thus, we use the double-pronged arrow connecting Step Three and Step Four. And finally, Step Five includes the discussion and application of your findings, which lead to new research questions. Each of these activities will be addressed in detail in later chapters of the workbook, but for now, let's do a brief overview of this graphic, step-by-step, followed by a focus on Step One and the development of the research question.

Step One: Developing your Research Question
The first line on the graphic shows the research problem, the question, and theory development as the first step in the research process. Each of these points will be discussed separately, although they integrally relate.

The Research Problem. According to our dictionary definition, a problem is something that is difficult to deal with or to understand (OUP, 2011). Primarily, your research should involve a problem that relates to an area of practice so that you can improve the way you and your colleagues deliver services. And, as in practice, the numbers of problems you can identify for one research study are not only infinitesimal, but the problems themselves are very complex (e.g., poverty, homelessness, child abuse, discrimination, work stress, mental illness). For example, the problem of poverty touches and is touched by many factors: lack of education and job opportunities; employee benefits; labor laws; public assistance; poor medical care; deteriorating housing; and crime rates, to name some. Research helps break down these massive problems into incremental, or smaller, parts to examine the individual pieces of the problem.

Note that not every problem we encounter in practice or in our everyday lives can be answered by research. Certain issues involve value judgments: Is capital punishment right or wrong? Is it more important to help older people who are poor or younger people who are poor? Although you may not be able to gather data to directly answer these questions, research can contribute objective knowledge that can better inform these types of decisions.

The Research Question. The next point, the research question, helps you identify and focus on the aspects of the problem that are of particular concern to you. Social work research questions seek to answer questions about the social world through the collection and analysis of data. For example, given the problem of poverty, you might want to know how the housing market influences poverty in a particular community. Or you might be interested in whether people who are poor tend to be more or less empathic with others. Or you may want to know what types of programs can improve the lives of people living in poverty.

What are the situations or questions in your field placement that are particularly problematic or intriguing to you? What more do you need to know about your client population or various practice interventions that would help you be a more effective social worker? From your natural curiosity, from your readings, and from the problems you encounter in your field placement beginning research questions will emerge. Not surprisingly, given the complexity of the human problems we face, the range of possibilities for good social work research questions is endless. One way to help you narrow down your research question is to make sure it is a socially important question for social work practice, that it has scientific relevance, and that it is feasible to conduct (Engle & Schutt, 2009). Think about the following characteristics of a good research question as you move through this step of the research process:

- Social importance. Will the answers to your research question make a difference in the social world? Does the question concern an important social problem with which social workers deal?
- Scientific relevance. Does your question fill a gap in the literature? Is it a question that has not been adequately answered by previous research? Does your question resolve contradictions about what we know about evidence-based practice? Does this question advance social theory?
- Feasibility given resources. Do you have the time and budget and other resources to be able to answer this question? Do you have access to an agency or a setting where you can carry out your project?

Example 2.1 presents some social work student projects and includes the type of agency where the project was implemented. This will help stimulate your ideas and recognize the scope of possible student research projects. Then use the Project Development Worksheet 2.1 to identify areas of social work interest to you and to reflect on various avenues that may lead to different questions that you can pursue for your research project.

Example 2.1.

SAMPLE STUDENT PROJECTS

RESEARCH QUESTION	AGENCY SETTING
Will a creative arts intervention produce a positive change in mood in adults who are court-mandated to participate in a parenting program?	Nonprofit child abuse prevention agency
What is the experience of staff members working with unaccompanied refugee and immigrant minors?	Residential home for children
Will youth express less acceptance of violence after participation in a nonviolence program?	Nonprofit after-school agency

RESEARCH QUESTION	AGENCY SETTING
What is the relationship between primary caregiver participation in patient care and expressed satisfaction with hospice services?	Hospice organization
Are female and/or African-American children more likely to be placed in more restrictive care following in-home counseling?	A national counseling organization
Are positive religious coping skills correlated with relief of everyday stress?	A local church
What post-incarceration services are available for recently released individuals?	A local church
Is there a difference in the level of compassion fatigue experienced by social workers and by nurses?	A hospital
What is the alcohol and substance use history of persons seeking homeless services?	Homeless shelter
Do children participating in social skills training increase the number of pro-social skills exhibited more than those who do not participate?	Day treatment program

Project Development Worksheet 2.1. DEVELOPING RESEARCH QUESTIONS	
THINK ABOUT YOUR EXPERIENCES AND PREFERENCES	
Where is your current or anticipated field placement:	
What are the topics of papers/projects for that you're doing or have done for current or previous coursework requirements:	
What population do you want to work with after graduation:	
What is your desired practice setting after graduation:	
What is your broad area of interest:	
DEVELOP POSSIBLE RESEARCH QUESTIONS IN WHICH YOU ARE INTERESTED	
About clients with whom you work or want to work:	
About social problems confronting the clients with whom you want to work:	
About social work interventions to address client problems:	
About the social policies that influence the lives of clients:	
About the practitioners or agencies who provide services	
Other practice issues:	

Don't be surprised if you have difficulty being able to complete Project Development Worksheet 2.1 with much detail or accuracy. You will need to conduct an extensive review of the literature before you finalize your research question and problem of interest and before you can thoroughly address how your question is socially important and scientifically relevant. The next two chapters, Chapters Three and Four, will help you move through the literature review process and ensure that your question is relevant for social work practice.

Theory. The next point on the first line of the graphic is "theory," which involves an attempt to describe phenomena or to explain relationships (why one factor is related to another). Following are several definitions of theory that you can add to your Terminology Worksheet that we hope you initiated in Chapter One (refer to Example 1.2).

- A theory is made up of concepts and propositions. (Fawcett, 1999)
- Propositions describe the relationships that might be logically expected among concepts. (Polit & Hungler, 1995, p. 97)
- "A theory is a set of interrelated concepts, definitions, and propositions that present a systematic view of essential elements in a field of inquiry by specifying relations among variables." (King, 1997, p. 23)

Think about the concept of poverty and all the factors that might influence why someone is poor and how poverty might impact that person's life. Some of these poverty-related factors are illustrated in Example 2.2 below. How do you think these identified factors might be related to each other? What are some theories that you have learned from your other courses that might explain how these factors relate to poverty? Would Social Learning Theory help explain why parenting style influences or is influenced by health and nutrition knowledge or behavior? Would any of the Empowerment Theories explain how employment opportunities are connected to poverty … or that poverty was connected to employment opportunities?

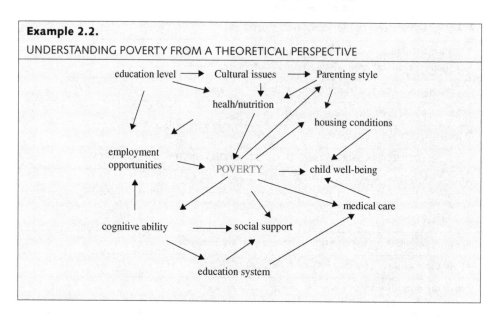

Example 2.2.

UNDERSTANDING POVERTY FROM A THEORETICAL PERSPECTIVE

Theory helps you to understand **why** these factors might be linked and the research question prepares you to investigate if any of these factors are indeed linked in the social world. In other words, theory requires that you delve deeper into the problem and begin to consider how the many pieces or aspects of the problem are related to each other. In social work practice, one of the reasons that it is important to understand these types of relationships is to be able to identify appropriate interventions and to test whether these interventions are effective. In this example, Social Learning Theory might suggest interventions aimed at helping parents learn how to model positive relationships and behaviors, whereas Empowerment Theory would direct your intervention to increasing employment opportunities. An appropriate social work research question based on these theories might be "How effective are parent education groups in helping parents provide good nutritional choices for their children?" or "What is the relationship between unemployment rates and household income in different neighborhoods?"

Example 2.3 is similar to Example 2.2; however, Example 2.2 shows the concept of poverty and the contributing factors, while Example 2.3 shows an intervention from a theoretical perspective. Let's imagine that this intervention is case management for persons experiencing domestic violence. As mentioned earlier, if a social worker wishes to develop a successful intervention, then he or she must consider the factors that contribute to domestic violence. The following shows the contributing factors and how the components of an intervention might relate to each other. For example, to assist someone experiencing domestic violence, we have to know the components that influence a participant's personal safety (ideas derived from theory). Understanding how these components relate to each other provides a theoretical basis that supports and guides the domestic violence intervention.

Example 2.3.

UNDERSTANDING A DOMESTIC VIOLENCE INTERVENTION FROM A THEORETICAL PERSPECTIVE

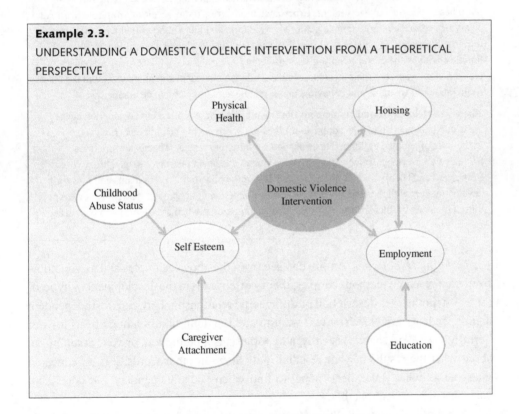

You will note that Social Learning Theory and Empowerment Theory are easily identified as formal theories that you have studied in other classes. It is important to know that you can use either an established or clearly identified theory for your research project *or* you can develop your own understanding of how client or agency characteristics and interventions and outcomes go together. At this juncture, the salient issue is that the theoretical basis of your project provides a rationale or the explanation of why concepts that you want to study might be related to each other. Some approaches to theory use from student projects are provided in Example 2.4.

Example 2.4.

THE USE OF THEORY IN STUDENT PROJECTS

Theory to Determine the Question/Hypothesis—Danielle learned about Ecological Systems Theory (Bronfenbrenner, 1979) in one of her classes. She believed that this theory helped her consider how multiple systems at micro-, mezzo-, and macro levels of intervention impacted child well-being in the family services unit of a military base in which she was doing her field placement. Ecological Theory suggests that the interaction among service delivery systems was important and that these system interactions contributed to child well-being. Eventually, Danielle used this knowledge to craft the following question—Do military families with a deployed member who participate in case management report less stress than families who do not participate in case management? Essentially, Danielle wanted to determine whether an intervention that linked multiple systems in an efficient manner could improve the overall stress level of military families with a deployed family member.

Theory to Guide Data Collection Instruments—Aiyshia was placed in a university counseling center and noted that female binge-drinking behaviors were appearing more frequently in women who sought services at the center. She thought about these behaviors within the context of her Gender Theory studies and wondered if a change in gender roles could be related to an increase in female binge drinking. Her theoretical explorations led her to the following hypotheses: Female college students experience more stress today resulting from role overload, awareness of sexism, more female autonomy, freedom, and more competition with male counterparts. Stress leads to binge drinking. Subsequently she developed a questionnaire that asked female clients in the center several questions about their roles as a student, parent, spouse/partner, employee, etc.; their awareness and experience of sexism among peers and in the classroom; and their thoughts and behaviors about female autonomy and male competition.

Theory to Help Craft and Implement the Design—Allen was placed in an adoption agency. He wanted to understand how adoptive families felt about having birth parents involved in the lives of adopted children. He developed a qualitative project. The agency operated from an empowerment framework, and Allen's field placement instructor helped him to use Empowerment Theory to craft questions and determine how to find participants and how to develop rapport with the respondents. After the completion of his project, participants were permitted to review results and then provide feedback regarding whether Allen "heard their voices."

Creating Hypotheses. As you can see from the above examples and as you know from your research methods courses, theory often leads to the development of hypotheses. A hypothesis is description of the specific relationship between the independent and dependent variables. You will want to add the definition of a hypothesis to your Terminology Worksheet. Basically, a hypothesis is a prediction, or your assumption, about what the results of your research will show. In other words, it is an educated guess about what you expect (hope) to find when your independent and dependent variables are studied together.

A hypothesis is generally written in present tense, but you will also see them in future tense. In the hypothesis, *High school students who attend an urban high school will show increased knowledge of birth control methods after a 2-hour intervention on contraceptives,* the independent variable is the 2-hour intervention, and the dependent variable is increased knowledge of birth control methods.

Is there always a hypothesis explaining the relationship between variables? Not always. In *qualitative* research, we allow meanings to emerge from the data rather than requiring a hypothesis. For example, the purpose of an exploratory study of a tribal life in a remote village is to explore an understudied phenomenon and to seek depth in understanding the experiences and attitudes of people there. A hypothesis may *emerge* from that exploration but is not necessary to begin with. Alternatively, quantitative research that is exploratory in nature can still use a hypothesis but leave the direction or focus open-ended. In general, however, these exploratory studies are often guided by a research question rather than a hypothesis.

Can you have more than one hypothesis in one research study? Yes, you have as many hypotheses as your research question requires. A research project evaluating a program designed to help offenders become employed is an example of a complex study with many hypotheses. The purpose of this study was to determine whether characteristics of ex-offenders (namely, educational level and severity of offense) were associated with employment outcomes. One portion of the study investigated the educational level of people enrolled in the program. Within this set, the first hypothesis was that people with a higher the level of education would have a greater likelihood of obtaining employment. The second hypothesis was that people with higher levels of education would search for employment for fewer days than those with lower levels. The third was that more highly educated persons would maintain employment longer once a job was found. Under severity of offense, the first hypothesis was that a person with a felony would be less likely to obtain employment; the second was that they would spend more time job-searching, and the third was that they would maintain employment for fewer days than those with misdemeanors.

Are there different types of hypotheses? Reread the above hypotheses and note the different way that the hypotheses are stated. Some hypotheses, referred to as *nondirectional* hypotheses, merely state the existence of a relationship. The hypothesis "The characteristics of ex-offenders (namely, educational level and severity of offense) are associated with employment outcomes" in the example above is a nondirectional hypothesis, meaning that the nature of the relationship, or how the two concepts are related to each other, is not specified. On the other hand, the statement that "people with a higher the level of education would have a greater likelihood of obtaining employment" is a *directional* hypothesis meaning that the direction of the relationship between the two concepts is stated—as the level of education increases, the likelihood of employment increases. A directional or nondirectional hypothesis is sometimes referred to as the research hypothesis, or the alternative hypothesis, to differentiate it from the *null* hypothesis. The null hypothesis states that there is no relationship between the concepts—that is, there is no relationship between type of felony conviction and ability to gain employment. Statements of the null hypothesis are very important in understanding statistical testing and will be discussed in more detail in Chapter Ten on Quantitative Data Analysis. For now, add these different hypothesis' terms to your Terminology Worksheet and use Project Development Worksheet 2.2 to begin thinking about possible hypotheses for your project.

Project Development Worksheet 2.2.	
DEVELOPING A RESEARCH HYPOTHESIS	
1. Think of a social work-related problem that is of interest to you. What are the concepts or variables that you would be studying in this problem?	
2. How do you think these variables are related to each other?	
3. State these relationships as non-directional, directional, or null hypotheses.	

Summary of Step One. Take note of the many multidirectional arrows that point to or connect the problem, question, and theory and that link to the different sections of the methods line. Research texts often describe this beginning part of the process as if it occurs in a linear fashion, moving from one step to the next. In reality, the beginning part of the research process is quite "messy;" it requires you to revisit and modify each of these sections several times before you have a research question and a theoretical understanding that is satisfactory and appropriate for scientific inquiry. We describe this part of the process as "iterative," meaning that you go back and forth between reviewing the literature and trying to identify and clarify the research problem and finding a theory (or developing your own) that helps you explain or understand the problem. You should expect to review new articles and to reread the ones you have throughout the entire research process and allow yourself the time to do so. Students who expect to finalize identification of their problem area and research question after an initial review of the literature often become needlessly frustrated when they realize that they need to revise their question several times in response to something new they have read or some feasibility issue or barrier in the agency setting.

During the question development phase of your project, you may want to keep a record of how and why your research question changes over time. This can help you understand the evolution of your project and how any new information has been integrated into your question.

Example 2.5 provides some examples of the evolution of a research question from a few student research projects.

Example 2.5.

THE EVOLUTION OF RESEARCH QUESTIONS

Scenario 1: Jay began her research class thinking that she wanted to study the effectiveness of English as a Second Language (ESL) class on recent immigrants ages 5 to 9. She focused on a child's ability to obtain a new language, and her initial review of the literature revealed several tools used to evaluate children's language acquisition. Her initial question focused on language: Do children participating in the ESL Program improve their ability to speak and understand English? She felt comfortable with her initial question but decided to reread some of the articles as well as review additional literature. After rereading the articles and the additional literature, she began to see that ESL classes had benefits that extended beyond language acquisition. Her original question was good but was constructed on her preconceived notions regarding program success. Additional readings and new articles helped her to explore additional areas and refine her question. She discovered that she was really more interested in the social and emotional impact of these classes on the participants. Consequently, her final question was: What are the social, emotional, and spiritual benefits of participating in ESL classes for children ages 5 to 9?

Scenario 2: Shelly wanted to see if a person's immigration status impacted his/her willingness to seek services from residential domestic violence shelter. Her original question was, "Does immigration status impact a person's willingness to leave his/her abuser and go to a domestic violence shelter?" She began to review literature and found literature related to immigrants and domestic violence. Shelly went to her course instructor and field agency to discuss her project. Both persons pointed out some of the methodological issues with using the shelter to draw her sample. One of these issues was that the shelter saw few immigrants. Shelly was really interested in her topic and was frustrated that she would have to rethink her sampling methods to answer her question. Shelly went back to the literature on immigrants and domestic violence and reread the articles while keeping in mind her agency's statements. She noticed that many articles discussed the lack of culturally competent services for immigrants. Shelly started to wonder if her agency provided culturally competent services. She also started to wonder if other organizations working with domestic violence services had staff trained and knowledgeable to work with immigrants experiencing

---

domestic violence. Her research question shifted from (1) examining immigrant status and willingness to participate in services to (2) examining the services available for this population. Thus, based on new knowledge and the recognition of the limited feasibility of her first question, she was able to transform her project into a community needs assessment.

In Example 2.5, you can see how each student had to be flexible to complete his or her project. In the first scenario, Jay constructed a research question and was able to modify it once new knowledge emerged. In the second scenario, Shelly's original question was based on her professional interest, but there were feasibility issues. She was able to modify her question so that it reflected her interest.

You will not be surprised to realize that, as you finalize your research question, different types of research questions reflect different research purposes. Before we move to the methods line in this graphic, let's do a quick review of what several research text authors refer to as the purpose or the goal of the research study (Engel & Schutt, 2009; Monette, Sullivan, & DeJong, 2011; Rubin & Babbie, 2011). These range from *examining* a topic in which little is known (exploratory), to *describing a phenomena* (descriptive), or *explaining "why or how" one social* condition is impacted by another condition or factor (explanatory). Exploratory research is closely linked with qualitative methods of inquiry. For example, one student was placed in a day treatment program for persons with serious mental illness. She wanted to understand how persons participating in the program defined and described their mental illness and how it shaped their identity. She had very little knowledge on how these specific persons described themselves. Conducting exploratory research using a qualitative method (in-depth interviews) was appropriate and helped her develop a beginning understanding of this area.

The information in Summary Content 2.2 summarizes the different purposes of research. Chapter Six on Quantitative Research Designs will provide exercises and worksheets to help you to strengthen and apply your understanding of these research purposes.

Summary Content 2.2.

RESEARCH PURPOSES

PURPOSE/GOAL OF RESEARCH	USED WHEN ...	SAMPLE QUESTION
Exploratory	• When a topic is new and the pertinent variables are unknown. • When we want to study a topic that is relatively unstudied and about which very little is known.	• How do people who are homeless get along in this environment? • What meaning do they give to their actions? • What concerns them?
Descriptive	• When pertinent variables are known and we want to explore further. • When we want to describe situations and events.	• What are the demographic characteristics of people who are homeless? • What are their needs? • How many people are homeless?
Explanatory	• When we want to explain "why" something happens. • When a "cause-and-effect" relationship is being investigated.	• What are the causes of homeless? • What is the relationship between homeless and mental illness? • What services have been most effective in helping people who are homeless?

Step Two: Making Decisions about Methods

The next line of the graphic highlights the methodological aspects of your project in regard to measurement (WHAT), design (HOW), and sampling (WHO). As in most research texts, this workbook discusses these three aspects in separate chapters. However, we think you'll find it helpful to envision the measurement, design, and sampling issues simultaneously to understand both the interaction and the unique contribution that each makes to the research project.

Measurement. Measurement concerns the "what" of your research project, as in "What variables are you going to measure?" In social work research, the variables are often: characteristics of individuals, groups, or organizations; the knowledge, behaviors, and attitudes of clients, families, or service providers; the interventions or services provided; or any types of strengths or weaknesses or experiences that we can observe in micro- or macro settings.

Most standard research texts discuss "conceptualizing" a variable, meaning to define the variable according to dictionary or standard use, and "operationalizing," meaning to define the variable very concretely or specifically so that a researcher knows exactly what is being measured or counted. Both *conceptualization* and *operationalization* are terms that you should add to your Terminology Worksheet. Additional exercises, examples, and worksheets to help you apply measurement aspects to your project will be provided in Chapter Nine (Measurement).

Sampling. "Who" you will study refers to the individuals or the groups from whom you will be collecting data. You will have an opportunity to consider the different ways to select the individuals or groups for your study and the implications of these selections in Chapter Seven (Sampling Methods). For now, it is important to note the distinction between "what" is being studied and "who" is being studied. Students sometimes get confused about the "what" and the "who" because these designations vary from study to study. For example, in the literature on work and family, gender (male or female) can be either the variable or the sample depending on how the researcher chooses to answer his or her research question. If the researcher is interested in investigating the level of parental satisfaction in a group of employed women, then parental satisfaction is the variable (the "what" that is being studied), and employed women is the sample. On the other hand, another researcher might wonder if parental satisfaction differs between employed mothers and fathers. In this case, both parental satisfaction and gender are variables, and the sample is employed parents. One way to think about this to remember that if everyone in a study is female or if everyone is employed, or if everyone is a parent, then that identified group of people who are being studied would be the sample. On the other hand, if you are studying parental satisfaction and you expect parental satisfaction to be different or vary within the group you have specified, then parental satisfaction is the variable. Example 2.6 can help you distinguish between the variable (what you are studying) and the sample (who you are studying).

Design. Research design is the "how" of the study, specifically the decisions the researcher makes about where, when, and how (in what format) to collect the data. As you know from your research methods courses, one of the most important methodological decisions you will make concerns whether you design your research project to establish a cause-and-effect relationship among your variables. Experimental designs such as randomized control group designs that collect data at

Example 2.6.

IDENTIFYING VARIABLES AND SAMPLES

1. What financial and social factors contribute to repeated homelessness among single mothers?				
	What?	• financial and social factors • homelessness factors	Who?	single mothers
2. How effective is the LEARN Program at increasing social adjustment for refugees?				
	What?	• LEARN Program • social adjustment	Who?	refugees
3. Does parental deployment increase mental health difficulties for children in military families?				
	What?	• parental deployment • mental health difficulties	Who?	children in military families

least twice during the study over a period of time (called *longitudinal*) are better able to establish causal relationships, whereas nonexperimental designs that collect data from sample participants at one point in time (referred to as *cross-sectional* studies) cannot. These are more terms for your Terminology Worksheet and will be revisited in more detail in later chapters.

Another design issue will be based on the nature of the question you are asking. If you are interested in the depth and detail of people's stories or different experiences, then you would consider a qualitative study. On the other hand, if your question concerns how well the data you collect from a small group of people can be generalized to larger groups of people, then you would consider a quantitative study. Qualitative studies use methods such as ethnography or participant observation and collect data in text format through techniques such as in-depth interviewing or focus groups or historical accounts. Quantitative studies use survey or experimental methods and collect data in numerical format, often through questionnaires (Holosko, 2006). As you know from your research texts, there are many advantages and disadvantages to each of these data collection types, which will be reviewed in later chapters. You can see from Example 2.7 how some of our students collected data to answer their research questions. Note the many different ways you can describe your data collection techniques. Deciding about research methods and techniques is one of the most important decision points in the research process, and the implications of these decisions need to be considered when planning your study. Example 2.7 provides a snapshot of how your research question connects to, and is reflected in, many design issues.

Step Three: Data Collection and Study Implementation

After you have made important research design decisions about what you will collect, from whom, and how, you are ready to begin the actual data collection step. The more thought and planning and review of the literature that you have put into these measurement, sample, and design decisions, the better chance that the actual data collection will proceed without incident. However, student research projects take place in settings and with people over whom students have little control. Challenges and unexpected changes are not uncommon at the beginning or during implementation.

Example 2.7.

RESEARCH GOALS, DESIGNS, AND DATA COLLECTION METHODS

QUESTION	PURPOSE/DATA COLLECTION TECHNIQUE	RESEARCH METHOD
What is the experience of staff members working with unaccompanied refugee and immigrant minors?	An exploratory qualitative study, cross-sectional, that collected data by face-to-face interviews.	Nonexperimental
Will youth express less acceptance of violence after participation in a nonviolence program?	An explanatory/ evaluative study, longitudinal, that collected data from one youth group by self-administered questionnaires.	Pre Experimental
How satisfied are primary caregivers with hospice services?	A descriptive study, cross-sectional, that collected data by mail survey.	Nonexperimental
Are female and/or African-American children more likely to be placed in more restrictive care following in-home counseling?	An explanatory study that collected data from agency records at the time of case closure.	Nonexperimental
Is there a difference in the level of compassion fatigue experienced by social workers and nurses?	An explanatory study, cross-sectional, that collected data by online survey questionnaires.	Nonexperimental
What is the alcohol and substance use history of persons seeking homeless services?	A descriptive study, cross-sectional, with data collected by face-to-face interviews.	Nonexperimental
Do children participating in social skills training increase the number of pro-social skills they exhibit?	An explanatory/ evaluation study, longitudinal, with data collected by researcher observation from and experimental and a comparison group.	Quasi-experimental

Anticipating possible barriers and thinking of alternative ways to answer your research question can help save time and avoid unnecessary stress during this step. Your research instructor should be able to help you address some of the challenges because of his or her experience supervising numerous projects. Even with instructor involvement, however, unexpected problems may still arise.

One of the most frequent challenges encountered during implementation is small sample size resulting from typically low client populations in some agencies or unanticipated changes in agency procedures or programs. In one student project, referrals to a residential treatment center were severely curtailed because of third-party payment problems at the beginning of the data collection and greatly reduced the number of clients available for the survey from 30 to 5. Staff changes within agency settings—particularly if the change involves a change in the student's agency supervisor—are another cause for disruption of student research projects. In another example, a research project to evaluate substance abuse group interventions had to be abandoned at the last minute because the agency therapist who was scheduled to run the groups went on extended sick leave, and the groups had to be postponed until after the student's field placement would end. If you experience a similar setback, then be aware that there are several ways for a student to salvage a research project that is being derailed. Often, a quantitative study using a questionnaire or survey can be revised into a qualitative study that interviews fewer numbers of people about the topic in which you are interested. This is what the student in the residential center did. He changed some of the original survey questions into open-ended questions and implemented a qualitative design. Also, rather than interview or survey clients, you can often obtain good information about the client problems in which you are interested by surveying the social workers or other human service staff who work with these clients.

Example 2.8 provides some examples of how students can overcome implementation barriers.

Example 2.8.

OVERCOMING IMPLEMENTATION BARRIERS

- Amber conducted her internship in a high school. She wanted to use secondary data to determine risk factors for truancy. The school was already conducting a truancy audit, so Amber's field instructor agreed to Amber's participation. However, during the project, Amber's field instructor was transferred, and her new instructor was hesitant for Amber to continue investigating her topic. In fact, the entire truancy audit was discontinued. Amber was discouraged but not deterred. She spoke with her research instructor, and they modified the question and data collection plan. Amber had access to published truancy statistics for the entire school system. She decided to interview school staff to assess attitudes and beliefs about truancy. She posited that a person's role in the school would influence his or her perception of truancy. She used the published truancy statistics to determine whether a person's beliefs were "correct."

- Susan wanted to study domestic violence survivors and their motivations for leaving abusive relationships. She planned to administer her instrument to incoming residents in domestic violence shelter during intake. Unfortunately, because of unforeseen circumstances, the shelter had to close, and clients were transferred to hotels throughout the area. This disrupted services and limited Susan's access to clients. Susan worked with other shelters and asked if she could train the counselors to administer the instrument to their clients. The shelters agreed, and Susan was able to collect data for her project.

- Peter, placed in a large public medical facility, wanted to understand substance use behaviors for veterans and their combat experience. He met with his field instructor and was informed that he would not be able to have access to client information without going through the organization's Institutional Review Board (IRB). His field instructor mentioned that an interdisciplinary team had just received IRB approval to implement and evaluate an intervention to help veterans stop smoking. Peter met with the chairperson of the team and was allowed to join the team and use the evaluation data as his project.

- Nicole did her second-year internship at a counseling organization. The agency asked her to conduct a client satisfaction survey. Nicole created a survey and mailed it to all clients who had received services within the past year. After 3 weeks and one follow-up letter, she had only received five surveys back. Nicole decided to modify her project; she believed that a qualitative project could provide rich data concerning the client's experiences seeking and receiving services. She contacted those who returned the surveys and asked them if she could conduct a telephone interview. Three participants agreed, and she was able to collect rich data regarding clients' experiences. Her question evolved from one that assessed client satisfaction to one that explored client experiences.

Step Four: Data Processing and Analysis

At this point in your research study, you should be aware of the different types of texts and resources needed to complete your project. Research methods texts present a general overview of the basic research concepts and activities and provide very basic introductions to statistical analysis. Research methods texts with which the authors are most familiar and that are referenced throughout this workbook include: Drake and Jonson-Reid (2007); Engel and Schutt (2009); Monette, Sullivan, and DeJong (2011); and Rubin and Babbie (2011). These research methods texts need to be supplemented by texts or resources that specifically address the whys and how-to's of data analysis. Statistical texts that the authors have used in this workbook include: Abu-Bader (2006); Rubin (2010); and Weinbach and Grinnell (2010). We assume that you are or will become familiar with the material in these different texts through the research courses in your social work program.

Data Processing. Research methods texts typically do not identify data processing as one of the major steps in the research process, opting instead to mention it briefly as part of data analysis activities (Rubin & Babbie, 2011). Texts devoted to statistical analysis tend to add an extensive "how-to" appendix on computerized data management systems or to incorporate instructions about data management throughout their discussions on various data analysis techniques. However, data management and data processing are important points to consider in the overview picture (Rubin & Babbie, 2011), not only to forewarn you of the amount of time required for this activity but to encourage you to do some preliminary work in this area prior to doing the actual data analysis. Note the bidirectional arrows between the data collection and data processing steps in the overview graphic. We recommend that you begin exploring and making these decisions as you finalize methodological aspects of your study and begin data collection.

The data processing or data management aspect of the research process is concerned with what happens to your data after they are collected but before they are analyzed. What type of computer software will be needed to enter, store, and analyze large amounts of data? How is the information from all the questionnaires or surveys or from your interview notes put into usable form for data analysis? Qualitative projects, in particular, require much time transcribing audiotapes or reviewing and rewriting handwritten notes. Although you can't process or manage your data until they are collected, the iterative nature of the research process means that you can prepare beforehand. For example, obtaining and learning one of the newer computer-assisted data management software systems for qualitative data early in the research process can be an incredible time-saver in the long run.

Statistical Package for the Social Sciences (SPSS) is one of the most common data management packages for quantitative research. You should find out from your instructor as soon as possible whether students will be required to use SPSS or some other data management system, how students are expected to access SPSS software (or qualitative data software) in your course, if there are computer labs with the required software available to you, or whether the software is available for download to your personal computer free of charge through your college or university.

Most data management software programs provide helpful tutorials that introduce you to the data processing requirements and take you through basic steps to get started on data analysis. If you are planning to use SPSS, then you can prepare your codebook and set up your SPSS file on the computer before data collection so that you can begin data entry immediately after you obtain data. Furthermore, thinking through the details of the data processing stage often helps to identify measurement or data collection problems that you might be able to avert. In the following chapters you will learn the range of data management resources available to you.

Data Analysis. Data analysis is the process of making sense of, or giving meaning to, the numbers or words that you gathered in the data collection phase and put into usable form in the data processing and management stage so that you can answer your research question. Statistics are the tools used for analysis of numeric data in quantitative studies; coding is the most frequently used tool for analyzing text data in qualitative studies. Whatever the type of data analysis used, the ultimate goal of the analysis is to answer your research question. The details of how to go about analyzing data for your project are presented in the subsequent Chapters Nine and Ten on Quantitative and Qualitative Data Analysis respectively.

Although the data analysis aspect of the research process is often the most intimidating for research students, as you can see from this Research at a Glance, it is only a fraction of the overall research project activities. You will have the opportunity to delve into the particulars of data analysis in later chapters of the workbook, and we hope that our discussion will help clarify and demystify these activities.

What we hope to emphasize in this chapter is that data analysis derives from the previous steps in the research process and is particularly connected to the decisions that you made earlier about your research question and those about the "what" of the study. The overall statistical strategy or coding scheme you choose will be strongly influenced by your research question. And, the decisions that you made about how to measure your variables—particularly in quantitative studies—will determine, to a great extent, the specific types of statistics you will use.

Data analysis will be less daunting as you begin to associate the terminology with more familiar language. That is why we are introducing it in this chapter. For example, some of the first decisions you will make in the data analysis stage will be whether to analyze one, two, or three or more variables to answer your research question. If you wanted to know how old the participants in your study were, then you could analyze the one variable of age. Or, you could analyze the relationship between two variables (age AND depression) to examine whether younger or older study participants tended to be more or less depressed. Or, you could analyze the relationship among three or more variables if you wanted to understand whether age and marital status was related to depression and educational level. In quantitative studies, the analysis of one variable at a time uses statistics referred to as univariate statistics. For the relationship between two variables, you choose from a group of statistics referred to as bivariate statistics, and for relationships among three or more variables, you choose from multivariate statistics. Note the language of these basic statistical terms. The "uni" in the word univariate means "one," and the "variate" means "variable" or "to vary." Thus, univariate statistics are used to analyze one variable at a time. Similarly, the "bi" in bivariate statistics indicates that two variables are analyzed, and the "multi" signals many variables. Example 2.9 illustrates some of the details regarding data analysis in one student project.

> **Example 2.9.**
>
> DATA ANALYSIS IN A STUDENT PROJECT
>
> Rebecca was interested in comparing the demographic characteristics of persons seeking services from two types of mental health clinics in her area. She suspected that those receiving services from Clinic A were wealthier than those who sought services from Clinic B. She asked each respondent to provide their annual salary and their race/ethnicity and to indicate where he or she was receiving services. To answer her research question about the relationship between demographic characteristics and type of mental health clinic, Rebecca would need to identify the following specifics for her research project.
>
> - **The sample is persons seeking services from mental health clinics.**
> - **The variables being studied and the values are:**
>   - o Demographic characteristic of annual salary is a variable that has values from 0 to 500,000.
>   - o Level of education is a variable that has values of less than high school, high school/GED completion, some college, college graduate, or more than college graduate.
>   - o Type of mental health clinic is a variable that has values of public or nonprofit or for-profit.
>
> Rebecca would use a:
> - univariate statistic to answer a question about one variable only, such as, "What is the average **income** of all cases in the study?"
> - bivariate statistic to answer a question about the relationship between two variables, such as, "What is the **relationship** between income and type of clinic?" or "What is the **relationship** between income and educational level?"
> - multivariate statistic to answer a question about the relationship among three or more variables, such as, "How does income and level of education determine services from different types of mental health clinics?"

Step Five: Discussion and Application

Once your data analysis is completed, your attention turns to evaluating and interpreting the results, the last point in the overview graphic presented above. At this stage, the full picture of your research comes into view. Students and new researchers often refer to this stage as the "ah-ha" moment when all the pieces of the puzzle come together and the impact of the decisions made and activities undertaken in earlier stages is clear. The primary issue here is the extent to which your study answered your research question. You will focus on not only what your findings mean within the context of the larger scope of the literature but, most importantly, the relevance of your findings to practice and their implications. Chapter Twelve (Write-Up, Presentation, and Dissemination of Results) will provide guidance and examples about interpreting, discussing, and applying your findings.

At this stage, you are also expected to raise new questions about your topic area that have not been sufficiently answered by your study or that have emerged as a result of your findings. If published in a refereed journal, your research project would become part of the literature and be used by other researchers to formulate research questions for subsequent studies. In fact, you might want to think about this final part of your research project as the beginning of someone else's (or your subsequent) research project!

INVOLVEMENT OF YOUR FIELD AGENCY

Of all the different research decisions that you will make, the decisions about how you will conduct your study require the most interaction with and cooperation from your field agency. Seldom do agencies allow students unlimited access to clients, client records, or employees. In some agencies, you will need permission from the agency director to conduct your study; in some, permission from your field supervisor is adequate; and in others, you will need to present your proposal to an internal review board for permission. Similarly, some agencies will permit you to administer questionnaires to or interview clients without restrictions; others—particularly schools and child-centered organizations—may automatically disallow children as research participants or require consent from parents or legal guardians. How much support or direction you get from your school or research instructor also will vary. Some schools have clearly articulated guidelines informing student researchers about what to expect when undertaking research in agency settings. Others may recognize that students will be conducting student projects in the field, but offer little guidance to either the field agency or the student on how to go about conducting these projects.

Whatever the conditions in your agency or whatever level and type of arrangement between the school and the field agency, communication between you and your field instructor is essential early in the project development, and the earlier the better. Use Project Development Worksheet 2.3 to guide your discussion with your field instructor.

Project Development Worksheet 2.3. QUESTIONS TO ASK FIELD AGENCY		
	QUESTION	RESPONSE
1.	Is there a person at the agency engaged in a research project who might be willing to incorporate a student project into the larger project?	
2.	What research questions are of interest to the agency?	
3.	What data are already routinely collected by the agency?	
4.	What is the agency's prior experience with student research projects?	
5.	What are the organizational restrictions and conditions that might apply to your project?	
6.	Whose permission is required to begin a research project and at what level must approval be sought?	
7.	Does the agency have its own human subject review process that you must go through?	
	Will you be allowed to conduct your study within your regular field hours or will your project require additional time spent at the agency?	

Additionally, for schools like ours that do not have formal arrangements with field agencies, we recommend that research instructors draft a letter of introduction for students to provide to their agency describing the general requirements of the research course and offering some idea of what might be expected from the field agency in relation to these requirements. A sample letter can be found at the end of this chapter.

We also strongly encourage you to outline in writing the specifics of your project—particularly how and when data will be collected—and ask for approval of the plan, in writing, from a person in authority at the agency. This is one of the more important strategies to prevent barriers to research projects discussed earlier. Use Project Development Worksheet 2.4 worksheet to outline the information that you should include in the written documentation from the agency regarding your research project. Although some agencies also want to see a copy of your research proposal, we have found that the arrangements with the agency need to be worked out before you finalize your research proposal.

Project Implementation Worksheet 2.4. ARRANGEMENTS WITH AGENCY	
Purpose of your research project	
Who from the agency will be aware of or is involved with your research	
The data you will be collecting	
How you will collect your data	
When you will collect your data	
How you have addressed protection of human subjects rights (IRB issues)	
The name and contact information for your course instructor	
Other information specific to your project	

ESTABLISHING PRINCIPLES FOR RESEARCH

The research process does not happen in isolation, especially when it is conducted in service organizations. Rather, the research process is interwoven with various practice activities. Many of the research steps that you read about in basic research methods texts often need to be modified to accommodate various client and agency requirements as the research process begins and unfolds. We present the following guidelines for practice–research collaborations for you to think about as you plan for your research project and to alert you to possible pitfalls that occur in agency-based research. The practice–research guidelines are intended to help you maneuver and coordinate your role as a social work student and a social work researcher through the various stages of your research project (*see* Secret, Abell, & Berlin, 2011, for more discussion about the following practice–research principles).

Because many of the research projects attempted by social work students depend on the cooperation of those who work in and run human service organizations, the first guiding principle concerns establishing a good practice–research relationship within agency settings prior to the onset of the actual research process. This first principle, labeled "*shared leadership*," derives from an awareness of and appreciation for both the practice wisdom that comes from years of experience in the field and for the scientific rigor that grounds good research. In other words, the shared leadership principle requires that we consider the insights and strengths that come from the practice side of the profession as well as those that are associated with the research side of the profession. Equal regard for practice and for research increases that likelihood that the research question will be relevant for social work practice and that the implementation of the project can avoid potential pitfalls and disruptions along the way. When social workers, who are trained to listen, communicate, and engage in various problem-solving approaches with clients, transfer their basic social work skills to the research arena, they enrich and sustain the practice–research collaboration through the entirety of the project. Ultimately, such an approach makes for a timely and satisfactory completion of your project.

A second principle of particular concern for student research projects is what we call the "*feasibility principle*," a principle similar to the social work mandate to "begin where the client is." This means that the selection of a research design needs to be appropriate to the programs' goals and client needs as well as the practitioners' experience and expertise. Moreover, your plan needs to be workable within the service setting and to include the use of data collection methods and instruments that resonate with the practitioner and that match the skill set and expertise of the researcher. Several workbook chapters provide examples and tools for helping you to understand the requirements for and implications of decisions made about each of these research activities.

A third principle, "*program and client first*," helps guide the implementation of the project. This principle underlines the need to continually reflect on and keep the needs of the client foremost as you implement the project. All researchers are required to follow specific procedures to honor and protect client rights during the implementation of a research project; these are outlined in the Social Work Research Code of Ethics. This guiding principle also suggests that you have a responsibility to make sure that the research project creates minimal disruption of the program and that service delivery concerns remain paramount in practice settings.

CONCLUSION

This chapter has provided an overview of the research process from start to finish. One of the themes of this chapter has been the iterative nature of research. Although the stages of research are provided in a sequential, linear fashion, that is not the way they occur in practice. Instead, one has to consider and weigh different aspects of the study, which will inform the other parts, and which in turn, will suggest revisions to the original aspects. This iterative process is necessary because of the complexity of research and the interlocking nature of its components. Although at times daunting and frustrating, this process can also be stimulating and interesting, especially when it relates to an area of practice in which you would like to deepen your knowledge and improve services to clients.

Now that you have an understanding of the research process, it is time to begin to investigate your topic by conducting a literature review. A good literature review is essential, as it is the foundation for your work and helps you make important decisions such as how to refine your question, define variables, select a measurement tool, and collect data. Developing a literature review can seem overwhelming for some students. There is an abundance of information, and students sometimes wonder which information to use and how to present it in the most effective way. Chapter Three will guide you through the literature review-writing process by showing you how to locate, evaluate, organize, and report your information. In summary, using the tools provided in Chapter Three will help to focus your work and reduce your research anxiety.

WEBSITES

Institute for Social Research (University of Michigan)
http://www.isr.umich.edu/home/
Society for Social Work and Research
http://www.sswr.org/
Social Psychology Network
http://www.socialpsychology.org/methods.htm#ethics
Center for Collaborative Action Research
http://cadres.pepperdine.edu/ccar/define.html
Analyzing, Interpreting and Reporting Basic Research Results
http://managementhelp.org/businessresearch/analysis.htm

Sample Letter

UNIVERSITY LETTERHEAD

School of Social Work
Xxxx
address

To: Agencies and Organizations   800-001-0001
        Involved with Social Work Student Research Projects   Fax: 800-800-008

From: Dr. xxxx name
        Associate Professor
        School of Social Work

Re: Student research projects in SLWK 706 and 707 taught by Dr. name

Date: September 19, 2012

The student research projects in this class are designed to help students understand the research process, learn how to conduct scientifically sound and socially relevant research, and use research knowledge to inform their practice.
I hope the projects will provide useful information to the agency where they are implemented, but the findings are not intended to be published or publicized. All policies for the protection of human subjects will be adhered to and ensured by the professor. It is not expected that the projects will have more than minimal risk for research participants.

Because the study will not be published and is not intended to produce generalized knowledge, formal IRB review and approval is not required unless specified by the professor.

The research projects are closely supervised by the professor.

If you have any questions or concerns about any of these student research projects, please contact me at mxxxxxxxx@xxx.edu or phone (800) 111-1111.

REVIEW OF THE LITERATURE

3

INTRODUCTION

This chapter discusses a key initial step in the research process: the literature review. First, we will define what a literature review is and why it is important. Then we will talk about the steps of the process, which include searching for and finding relevant literature and reading the literature to critically appraise it. Finally, we will give attention to the actual writing and the referencing of your literature review, which will set the stage for your own research.

DEFINITION AND PURPOSE

The literature review is a standard component of any research and is found at the beginning of any published research-oriented document, such as a journal article, dissertation, or grant application. The literature review is where you make extensive references to the existing theory and research that have influenced your choice of topic, a problem to be researched, and the methodology you will adopt for your study (Ridley, 2008). The literature review is also where you position your own research in relation to the existing research. You are demonstrating to the reader that a gap exists in the published material and that your study attempts to fill it. "It is your opportunity to engage in a written dialogue with researchers in your area while at the same time showing that you have engaged with, understood and responded to the relevant body of knowledge underpinning your research" (Ridley, 2008, p. 2).

WHY CONDUCT A LITERATURE REVIEW?

Most research texts advise you to conduct your literature review *before* you refine your topic of study and develop your methodology. Performing a literature review early ensures that your work will be original and not a duplicate of existing research. However, students (and researchers) sometimes resist doing this important step before planning their study because they do not appreciate the connection between what they want to study and what other people have studied. As we shall see, the literature review is critical for many reasons.

1. To learn more about your topic area.

As discussed in the first two chapters, students come to their topic area with various levels of preparation and knowledge. Your topic may be one in which you have had a great deal of work experience and to which you have already devoted a lot of your graduate study. For example, you may have written many papers on your topic and may have chosen classes that inform your area of interest. At the other extreme, you may have no knowledge about a particular topic area, but the personnel at your internship may have an urgent need for research on this topic. A search of the literature will familiarize you with the topic area and the existing research in this area.

2. To discover whether a study is worth doing.

Consider the following example of how a literature review can determine whether an area of research needs attention. A social worker at a health clinic wanted to research why Latinas in the area seemed reluctant to access the free-of-charge cervical cancer and breast cancer screening services offered at her clinic. She and her director decided that they wanted to conduct focus groups of Latina consumers and their health-care professionals to learn how the women perceived the screenings (specifically the barriers and facilitators to having the Papinalou test and the mammogram). However, a literature review indicated that 10 qualitative studies with a similar purpose to theirs had each been conducted in the areas of Latina breast cancer screening and Latina cervical cancer screening, and the results of these studies tended to have common themes. As a result of the literature review, the health clinic personnel found the information needed to make their services more responsive to Latinas. The literature review demonstrated that they did not need to conduct a study of their own because the topic was already well-covered in the research literature. Another example has to do with a student researcher who was placed at an alternative school setting. She and her team of researchers wanted to conduct focus groups to better understand the experiences of parents with children who had been diagnosed with pervasive developmental disorders. After a preliminary search, they found many qualitative studies that had used focus groups (as well as semi-structured, face-to-face interviews) to address this very topic. Therefore, it became more worthwhile to turn their attention to another area of study.

3. To get ideas for how to do your study.

In addition to determining whether the general idea for a research project is sound, reading studies on related research can give you ideas about how to more specifically implement your research. For example, a student researching client preferences for incorporating spiritual interventions in a community mental health setting came across an article entitled "Empirical Assessment of Spirituality in Counseling" (Standard, Sandhu, & Painter, 2000). In addition to providing her with material for her literature review, the article provided her with a questionnaire for her research.

4. To build a justification for your study.

An important part of a literature review is critiquing the state of the literature—both in a "big picture," macro way and through a microlens. Comprehensively examining the studies that compose this literature (*see* Reading the Literature) allows you to identify gaps in the literature and methodological limitations of existing studies. For example, using the macrolens to investigate sexual abuse treatment (including the impact on the nonoffending caregiver) research shows that treatment outcome studies have been conducted with preschool and school-age children, but they have not been conducted with adolescents. Therefore, research into caregiver involvement in sexual abuse treatment of adolescent victims is needed.

The most efficient way to begin your literature review is to seek out the systematic reviews and meta-analyses that have been done in your area of interest. These reviews aim to comprehensively locate and synthesize the research that bears on a particular question and will act to distill a large body of knowledge so that you can gain a sense of the current research status of your topic. Because systematic reviews are specialized types of literature reviews requiring clearly identified organized, transparent, and replicable procedures at each step in the process, we will discuss them in detail in the next chapter. Chances are, it will also be necessary for you to look for the individual studies that pertain to your area. You are probably most familiar with this more generic type of literature review that is the subject of this chapter.

STEPS OF THE LITERATURE REVIEW

The steps of the literature review involve the following:

1. the literature search
2. reading the literature
3. writing the review
4. referencing

Although delineated separately, these steps are actually an "interconnected and cyclical processes. The literature searching, reading and writing feed into each other constantly; and all the other activities, such as formulating research questions and justifying the research problem, influence and are influenced by the literature searching and reading, providing inspiration for the writing. Your writing in turn helps you discover and clarify your ideas and can result in the refinement of the focus of your research and the content of your review" (Ridley, 2008, p. 80).

Step One: Searching the Literature

There are two main sections to a literature review: the introduction and the main section. Each requires a different approach. The introduction to the literature review is narrowly focused on establishing the problem you will address and why it is important to study. Part of its importance involves the prevalence of the problem. Here, you need to present some government statistics generated from federal agencies, such as the Centers for Disease Control and the Department of Health and Human Services, or those produced by a reputable national organization, such as the Guttmacher Institute (for reproductive and sexual health) to demonstrate the scope and severity of the problem. FedStats.gov is a helpful resource for finding rates from the federal government. Be careful not to use prevalence rates from articles that cite the information; these are referred to as secondary sources and you will want to use primary sources. Another source to avoid is websites of special interest groups, as information presented may be biased toward a particular viewpoint.

Another critical part of this first part of the literature review is to introduce the nature of the problem. For example, one of the authors has written about and studied child sexual abuse treatment. In the introduction section to these articles and chapters, she typically summarizes the symptoms that children who have been sexually abused may suffer at both the short- and long-term. Although unsettling, this information provides evidence that the topic is worthy of focus. As the introduction to your topic will only take a page or so, you should limit your efforts when pursuing this part of the literature review. One of the authors learned this lesson when she wrote her dissertation proposal on the risk factors associated with adolescent pregnancy. She relentlessly tracked down all the research she could find on the consequences of teenage pregnancy and becoming a parent in terms of educational and income status and the impact on the cognitive, social, and emotional impact on the child. Although this is important research, she lost sight of the fact that these consequences only needed to be outlined briefly to convey that adolescent pregnancy was important to study. She spent far too much literature review time and effort on the consequences of adolescent pregnancy when she should have been working more productively on the antecedents, or risk factors, that lead to adolescent pregnancy, which was the actual topic of her dissertation.

Along these lines, you can limit or carve out the literature, in some way being explicit about this when you write the literature review. Just because some areas have received a lot of study doesn't mean you need to address every facet of the research. For example, if you are interested in group treatment for sexual abuse survivors, you should focus on group treatment with this population, rather than examine every study that has to do with survivors of sexual abuse. In other words, the main part of the literature search should have to do with the actual topic of your research.

Formulating Key Terms. When formulating search terms, it is helpful to consider synonyms in terms of each category of your research. These might include the characteristics of the participants, the type of study, the intervention, and the outcome. For example, consider a study on a program for preventing pregnancy in teens who are already parents. Synonyms for teenage parents are *adolescent parents*, *adolescent* (or *teen*) *pregnancy*, or *adolescent* (or *teen*) *childbearing*. A synonym for pregnancy prevention with teen parents is *secondary pregnancy prevention*. Other terms for the outcome are *repeat* or *subsequent childbearing*. Intervention research can also be called *treatment outcome research, controlled research, experimental research*, or *evaluation*. These are all important terms for you to include in your Terminology Worksheet,

Using Library Databases. After you have brainstormed key words, it is time to use the expertise of a research librarian. It is common for an information specialist to be assigned to a social work program. This research librarian can help create search strings for each of the databases you are interested in searching. They will amplify your search terms by combining them with Boolean operators appropriate to each database. (Boolean operators are special instructions that clarify the search task for a given database.) Because social work is a diverse, interdisciplinary field, it potentially uses a variety of electronic databases as noted in Summary Content 3.1.

> **Summary Content 3.1.**
>
> DATABASES THAT MAY BE RELEVANT FOR SOCIAL WORK RESEARCH TOPICS
>
> 1. **Medline/PubMed**: biomedical and health sciences, especially if student research has to do with health or mental health
>
> 2. **Cumulative Index to Nursing and Allied Health Literature** (CINAHL): nursing
>
> 3. **PsychInfo** (Psychological Abstracts): psychology
>
> 4. **Social Services Abstracts:** social work, human services, and related areas, including social welfare, social policy, and community development
>
> 5. **Social Work Abstracts:** social work and other related journals on a variety of social work topics
>
> 6. **Dissertation Abstracts Online:** dissertations and some theses

You will not necessarily use all the databases listed here. In fact, it is quite possible you may include others that are relevant to your topic. For example, if your project involves older adults, then you would likely include *AgeLine*.

Application of Key Terms to Databases. This section involves the systematic application of key terms to each database. Written here are the steps to fill out the worksheet that allows you to do this. A sample of the complete worksheet is included on the topic of mental health treatment with military families.

1. *Enter the search terms and correct Boolean operators for each database.*
2. *Record the number of "hits," or the number of articles that come up when you put in the terms for each database. If you are inundated with "hits" (let's say more than 200), your search terms may be too broad. On the other hand, you may have no hits on the various databases or very few; in this situation, there may not be studies in the area you have chosen, but another possibility is that you have not included the appropriate search terms or you may have made your terms too narrow. A revised version of the terms may lead to finding more studies.*
3. *Screen the titles and abstracts of the study.*

Typically at this point you may screen out articles that do not fit your criteria just by skimming the title and the abstract of studies. See Summary Content 3.2 for a description of the four different types of articles you will encounter.

4. *Download articles that seem to fit the criteria for your literature review. Use interlibrary loan (ILL) to get the articles not available by download.*

When thinking about which articles to collect, students often shy away from using their university ILL services, preferring the convenience of downloadable articles. As discussed in Chapter Three, relying on downloadable articles means you limit the information you receive and may result in a biased review.

Summary Content 3.2.

TYPES OF ARTICLES

1. Reviews

We have talked about high-quality reviews, such as systematic reviews and meta-analyses. You will also run across articles that present basic reviews of the literature on a particular topic. Although subject to bias, these more general reviews can be helpful in offering an overview of a topic and providing you with a list of studies that have already been done in your area.

2. Theoretical Articles

As the name suggests, a theoretical article may discuss the theory underlying a topic or the application of theory to a population or problem. The student project we have been following about spirituality interventions in a community mental health agency used "Advances in the Conceptualization and Measurement of Religion and Spirituality: Implications for Physical and Mental Health Research" (Hill & Pargament, 2003) as a theoretical article.

3. Quantitative Articles

Quantitative studies, at their most basic level, involve numbers. They assess groups of people in ways that produce numerical data. Large sample sizes, standardized measurement instruments, and attempts to obtain random samples characterize quantitative studies. Any *intervention research* falls under the category of quantitative study.

4. Qualitative Studies

Qualitative studies are those that involve narration and textual data rather than numbers. They seek to obtain depth of information rather than breadth. They are characterized by small sample size, typically focus groups or individual face-to-face interviews, and are not concerned with generalizability of results to the greater population.

In the student project we have been following, "Exploring the Consumer's and Provider's Perspective on Service Quality in Community Mental Health Care" (2004) is what is called a *mixed-method* piece of research, meaning it has both quantitative and qualitative aspects.

Both quantitative and qualitative articles have a recognizable format that includes a methods section and a findings or results section. If you can't find a methods section or a findings/results section in the article that you are reviewing, it is probably a review or theoretical article rather than a quantitative or qualitative article.

Often students ask how many references are required. Although this may be dictated by your instructor's requirements, your literature review should be as comprehensive as possible, as long as it is also focused on your topic area. The literature should also be recent. Having a lot of references that go back before the last decade (unless they are seminal works on the topic) may outdate your review.

After you have screened out articles from reading the titles and abstracts, you are left with those that you need to look at in full-text. Note how the number of screened titles, downloaded articles, and articles retrieved through ILL match the number of hits on each search. Keeping a chart (*see* Example 3.1 below and Project Development Worksheet 3.1) helps ensure that you are conducting a thorough search. It is also a document that can be incorporated into your final paper to demonstrate that you have followed a standardized process for finding relevant articles.

Example 3.1.

DATABASE SEARCH (TOPIC: MENTAL HEALTH TREATMENT OF MILITARY FAMILIES)

DATABASE	SEARCH TERMS	QUALIFIERS	NO. OF HITS	NO. SCREENED OUT AFTER READING TITLES AND ABSTRACTS	NO. DOWNLOADED	NO. ILL
PsycInfo	Military and (spouse and child*or famil*) and (counsel* or treat* or intervention)	English Peer-reviewed empirical 1994–2009	48	40	6	2
Social Services Abstracts	Military and (spouse and child*or famil*) and (counsel* or treat* or intervention)	N/A	66	63	2	1
CINAHL+	Military and (spouse and child*or famil*) and (counsel* or treat* or intervention)	Peer-reviewed research articles	66	53	7	6
Academic Search Complete	Military and (spouse and child*or famil*) and (counsel* or treat* or intervention)	Peer-reviewed journal articles	36	27	9	0
Medline/ PubMed	Military and (spouse and child*or famil*) and (counsel* or treat* or intervention)	N/A	52	42	8	2
Social Work Abstracts	Military and (spouse and child*or famil*) and (counsel* or treat* or intervention)	Peer-reviewed	4	3	1	0
Consumer Health Complete	Military and famil* and (counsel* or treatment)	English	19	17	2	0

Project Development Worksheet 3.1.

DATABASE SEARCH (TOPIC)

DATABASE	SEARCH TERMS	QUALIFIERS	NO. OF HITS	NO. SCREENED OUT BASED ON ABSTRACT AND TITLE	NO. DOWN-LOADED	NO. REQUESTED FROM ILL
PsycInfo						
Social Services Abstracts						
CINAHL						
Social Work Abstracts						
Dissertation Abstracts						

5. *Read the articles and find other relevant studies.*

You will find that many of the research articles you download or order from ILL have varying degrees of usefulness. Some articles, upon closer examination, are off your topic area and are not useful for your review. But other articles will not only offer important information, they will lead you to other important articles that you will want to obtain. Indeed, you often find more relevant articles through this "snowball technique" (Ridley, 2008) than through database searches.

Step Two: Reading the Literature

You can easily become overwhelmed by the amount of information you collect for your literature review to the point that you can forget what you have read and what you have not! This section provides an organizing framework to help you funnel the information you find in articles into a cohesive literature review. We will also teach you in this section how to read research and critically appraise articles so that you can report on the state of the research and how your research can address previous studies' limitations.

Organizing Framework. The organizing framework presented here consists of three parts (adapted from Ridley, 2008):

1. an introduction
2. a discussion of the historical context of the problem and relevant theories
3. an analysis of the previous research on the topic
4. culminating in the gaps of the research and the need for your study

As you read articles, you should immediately jot down some ideas about how they may fit into these sections, which are detailed further in Summary Content 3.3 and provides room for you to write in your own notes regarding your project. Without a way to organize the material you are reading, it is easy to become overwhelmed and spend a lot of effort reading and rereading articles, which is an inefficient use of your time. By having this framework in mind, you can easily weed out the studies that do not belong and jot notes about what to do when you uncover information in relevant studies. In this way, you are reading studies with a purpose in mind, which will greatly contribute to the actual writing of the review. Remember to put the author's last name and the year of the article/book when you write notes and put in quotes and provide a page number for any material you have transcribed directly. In this way, you can guard against plagiarism and can trace back to the articles you have used. Taking the extra time to do this is important because tracking down page numbers and trying to find where you read what later can take up hours of unnecessary time.

Summary Content 3.3.

HOW TO ORGANIZE A LITERATURE REVIEW

SECTION OF LITERATURE REVIEW[1]	YOUR LITERATURE REVIEW
Introduction (Statement of the Problem) • Key terms and concepts are defined • Establishes the scope and significance of the problem you are studying, substantiated with data from a reliable primary source, such as a federal agency.	
LITERATURE REVIEW PROPER	
Historical Context • Statement of the historical context of the problem and its study	
Theories • Discussion of theories involved in the study of this topic	
Presentation and Analysis of Previous Related Research	

Source: Adapted from Ridley (2008)

Reviewing Research Studies. A critical piece of becoming conversant in your topic area is to review in detail the research studies related to your topic with a chart similar to the one offered below (*see* Example 3.2). Although admittedly time-consuming, going through the process of deconstructing the articles will help you understand the literature in an in-depth way. It will also help you write your literature review because you will be able to see the themes that emerge from content analysis of the categories. For example, you may, on the basis of such a review, decide to organize your studies in a matrix by their purpose, their theoretical orientation (such as ego psychology), or their research designs. An added benefit of such a review is that it can make you feel much more confident about reading academic literature. A final advantage is that the table produced from this effort can become part of the paper. You will find that many published literature reviews have similar charts included.

Example 3.2.

RESEARCH ARTICLE SUMMARY—TOPIC: COLLEGE PREPARATION PROGRAMS FOR LOW-INCOME AND ETHNIC MINORITY STUDENTS

AUTHOR(S) (YEAR) PURPOSE AND HYPOTHESES	RESEARCH DESIGN SAMPLING INFORMATION (DEMOGRAPHIC INFORMATION, SAMPLING TECHNIQUE)	MEASURES	RESULTS	LIMITATIONS
Engle et al. (2003) Purpose: to provide an intervention to academically at-risk students in form of counseling (group and ind.), and required study time	• Quasi-experimental • *n* = 91 participants • Academically at risk–on probation (GPA between 1.25 and 2.0) • Midsized comprehensive university • Those on probation after F09 were sent info on program—registration form and appt needed • Mostly White and female with less than 30 credits	• IV: program membership • DV: Grade point average (GPA) Attrition—student that did not return following semester • LASSI—study skills measure • Rosenberg—self-esteem measure	• 69% of program students were in good academic standing compared to 43% control • 55% of participants in the program returned to school vs. 28% control • GPA increased overall in those in the program • Semester after intervention: 72% vs. 56% control had GPA above 2.0 after semester after intervention	• Unable to determine causality Attention from counselors vs. actual counseling session • Was no self-report increase of study skills • Random assignment was not available • Participant mortality
Grant-Vallone et al. (2004) Purpose: To examine the relationship among self-esteem, family support, peer support, and using programs that are available and academic and social adjustment and commitment to college	• Two surveys (demographics and experiences of support services) mailed out to juniors and seniors involved in a college support program, requirements for programs were financially disadvantaged or first generation • 118 responses for survey one • 73 responses for survey two • 76% female, 24% male • average age: 32 years old	• Paper survey Predictor variables: • self-esteem • student adjustment • social support • program support and utilization Outcome variables: • attachment and commitment	• High level of academic adjustment and motivation was reported • Fairly high levels of social adjustment, but less satisfied with social environment on campus • High level of satisfaction of being in college • Support of specific programs helps in success in college career, Example of services: • academic, personal life, mentoring	• Small sample size and from one university • Based on self-report surveys

Study	Method/Sample	Findings	Limitations

Inkelas et al. (2007)
 	
Purpose: To examine the role of Living/learning (L/L) programs in the experience of the academic and social transition to college for first generation college students.
	• 33 post-secondary institutions in U.S. and DC
	• $n = 1335$ first-generation students, freshman or sophomore
	• Random sample of students in L/L program
	• Matched sample for control group-gender, race/ethnicity, SES
	• Internet survey with 258 items in 40-item sets
	• Perceived ease of academic transition
	• Perceived ease with:
	  • communicating with instructors outside of class
	  • finding academic help
	  • forming study groups
	  • perceived ease of social transition to college
	  • getting to know others in the residence hall
	  • making new friends
	  • getting along with roommates
		• L/L programs are beneficial for first-generation students
		• Those in L/L program were more likely to perceive easier academic and social transition to college
			• Student age was 17 to 22, and a lot of first-generation college students are older and start at a community college opposed to a 4-year university
			• Study was administered to those still in program, and the full effect of the program may not be realized

Oseguera et al. (2009) Purpose: to show the first and third-year experiences for students who are receiving the scholarship opposed to those who are not.	• Second year (2001–2002) • Hispanic recipients of the Gates Millennium Scholarship (GMS) • Control group-students that applied for scholarship but were not chosen to receive it. • $n = 375$ eligible respondents to survey • Mostly of Mexican American origin • Survey at end of first year and third year. Selected for profile: • pre-college factors and pull factors • initial commitments • college academic and social experiences • cognitive and noncognitive outcomes • final commitments	• A similar rate of attendance for recipients and nonrecipients for first year • By the third year the recipients had more positive college outcomes that nonrecipients	• No information on Latino subgroups • Students attended all types of college (public vs. private) • No information that shows that receiving the scholarship allows the student to participate in college life more • No information on college completion rates

Reading and organizing your literature is a critical step in the research process. The more thorough this process is, the better your overall project will be. Use Project Development Worksheet 3.2 below to organize the literature for your project and then refer back to the worksheet as you begin to write your literature review. We added a column for you to note where you might cite the article when you write your literature review and other sections of your research project. Following Project Development Worksheet 3.2 are multiple choice questions testing your knowledge.

Project Development Worksheet 3.2.

LITERATURE REVIEW ORGANIZATION

AUTHOR(S) (YEAR) PURPOSE AND HYPOTHESES THEORETICAL ORIENTATION	RESEARCH DESIGN SAMPLING INFORMATION (DEMOGRAPHIC INFORMATION, SAMPLING TECHNIQUE)	MEASURES	RESULTS	LIMITATIONS	USED WHERE IN YOUR WRITE-UP

Exercise 3.1.

TEST YOUR SKILLS

Vignette/Scenario # 1: Marcus

Marcus, a first-year MSW student, is considering topics for his research proposal assignment and thinks he might want to do a research project on fatherhood. He has reviewed several articles that he has used for papers in other courses to identify the gaps in the literature. Below are excerpts from a few of the articles he has reviewed.

Article 1: Families and incarceration: An ecological approach

"The broad ecological perspective adopted by this study also recognizes that the father's family system is embedded in a sociocultural network that stigmatizes individuals in the criminal justice system (Arditti et al., 2005). The framework of responsible or active fathering, which has guided much recent father involvement research, has not yet been refined for such marginal families. As Arditti et al. (2005) suggest, it is unclear how the notion of responsible fathering applies to the difficult situation of father identity construction and father involvement for incarcerated fathers."

Article 2: Fathering behind bars in English prisons: Imprisoned fathers' identity and contact with their children

"What this group of fathers had in common was a history of complex couple relationships: the majority of the men in this sample had never been married to the mother of their child. Divorced, separated, cohabiting, and casual dating relationships were the norm. The study has shown that father–child visitation is related to pre- and in-prison partnership quality but that imprisonment also imposes an additional strain on these relationships. Some men had poor relationships with the mother before they came to prison, but for some the imprisonment aggravated or provoked a deterioration of the relationship. Both pre-prison couple status and the relationship quality before and since imprisonment were associated with whether the father was visited by the child or not. In essence a good relationship with the child's mother is usually critical for maintaining access to children (Clarke et al., 2005, p. 239)."

Article 3: Low-income fathers and "responsible fatherhood" programs: A qualitative investigation of participants' experiences "Although this study provides insight into low-income, nonresidential fathers' perspectives on the services of a particular RF program, there also are limitations that leave other relevant and important questions unanswered. For example, because little demographic data were collected from participants, we are unable to extensively describe the participants' family relationships, particularly the nature of their relationships with the mothers of their children. Recent research revealed that many parents in supposedly "single-parent" families are either romantically involved or cohabiting, especially around the time of a child's birth. Additional research on the fathering experiences of low-income men involved in a variety of relationship and family constellations is an important next step. Such work would hold particular implications for program development and service delivery, because the needs of fathers who have and have not continued romantic involvements with the mothers of their children are likely to differ considerably (Anderson et al., 2002, p. 154)."

1. Which article would you choose if you were looking for a theoretical framework to guide your study about incarcerated fathers and children?

   a. Article 1 (An ecological approach)
   b. Article 2 (Imprisoned fathers' identity and contact with their children)
   c. Article 3 (A qualitative investigation of participants' experiences)
   d. None provides a good theoretical framework
   e. All would probably provide an equally good theoretical framework

2. Low-income fathers and "responsible fatherhood" programs: A qualitative investigation of participants' experiences. Based on the title of this study, which of the following statements would you say is true?

   a. This study can be generalized to other low-income fathers.
   b. The study used a quasi-experimental research design.
   c. This study established a cause-and-effect relationship between the income of fathers and their level of responsibility for their children.
   d. None of the above

3. The statement, "Father–child visitation is related to pre- and in-prison partnership quality," is an example of. . .

   a. hypothesis
   b. operational definition
   c. theory
   d. social research question
   e. concept
   f. none of the above

4. The statement, "The broad ecological perspective adopted by this study also recognizes that the father's family system is embedded in a sociocultural network that stigmatizes individuals in the criminal justice system," is an example of. . .

   a. hypothesis
   b. operational definition
   c. theory
   d. social research question
   e. concept
   f. none of the above

5. "It is unclear how the notion of responsible fathering applies to the difficult situation of father identity construction and father involvement for incarcerated fathers." Is an example of. . .

   a. hypothesis
   b. operational definition
   c. theory
   d. social research question
   e. concept
   f. none of the above

6. Which statement best describes the practice implications for Article 2: *Fathering behind bars in English prisons: Imprisoned fathers' identity and contact with their children.*

   a. Children can benefit from programs to help incarcerated fathers improve their relationships with the mothers of their children.
   b. Incarcerated fathers should be encouraged to marry the mothers of their children.
   c. Children's visitation with their fathers should be limited to those families where there is a good relationship between the parents.
   d. We need more information about the pre-prison couple status and relationship quality before we can make any statements about practice implications.

Sources: Anderson, E.A., Kohler, J.K. & Letiecq, B.L. (2002). Low-income fathers and "responsible fatherhood" programs: A qualitative investigation of participants' experiences. *Family Relations*, 51 (2), 148–155.
Clarke, L., et al. (2005). Fathering behind bars in english prisons: Imprisoned fathers' identity and contact with their children. *Fathering*, 3 (3), 221–241.

Step Three: Writing the Literature Review

If you have used a framework, such as Ridley's (2008) above, writing the literature review may not be so intimidating. You may have already organized your reading around the salient sections necessary to a strong literature review. Simply thinking about your review in this way can help reduce the anxiety of figuring out what should be put down.

Structuring Your Literature Review. When you begin the literature review proper, it is often helpful to describe how you will organize your writing so the reader knows what to expect and can follow the logic of your argument. While you are writing, begin using headings and subheadings—a hallmark of successful graduate school papers—to help you structure your literature review, recognizing that the organizing system may change over time. Students sometimes create their own formatting versions of headings and subheadings, but the APA reference manual has guidelines (*see also* website listing at the end of this chapter).

The use of an outline, such as Example 3.3, to guide writing is often recommended. However, for some students, writing from an outline is helpful, whereas for others, particularly those who don't discover their organizational system until they are well into writing narrative, outlines are onerous tasks. Although some people find it easier to outline what they have already written, discovering as they go along whether their writing and the points made follow a logical progression, we encourage you at a minimum to use the general outline that we presented in the summary content on organizing your literature review above.

Example 3.3.

LITERATURE REVIEW OUTLINES

Topic Outline Example #1: Examining the Effects of a Group Intervention for Homeless Women living in Shelters

I. Homelessness
   a. General stats
   b. Stats of homeless families
   c. Common characteristics of homeless women
      i. Trauma
      ii. Stress
      iii. SA
   d. Impacts of those characteristics on well-being
      i. Relationships with self/others
      ii. Environmental mastery
      iii. Life purpose
II. Group Therapy
   a. Definition
   b. Effective uses
      i. Range of issues
      ii. Populations
         1. gender
         2. voluntary/involuntary
III. Homeless population and group intervention research
   a. Trauma
   b. Stress
   c. SA
IV. Dearth of research on homelessness and overall psychological well-being
   a. Overview of psychological well-being as multidimensional construct
      i. Ryff construct
   b. Question and hypothesis

Topic Outline # 2: The Relationship Between Rape and Substance Abuse and Use on College Campuses

I. Introduction

II. Definition of Rape
   A. Prevalence in the United States
   B. Prevalence in Virginia
   C. Negative consequences of rape
      1. Pregnancy
      2. Sexually transmitted disease
      3. Physical injuries
      4. Emotional distress
   a. Posttraumatic Stress Disorder
   b. Depression
      5. Lack of reporting

```
III. Substance Use
    A. Alcohol
        1. Definition of binge drinking
        2. College environment
    B. Illegal drugs
        1. Marijuana
        2. Cocaine
        3. Ecstasy
        4. Polydrug use

IV. Effects of Alcohol on Sexual Assault
    A. Alcohol Myopia Theory
        1. Cognitive functioning
        2. Interpreting cues
    B. Resistance
        1. Planning escape
        2. Resisting verbally
        3. Resisting physically
    C. Communication
        1. Verbal
        2. Nonverbal

V. Connection to Social Work
    A. Prevalence of sexual assault
        1. Emotional response
            a. Depression
            b. Posttraumatic Stress Disorder
        2. Health issues
            a. Pregnancy
            b. Sexually transmitted disease
            c. Injuries
    B. Substance abuse
        1. Pre-assault drinking
        2. Post-assault drinking
    C. Rape prevention programs
        1. College campus
        2. Community
VI. Conclusion
```

Reviewing and Integrating the Research. The bulk of the literature review centers on research studies related to your topic. Indeed, as an introduction to this section, you can present your search terms and the databases used, referencing Project Development Worksheet 3.1 that you conducted above. As you discuss the studies that have been done, refrain from simply lifting the information from the table you have filled out and providing this level of detail to the reader. This essentially represents an annotation of each study, one after the other. The problem with this approach is that it does not offer sufficient integration and synthesis of the literature.

Integration and synthesis of the literature is challenging. Often you will find some studies in your area that report statistically significant positive results and others that do not. (*See* Chapter Nine for more discussion on statistical significance.) Additionally, there are a variety of outcomes typically provided in studies. For example, interventions for adolescent parents may try to positively influence teen parenting behavior, teen psychosocial adjustment, educational and employment attainment, and repeat pregnancy. Synthesizing a variety of outcomes is hard because when researchers report statistically significant findings for some dependent variables they included in their studies but not others, how are you to make heads or tails of this variation? Example 3.4 shows how one student synthesized the literature to build an argument for the need for interventions for refugee minors:

Example 3.4.

TWO EXAMPLES OF INTEGRATION OF THE LITERATURE FROM ONE STUDENT PAPER

Note how the theme is supported by three different articles

There is a large amount of research supporting the prevalence of psychological and behavioral issues refugee and immigrant children are faced with after migrating to a new country (Ellis, MacDonald, Lincoln, & Cabral, 2008; Derluyn & Broekaert, 2007; Heptinstall, Sethna, & Taylor, 2004).

Note how a series of statements, supported by many articles, lead to one conclusive statement

- Many studies have been conducted examining the effectiveness of various therapies and interventions in the treatment of refugee minors who experience emotional and behavioral disorders (Silove, Steel, Bauman, Chey, & McFarlane, 2007) such as cognitive-behavioral therapy (Hinton, Pham, Tran, Safren, Otto, & Pollack, 2004; Paunovic & Ost, 2000).
- Children migrating without the support and protection of a primary caregiver are at even greater risk for emotional well-being (Derluyn & Broekaert, 2007).
- Because of their exposure to traumatic events and post-migration stresses a high percentage of unaccompanied children suffer from Posttraumatic Stress Disorder, (Hepinstall et al., 2004; Khamis, 2005).
- Ellis et al. (2008) suggests that because of these high numbers there is an urgent need for research to study post-resettlement factors that are involved in "the development and maintenance of these mental health problems in child and adolescent refugees," (p. 185).
- **The implications, therefore, for social service and mental health workers to have some knowledge and preparedness in working with unaccompanied minors are great.**

Synthesis can also be challenged by the fact that studies often have very different methodologies in terms of research designs, sampling procedure, and sample size. Without a systematic analysis, it is impossible to factor in all these variables simultaneously. In truth, the optimal way to synthesize studies is to conduct a meta-analysis and to perform statistics that enable you to quantitatively summarize the results. We discuss this topic further in Chapter Four. However, such a methodology is beyond the scope of a Bachelor's or Masters student. This raises an important question: If the means to optimally analyze and integrate the existing research are beyond your level, then what should you do?

We emphasize again the importance of including systematic reviews/meta-analyses in your literature review. If this work of synthesis has already been done in your area, then including these findings in your literature review will be much more meaningful than your embarking on a review of this literature with inferior methods.

Also, your Project Development Worksheet 3.2 that organizes the research studies can enable you to find themes in studies, so that you can write about patterns in sampling, research designs, results, and weaknesses of studies (Pan, 2008). At the same time, you can further discuss where there are contradictions in the literature and inconsistent results. These may bolster your argument that your study is worth consideration.

Micro-Issues and Technicalities. As well as the global issues attendant to writing, there are also the finer details: paraphrasing other people's ideas; using paragraphs; and transitioning effectively to enhance the flow of the reading experience. Remember, your goal is to make it easy for the reader to follow your argument. Rather than present your reader with a set of ideas that may or may not be connected, take the time to explain your thought process in straightforward and simple steps. In this way, your reader will have an easier time following your work.

Paraphrasing. Because so much of a literature review involves building on and positioning yourself among the research tradition on a topic, you have to describe the ideas and work that have gone before you and reference these works properly. Otherwise, you may be guilty of plagiarizing— presenting ideas and statements as your own without crediting the correct source. Recall that if you use more than three words in a row of another person's writing, then you have to not only cite that person, you also have to put quotes around that material and provide the page number of the passage from the original document.

As much as possible, it is important to paraphrase what other people have written, rather than quoting them exactly. Students often feel insecure about their own writing. When they come across an elegant turn of phrase, they much prefer to use the authors' words than rely on what they believe to be their own clumsy language. An occasional brief quotation may enhance the level of articulation in your own work, but a literature review that is strung together by quotes made by other people is not only difficult to read, it conveys the author's lack of understanding of the material being presented.

Paragraphs. It is much better to write short paragraphs than to have a whole page of text that is unbroken. A solid block of text is daunting to the reader and almost always has more than one idea embedded within it. At the same time, avoid one and two-sentence paragraphs and strive to include at least three sentences, if not more. Each paragraph should flow from a topic sentence that identifies and helps focus on a particular topic for that paragraph. You should be able to identify a topic sentence or a theme for each paragraph. See if you can identify a topic sentence in some of the paragraphs from your literature review in Project Development Worksheet 3.3.

Project Development Worksheet 3.3. PARAGRAPHS	
PARAGRAPH	TOPIC SENTENCE

Transitions. For the reader to follow the logic of your arguments and how one idea builds on the next, transitions are required. Transitions are cues to the reader that the idea they are about to read relates to something else in your paper. They help create a flow of ideas, in which one idea naturally leads into next. Transitions occur between sentences, as well as paragraphs, and different sections of the literature review. Use Project Development Worksheet 3.4 to ensure the apt use of transitions in your own work.

Project Development Worksheet 3.4.
Look at one paragraph in the literature review you are preparing. Write three transitional words that you used between the sentences.   1.   2.   3.
Look at three paragraphs of your literature review. Write the transitional words between your paragraphs.   1.   2.   3.
Look at different sections of your literature review. Write the transitional sentence between three sections of your literature review.   1.   2.   3.

References. Another critical piece to writing the literature review involves citing other researchers and authors and providing reference to their work. There are many important reasons for this practice (Ridley, 2008, p. 97):

1. Acknowledging and showing respect for other researchers' contributions to the field
2. Establishing the location of your work within a particular field
3. Providing justification and support for your assertions and arguments
4. Creating a niche for your own research by showing how you wish to extend or challenge previous studies
5. Comparing, contrasting, and evaluating the work others have done in the field
6. Illustrating your own understanding of the subject matter by demonstrating that you have read widely and are able to select relevant information to contextualize your own research
7. Enabling readers to track down your source texts easily if they wish to find out more information
8. Allowing the accuracy of your work to be checked
9. Avoiding plagiarism

Summary Content 3.4 offers some general guidelines for referencing information in your literature review.

Summary Content 3.4.
REFERENCING HOW TO'S
1. Rely on primary sources: Make sure that you are not getting your information from websites of special interest groups or secondary sources but, rather, the governmental agencies or the researchers that have actually collected the data.   2. Be recent (center on the last 5 years or so, with the exception of seminal works).   3. Be comprehensive.   4. Rely heavily on the academic literature (peer-reviewed journal articles).

To conclude the chapter, we have included a checklist in Project Development Worksheet 3.5 for preparation of the literature review. *This checklist can be used to check your own work and to use for peer-review of classmates' literature reviews.*

Project Development Worksheet 3.5.
CHECKLIST FOR PREPARING A LITERATURE REVIEW

- Does the introduction establish the importance of the topic and the problem being studied (U.S. prevalence statistics and the consequences of the problem) using up-to-date references?
- Are new terms defined?
- Is there a stated organization to the literature review?
- Are there subheadings that follow the organization of the literature review?
- Does the author explore systematic reviews and meta-analyses that have been done as an initial discussion?
- Are other studies covered logically and do they flow from the initial discussion?
- Is there sufficient summarizing of the research literature rather than "a recipe card index" approach?
- Does the literature review seem comprehensive of the studies?
- Does the literature review include updated work?
- Are there good transitions between paragraphs?
- Are there good transitions between sentences?
- What is the quality of the references?

CONCLUSION

This chapter has explored the crucial role of the literature review for a research project. It also has discussed the way in which you search the literature and analyze studies for integration. Although the literature review can be one of the most difficult pieces of the paper to write, there are certain suggestions that we have offered that will make the process go more efficiently and lead to a literature review that summarizes the scholarly discussion in your area and paves the way for your research. In the next chapter, we discuss systematic reviews, a more sophisticated evolution of the literature review. Through finding and understanding systematic reviews, you will usually find that you can shortcut a lot of literature searching and reviewing and instead rely on the findings of relevant systematic reviews in your own literature review.

WEBSITES

Purdue Online Writing Lab
http://owl.english.purdue.edu/owl/resource/560/24/
APA style
http://apastyle.org/
Literature reviews
http://www.unc.edu/depts/wcweb/handouts/literature_review.html

SYSTEMATIC REVIEWS

4

A *systematic review* aims to comprehensively locate and synthesize the research that bears on a particular question. It uses organized, transparent, and replicable procedures at each step in the process. This chapter will detail and provide examples of systematic reviews and how you are to locate and understand them. We will describe how they can be used as part of your literature review, a topic that has been elaborated upon in Chapter Three. This chapter will also discuss meta-analysis (the synthesis of quantitative findings) and meta-synthesis (the synthesis of qualitative findings). Because meta-synthesis represents a valid research project that can be completed by research students, we will also detail the procedures for this kind of study.

HOW ARE SYSTEMATIC REVIEWS DIFFERENT FROM LITERATURE REVIEWS?

The most efficient way to begin your literature review is to seek out the systematic reviews that have been done in your area of interest. These will act to distill a large body of knowledge so that you can gain a sense of the current research status of your topic. But how do *systematic reviews* differ from the literature reviews included in your research proposals and the "research papers" that are requirements for other classes? "Research papers" for other classes and literature reviews involve the same process of researching the literature in a particular area. Summary Content 4.1 elaborates upon how literature reviews differ from *systematic reviews* in three essential ways: bias, transparency, and methods of synthesis.

META-ANALYSIS

Systematic reviews often contain a meta-analysis. A *meta-analysis* uses statistical methods to combine *quantitative* results from multiple studies to produce a single, overall summary of empirical knowledge on a given topic. As a result, meta-analysis is a powerful tool that allows us to understand a body of research. If a systematic review lends itself to *combining* quantitative results of two or more primary studies, then it can (and often should) include meta-analysis. To combine studies quantitatively, it is necessary to obtain measures that are comparable across studies. For

Summary Content 4.1.

DIFFERENCES BETWEEN LITERATURE REVIEWS AND SYSTEMATIC REVIEWS/META-ANALYSES

PRACTICE	LITERATURE REVIEWS	SYSTEMATIC REVIEWS
Bias	Students rely on full-text articles rather than requesting nonavailable articles from their interlibrary loan service. Limited searches of different databases (e.g., only relying on *Social Work Abstracts*). As a result, "a convenience sample" of articles is collected.	Comprehensive search for articles to avoid publication bias (studies with positive results are more likely to be published).
Transparency	Unknown how studies were located and selected and why certain ones were included in the discussion and others left out.	Lays out a detailed protocol in advance so readers can track the procedures and process of the study.
Method of synthesis	Rely on vote counting (dividing statistical significance of studies into positive, null, and negative results, and the group with most "votes" is "the winner"). This fails to take into account sample size (statistical significance increases with sample size), and it can't handle the complexity of multiple outcome measures across studies (e.g., when studies involve depression, anxiety, behavioral acting out, and other domains of functioning). Can't determine the samples or types of treatments or their delivery that contribute to outcomes.	Quantitative synthesis (meta-analysis) pools all the studies together quantitatively for each outcome measure, adjusting for sample size, and telling us the strength or magnitude of the relationship. The use of moderator analysis to assess the influence of participant, treatment, or study design characteristics that influence the outcomes.

example, suppose we had a set of studies that measured distance in a variety of ways—miles, number of footsteps, hours traveled, and so forth. To make sense of these studies collectively, we would need to make the various measurements compatible with each other. This is sometimes referred to as standardization. To obtain such comparable or standardized measures across studies, researchers use an *effect size* (ES). Effect sizes tell us the strength or magnitude of the relationships between variables. In other words, ES are statistical tools that allow comparison of different measures, like kilometers, hours traveled, and number of footsteps. The most commonly used effect size, used for studies that test intervention effects and report differences (e.g., between treated and untreated groups) in terms of average scores of a scale used to assess a construct, is the *standardized mean difference* (SMD). The SMD, also known as *Cohen's d* (Cohen, 1969), is the mean difference divided by the pooled standard deviation of the two groups. Presented in Summary Content 4.2 are Cohen's (1988) standards for interpreting the SMD and whether it represents a small, medium, or large effect. More desirable is a large effect, but medium effects and even small effects can be important for social science research when results represent improvement in human suffering.

Summary Content 4.2.			
INTERPRETING EFFECT SIZES			
ES METRIC	SMALL EFFECT	MEDIUM EFFECT	LARGE EFFECT
SMD	0.2	0.5	0.8

A comparable process to *meta-analysis* (which is for *quantitative research*) exists for *qualitative* research. Called *meta-synthesis*, it is a recent methodology designed to systematically review and integrate results of primary qualitative studies that have been conducted on a particular topic using qualitative methods (Finfgeld, 2003; Sandelowski & Barroso, 2006). Meta-synthesis is also a valuable way to build knowledge in a particular area of study. By drawing on all the relevant studies at once, it may offer new interpretations of findings. Thus, the knowledge of a given subject may become more substantive than if only individual studies were examined (Finfgeld, 2003). Meta-syntheses have been undertaken in health-related areas and are most common in the field of nursing (*see*, for example, Yick [2008] and Nelson [2002]), but social work could also gain from such knowledge-building. Indeed, we believe that a meta-synthesis embedded within a systematic review is a viable student research project, and we will offer more detail about such a project later in this chapter.

HOW TO FIND SYSTEMATIC REVIEWS

Two international, interdisciplinary collaborations of scholars, policymakers, practitioners, and consumers are the go-to sources for high-quality systematic reviews, the Cochrane Collaboration and the Campbell Collaboration. The Cochrane Collaboration synthesizes results of studies on effects of interventions in health care. Your institution might have a subscription to this database; if so, it is best to access the database this way. The Campbell Collaboration synthesizes results of research on interventions in the fields of social care (education, social welfare, and crime and justice). Your institution may or may not have a subscription to The Campbell Collaboration, but accessing it through Google will still allow you to view and download the reviews.

As the Cochrane and Campbell Collaborations collect high-quality systematic reviews, these should be the first databases to search on your topic. If there are no reviews in the Cochrane and Campbell Collaboration databases related to your topic, then you can move on to other relevant academic databases, entering as your topic search terms "systematic review"/"meta-analysis." If you find one high-quality review that is exactly in your area, you may not need to go much further in locating individual studies. However, more commonly you will find related reviews rather than one that is completely on target for your topic. The following reviews in Example 4.1 show the kind of information they can provide, which are relevant for both practice and student research. In Project Development Worksheet 4.1, you are asked to locate systematic reviews on topics involving your project.

Example 4.1.

INFORMATION GLEANED FROM SYSTEMATIC REVIEWS

- Social information processing interventions are able to reduce aggressive and disruptive behavior in school-age children at about a 25% reduction over control groups (Wilson & Lipsey, 2006a, 2006b).
- Sex education programs do not have consistent effects on teenagers' sexual behavior, but abstinence-focused programs appear to increase pregnancy rates (Scher, Maynard, & Stagner, 2006).
- Approaches to improve parental involvement with children's school performance lead to a positive impact on academics, particularly reading (Nye, Turner, & Schwartz, 2006).
- Prison-based therapeutic communities are consistently effective in reducing drug use and recidivism, and correctional boot camps are not (Wilson, MacKenzie, & Mitchell, 2005; Mitchell, Wilson, & MacKenzie, 2006).
- Including nonoffending parents in treatment for their children's sexual abuse offers benefits for children's outcomes (Corcoran & Pillai, 2008).
- Welfare-to-work programs have had consistent, small effects on participants' employment and earnings in the United States (Smedslund et al., 2006).
- Case management for people with severe mental illness does not offer benefits over usual care in terms of improvements in mental state, social relations, or quality of life, and it increases rates of hospitalization (Marshall, Gray, Lockwood, & Green, 1998), whereas Assertive Community Treatment (a type of specialized, intensive case management) prevents hospitalization and is associated with higher client satisfaction than comparison care (Marshall & Lockwood, 1998).
- After court-mandated batterer intervention, official reports of domestic violence decreased but victim reports did not (Feder, Austin, & Wilson, 2008).
- Children in kinship foster care experience better outcomes in terms of behavioral development, mental health functioning, and placement stability than do children in non-kinship foster. However, the latter were more likely to be adopted and to utilize mental health services. Both groups of children had equivalent re-unification rates with biological parents (Winokur, Holtan, & Valentine, 2009).
- Programs for juvenile offenders to reduce recidivism are just as effective for minority as for majority youth (Lipsey, Wilson, & Soydan, 2003)

Project Development Worksheet 4.1.

LOCATING SYSTEMATIC REVIEWS FOR YOUR PROJECT

1. If you have a topic that is in the area of health or mental health, go to the Cochrane Collaboration website. Under search terms, type in your topic area and see the results.
   Write down the references that seem relevant to your topic:

2. If you have a topic that is related to social services, education, or criminal justice, then go to the Campbell Collaboration website. Go to each of the "libraries" for these groups and type in search terms or browse the topics on which reviews have been conducted.
   Write down the references that seem relevant to your topic:

Because systematic reviews can be difficult to read and understand, Summary Content 4.3 shows you how to find key information in a systematic review, followed by an example summary of one that was done by a student for her research topic on elderly depression (*see* Example 4.2). After that, Project Development Worksheet 4.2 is provided so that you can do a summary of a systematic review that is relevant to your research project.

Summary Content 4.3.

HOW TO FIND KEY INFORMATION IN SYSTEMATIC REVIEWS/META-ANALYSES
Note: Outline is in italics and regular print indicates directions.

Author and Purpose Find this information following the literature review and before the methods section.	Inclusion Criteria Typically at the start of the methods section.	Results (Main effect sizes and moderator analysis)	Limitations
• Report authors' last names and the date of the publication. • Paraphrase (if possible) the purpose of the systematic review or meta-analysis.	*Studies*: • Was the published literature the only focus or was there an attempt to also find the unpublished studies? • What kind of designs were included (typically either randomized, controlled trials only or randomized, controlled trials and quasi-experimental designs)? • Were there date parameters set on the search for studies? *Intervention* (if intervention research): • Theoretical framework of the intervention • What was the intervention compared to? *Participants*: • Target population for intervention *Outcomes*: • What measures were used to assess outcome (dependent variable)?	• *Total* N *of studies* included in the review (find in the results section) • *Main effect size* (find in results and/or discussion/ abstract) • Evaluate in terms of Cohen's framework for effect sizes. • Paraphrase what overall effect size means. *Moderator analysis:* Were there characteristics of the participants, the intervention, or the studies that influenced the effect size?	Note any limitations you encounter and include those that the author mentions in the discussion section.

Example 4.2.

SUMMARY OF SYSTEMATIC REVIEW

Reference: Mead, G.E., Morley, W., Campbell, P., Greig, C.A, McMurdo, M., & Lawlor, D.A. *Exercise for depression*. Cochrane Database of Systematic Reviews 2009, Issue 3. Art. No.: CD004366. DOI:10.1002/14651858.CD004366.pub4

Author/Purpose

Author: Mead, G.E., Morley, W., Campbell, P., Greig, C.A, McMurdo, M., & Lawlor, D.A.
Purpose: To determine whether exercise is effective in the treatment of clinical depression.

1. Participants:
Adult men and women (age 18+ years) with depression (as determined by criteria from original studies) except for postnatal depression.

Inclusion Criteria

2. Intervention:
Studies that compared exercise (any type) with either no treatment, placebo, or other type of inventions (pharmacotherapy, psychotherapy, or alternate intervention) OR studies that compared an intervention plus exercise with another intervention that did not include exercise.

3. Design:
Experimental, "allocation of participants to intervention and comparison groups is described as randomized." (p. 3)

Results

4. Outcome measures:
Depression symptoms at the end of treatment.
$N = 25$

Exercise is superior to no treatment and comparable to both cognitive therapy and antidepressants.

Whereas aerobic exercise was effective, mixing aerobic exercise with resistance training was even more powerful in combating depression.

Project Development Worksheet 4.2.
SUMMARIZING A SYSTEMATIC REVIEW
ARTICLE REFERENCE:

AUTHOR AND PURPOSE	INCLUSION CRITERIA	RESULTS (MAIN EFFECT SIZES AND MODERATOR ANALYSIS)	LIMITATIONS

By summarizing the available systematic reviews that relate to your topic, you will have no need to examine the individual studies that make up these reviews. (*See* Chapter Three). For example, one of the authors recently did a study on interventions for adolescent suicide. There were many reviews and meta-analyses that already related to this topic—namely, concerning self-harm and actual suicide—although a systematic review on only interventions for adolescents who were suicidal had not been conducted. Therefore, the literature review portion of her study read as follows with no need to locate and review individual studies (*see* Example 4.3):

Example 4.3.
WRITING SYSTEMATIC REVIEWS IN THE LITERATURE REVIEW: ADOLESCENT SUICIDE INTERVENTIONS

"A Cochrane Collaboration systematic review was conducted on interventions for people who had committed an act of self-harm (Hawton et al., 1999). Only randomized, controlled trials were included, and samples comprised both adults and adolescents. Results of the 23 primary studies were not analyzed separately for adolescents, and only two studies actually involved teen samples. The review concluded that there was 'insufficient evidence' to demonstrate the effectiveness of interventions for those who had committed acts of deliberate self-harm.

Another, more recent systematic review focused solely on mortality from suicide when psychosocial interventions were implemented with people who had committed self-harm (Crawford, Thomas, Khan, & Kulinskaya, 2007). Only randomized, controlled trials were included. There was no mention of whether samples were to be limited by age, so presumably studies with adolescents could be included. With these inclusion criteria, 18 trials were meta-analyzed. Results indicated that psychosocial interventions did not reduce suicide rates over control group conditions, which typically offered some care. Results were not provided separately for adolescents. One problem with 'completed suicide' as an outcome is that it is infrequent enough 'to limit is usefulness as an outcome measure … in spite of its obvious importance' (Tarrier , Taylor, & Gooding, 2008).

Another systematic review centered only on cognitive-behavioral interventions to reduce suicidal behavior (Tarrier et al., 2008). The researchers argued for including the spectrum of suicidal behavior to include 'completed suicides, suicide attempts, suicide intent and/or plans, and suicide ideation' as a possible continuum may lie 'from ideation, through intent and planning, to action' (Tarrier et al., 2008, p. 79). Only published experimental and quasi-experimental studies from 1980 were included. Seven of the 28 studies involved adolescent samples. Although the effect size for the studies involving adult samples was statistically significant, the effect size for the adolescent studies were not. Therefore, it appears that cognitive-behavioral interventions for suicidal youth was not effective; however, the sample size of seven studies was small.

More recently, a literature review was published on interventions for suicidal youth (Daniel & Goldston, 2009). Twelve published studies were included (five were quasi-experimental designs and seven were randomized controlled trials). Meta-analysis was not performed; each study was only discussed in terms of statistical significance. The conclusion of Daniel and Goldston (2009) was as follows:

… it appears that interventions for suicidal youth have been in general more successful at affecting aspects of service utilization and delivery (e.g., compliance with medical recommendations, aftercare utilization, reduced hospitalization, decreased time to outpatient appointments) than in reducing rates of suicide attempts per se (p. 259).

The authors complained about the diversity of outcomes in terms of suicide attempts, suicidal ideation, and severity of suicidal ideation in being able to determine the effectiveness of studies.

A final study of relevance here is a meta-analysis on psychotherapy for child and adolescent depression (Weisz, McCarty, & Valeri, 2006). Dissertations were included, along with the published research. Weisz et al. (2006) located 35 studies and found a small overall effect size for improvement of depression at posttest, but a negligible impact on suicidality."

This example demonstrates how the use of systematic reviews covers an area of knowledge in an in-depth way to set the context for your own study, without having to look into individual studies, a labor-intensive and time-consuming process. Of course, your ability to do this will depend on the availability of systematic reviews in your topic area.

STEPS IN A SYSTEMATIC REVIEW

As well as understanding systematic reviews and including them in your literature review, we also discussed that a meta-synthesis embedded within a systematic review makes a viable research project. The following meta-syntheses have been conducted by our students:

- Adolescent dating violence
- Latina breast cancer prevention
- Latina cervical cancer prevention

- Depression in the elderly
- Parents of children with autism-spectrum disorders
- Living with bipolar disorder

With these examples in mind, Project Development Worksheet 4.3 asks you to consider some topics that may be worthy of meta-synthesis, and Project Development Worksheet 4.4 helps you determine whether these topics are viable in terms of the number of qualitative studies available.

Project Development Worksheet 4.3.

POSSIBLE TOPICS FOR META-SYNTHESIS

Thinking about some of the research topics you named in Chapter Two, name the ones here that might lend themselves to qualitative study:
1.
2.
3.

Basically, a guideline is that a topic studied qualitatively will lend itself to systematic review if there are sufficient numbers of studies already collected. How many are sufficient? We would estimate that at least seven qualitative studies published on your topic are needed to conduct a meta-synthesis.

Project Development Worksheet 4.4.

DETERMINING TOPICS WITH SUFFICIENT STUDIES

Take one of the topics named above and run search terms for that topic (*see* Chapter Three) crossed with the term "qualitative" in a couple of different databases, such as Medline and Psychinfo. How many studies come up that seem to be the focus of your topic and are qualitative studies? _____
Does this topic seem to warrant study through meta-synthesis? _____

The systematic review process involves several stages. To help illustrate the stages, each one is accompanied by an example from the student meta-synthesis on the experience of elderly depression. Note that if you decide to conduct a meta-synthesis for your research project, these are the steps you would follow.

1. Develop a set of clearly formulated objectives and specific, answerable research questions or hypotheses.

Example of research question: How do older adults experience depression, and what is helpful for coping and recovery?

---

2. Form a review team that includes people with the diverse skills necessary (including substantive, methodological, and technical expertise).

Example: A group of three students in the advanced research sequence with the research instructor as advisor to the project.

3.	Create explicit inclusion and exclusion criteria that specify the problems or conditions, populations, interventions, settings, comparisons, outcomes, and study designs that will and will not be included in the review.

> *Example: The inclusion criteria for the research project on elderly depression was as follows:*
>   *A. Studies: qualitative studies*
>   *B. Participants: Older adults (defined as 60 years and older) with depression, determined either through self-report or clinical diagnosis.*

4.	Develop a written protocol that details in advance the procedures and methods to be used.

The methods section of the meta-synthesis stands as the protocol.

5.	In collaboration with information specialists, identify and implement a comprehensive and reproducible strategy to identify all relevant studies. This includes strategies to find unpublished studies.

> *Example: With the social work reference librarian and a specialist on the Medline databases, appropriate search terms and Boolean operatives were crafted for each relevant database.*

6.	Screen titles and abstracts to identify potentially relevant studies.

> *Example: The databases Ageline, CINAHL, Dissertation Abstracts, Dissertations and Theses, PubMed/Medline, Psych Info, Social Services, and Social Work were searched, yielding 402 potential studies.*

7.	Retrieve published and unpublished reports on potentially relevant studies.

> *Example: After looking at the titles and abstracts and eliminating repeated articles, 79 studies remained. These studies were downloaded or requested through the university's interlibrary loan service and divided among the research team to read through the whole article.*

8.	Determine whether each study meets the review's eligibility criteria. Two reviewers judge each study, resolve disagreements (sometimes with a third reviewer), and document their decisions. The reason that more than one person is involved in this process is to increase *reliability*. Reliability is discussed in Chapter Eight, but basically the idea here is that decisions should be made consistently. We will go to an example of a systematic review on cognitive-behavioral (CBT) interventions for parents who have physically abused their children to illustrate the point. One person on the team, if operating alone, may start to make certain decisions. For example, she may decide that CBT means that cognitive-oriented techniques, as well as basic behavioral techniques (the latter are called parent training) need to be included for a study to be part of the review. Another member of the team, if working independently, may decide that *either* parent training or more cognitively oriented treatment may be included. Thus, these team members will make different primary study selections based on their interpretation of what CBT means. That is why a parallel process is required—so that there is consistency in the selection process of primary studies.

> *Example: The main reasons for study exclusion were because studies were quantitative rather than qualitative, because the focus was not depression, and because not all of the participants in the studies were depressed and the results were not reported separately for those that were. Although there are supposed to be two reviewers judging each study, in the interest of time, the studies were divided between the student researchers.*

9. Reliably extract data from eligible studies onto standardized forms. Assess inter-rater reliability, resolve disagreements, and document decisions.

> *Example: A form was adapted from Paterson et al. (2001) by the research instructor for the purpose of this study. Data was collected on study participants, the research method, the data analysis procedure, and the findings of primary studies. One member of the student research team coded each study, and then it was double-coded by either the research instructor or an additional trained graduate student.*

10. Systematically and critically appraise the qualities of included studies. As before, this should be done by two raters, who resolve disagreements and document decisions.

> *Example: As part of data extraction, methodological qualities of studies were coded in the same as above.*

11. Describe key features of included studies (in a narrative, tables, and/or graphs).

> *Example: A table was created (see a section excerpted here in Example 4.4) to display the methodological and participant details of the primary studies.*

Example 4.4.

DEPRESSION IN OLDER ADULTS META-SYNTHESIS: METHODOLOGICAL FEATURES OF PRIMARY STUDIES

AUTHOR & PURPOSE	DESIGN	DATA ANALYSIS	SAMPLE INFORMATION
Bayer (2007) To explore the role of family relations in symptoms of depression in older adults receiving outpatient mental health services in a rural area.	In-depth interviews	Ethnography	$N = 14$ All living at poverty level in rural area, receiving outpatient mental health services Average age: 73.5 years Gender: Male (2); Female (12) Race: Caucasian (6); African-American (8) Education: High school (3); less (9) Participants recruited at outpatient group meeting at a hospital in rural Louisiana.

AUTHOR & PURPOSE	DESIGN	DATA ANALYSIS	SAMPLE INFORMATION
Black, White, & Hannum (2007) To explore the lived experience of depression, sadness, and suffering in elderly persons ages 80 years and older; to understand the meaning of depression and how it is experienced and expressed	Formal ethno-graphic interviews and infor-mal con-versation	A "bottoms-up" theoretical framework Social constructivist: 1. phenomen-ology and the soci-ology of knowledge 2. conceptuali-zations from cultural anthropology 3. African-American religious studies and the psych-ology of religion	$N = 20$ All African-American women Split evenly (10 & 10) according to health status (excellent/good & fair/poor) Data collected from research funding by the National Institute on Aging ($N = 120$)—this sample was stratified; this study used the stratified groups of women and health status.
Dekker, Peden, Lennie, Schooler, & Moser (2009) To illustrate the experi-ence of depression in older adult patients with heart failure.	Semi-structured interviews	Inductive Approach, ATLAS ti (version 5)	$N = 10$ All with heart failure Gender: Female (5); Male (5) Mean age: 63 years 20% Minority 70% Married 70% have some college educa-tion or greater Purposeful sampling of outpa-tients in a clinical trial of bio-feedback and cognitive therapy in patients with heart failure.

12. Synthesize findings.

In meta-synthesis, the findings, extracted from the primary studies, comprise the data to be analyzed. Because a meta-synthesis involves synthesizing qualitative data using qualitative methods, the process of data analysis is similar to what is discussed in Chapter Ten. Tables can be enormously helpful, both in figuring out how to ana-lyze and how to present the data. Used as an example here is the student meta-synthesis that was done on elderly depression.

The first step is to figure out the very broad categories under which data can go. This takes a "stepping back" approach rather than becoming overwhelmed with all the separate pieces of data (which is very easy to do when first looking at any quali-tative data). In the elderly depression meta-synthesis, the studies from the primary studies could be sorted out around four broad themes:

- people's experience with depression
- their perspectives on how the depression came about

- their ideas about what was helpful for recovery
- the barriers they saw to formal treatment

The following table (Example 4.5) illustrates how each of the study's findings fell into one of these themes.

Example 4.5. MAIN IDEAS OF PRIMARY STUDIES ACCORDING TO THEME				
AUTHOR	**CAUSES**	**EXPERIENCES**	**RECOVERY**	**BARRIERS**
	MAIN FINDINGS			
Bayer (2007)	• Memory problems • Long-term physical illness • Family problems • Grief from losing parents, spouses, children, and friends; anniversaries of deaths		• Spirituality, going to church • Having social outlets with loved ones, friends, and supportive family • Talking with others about depressive symptoms • Hobbies such as fishing and quilting	
Black, White, & Hannum (2007)	• Lifelong poverty • Poor relationships • Early experiences of grief	• Sadness and suffering • They often have feelings of "no way out" • Diminishment of personal strength • Physical strength that is decreasing because of the difficulties that occur throughout life	• Faith in God convinced participants that negative situations would improve or they would have the strength to bear them. • Primary means to prevent or resolve depression was religious beliefs. • One must fight depression with all the strength that remains in their body. • Depression is prevented or resolved by personal responsibility.	
Dekker, Peden, Lennie, Schooler, & Moser (2009)	• Financial difficulties as a stressor • Health issues as a stressor • Family problems as a stressor • Loss as a stressor	• Negative thinking or self-critical thoughts • Emotional symptoms of sadness • Depression also described in terms of somatic symptoms of changes in appetite, sleep, and energy	• Distraction through spirituality/religion • Family and friends as social support • Involvement in activities • Positive thinking to cope with depression • Participants used antidepressants most often	

AUTHOR	CAUSES	EXPERIENCES	RECOVERY	BARRIERS
Givens et al. (2006)		• Resistance to view depression as medical illness		• Fear of addiction • Past negative experiences with medication to treat depression are an obstacle to treatment • Concern that natural sadness may be inhibited by antidepressants
Hedelin & Strandmark (2001)	• Depression was caused by specific life events or series of traumatic events.	• Fear • Self-blame for their illness • Meaningless, emptiness, hopelessness • Alienation • Diminished vitality • Physical pain	• Fighting illness	• Giving up/ giving in
Hostetter (2003)		• Feeling useless • Sadness • Experience loneliness • Not confiding in others about depression • Sleep changes • Decline in physical mobility • Less energy and/or ability to motivate self • Aggravation of feelings with chronic pain	• Have to keep busy • Feelings of depression distractible	
Orr & O'Connor (2005)	• They didn't see a cause behind the depression.	• Perceived powerlessness over the depression. • Participants were disconnected from the depression experience, using "you" instead of "I".	• Participants developed alliances with doctors as a way to control the depression.	
Pollitt & O'Connor (2008)			• Some patients made friends in the hospital. • Respondents reported benefiting from feeling useful, being given or undertaking tasks. • Thinking positive • Able to make the best of it • Coping strategies were being assertive.	

AUTHOR	CAUSES	EXPERIENCES	RECOVERY	BARRIERS
Proctor, Hasche, Morrow-Howell, Shumway, & Snell (2008)	• Financial difficulties • Some participants did not know how depression was related to other aspects of their lives. • Health • Loneliness	• Participants had difficulty identifying their symptoms as depression.		• Depression is a normal part of life.
Ugarriza (2002)	• Could not give reason for depression • Didn't know • Most said depression was a result of changes in their health. • Depression caused problem related to ADLS. • Loss of function contributed to depression. • Problems related to physical illness and pain. • Death of family members, most often husband.	• Fear they would not recover the ability to accomplish things • Feared depression was permanent • Felt hopeless • Poor appetite or eating habits • Feared they would suffer physical damage or ill health	• Talking to psychiatrist/doctor • Therapy/group/occupational/ movement/art • Best treatment is use of medication	
Wilby (2008)	• Poverty • Medical problems, feeling tired, having chronic conditions such as diabetes • Chemical imbalance (hereditary) • History of childhood abuse, including sexual and physical	• Disappointment, specifically in inability to attain goals, meet expectations for one's self • Lack of self-worth, not being good for anything • Hopelessness, that one would not get better		• Dissatisfaction with prior treatment • Withdrawal and hopelessness—it's just the way things are. • Other people caused the depression, therefore saw no need for seeking treatment • Minimization of symptoms

AUTHOR	CAUSES	EXPERIENCES	RECOVERY	BARRIERS
Continuation of Wilby (2008)	• Loss and complicated grief, specifically loss of spouse, friend, or family member • Loneliness, not being around others			• Faith—no need for treatment • One should be able to solve the problem themselves.
Wittink, Barg, & Gallo (2006)			• Patients feel any discussion of emotional issues will lead to referral to a psychiatrist. • Physicians focus mostly on the physical issues and tend to ignore emotional ones.	• Patients feel any discussion of emotional issues will lead to referral to a psychiatrist. • Physicians focus mostly on the physical issues and tend to ignore emotional ones.

A second step is to take each of these broad themes in turn and then develop categories within each of these areas.

An example is provided here in Example 4.6 from the elderly depression meta-synthesis. Participants' perspectives on the causes of their depression could be organized into biological/medical; grief and loss; financial; relationship problems; trauma; and loneliness. These categories are ranked according to the frequency of their presentation in the primary studies.

Note that not all qualitative researchers agree that *frequency* should be a principle of data analysis as they view counting as a quantitative exercise. Generally speaking, a continuum of qualitative data analysis exists. On the extreme quantitative end of the spectrum is content analysis, or simply counting the appearance of certain words or phrases or entities; at the other end is a more interpretive, theoretical approach, and more attention is brought to bear on accounting for all participants' perspectives. As discussed in Chapter Ten, our perspective is that a step beyond merely counting the appearance of certain words or phrases is useful, and most social work students are more than capable of formulating categories that take the data to a higher level of meaning. At the same time, we also believe that some ranking and documenting of how many studies addressed a particular theme is important information to share with a reader of the research.

Example 4.6.

CAUSES OF ELDERLY DEPRESSION

THEMES	FINDINGS	STUDIES
Biological/ Medical	• Most said depression was a result of changes in their health. • Depression caused problem related to ADLS. • Memory problems • Loss of function contributed to depression. • Medical problems, feeling tired, having chronic conditions such as diabetes • Problems related to physical illness and pain • Chemical imbalance (hereditary)	Bayer (2007) Dekker et al. (2009) Proctor et al. (2008) Ugarriza (2002) Wilby (2008)
Grief/Loss	• Loss and complicated grief, specifically loss of spouse, friend, or family member • Early experiences of grief • Anniversaries of deaths	Bayer (2007) Black et al. (2007) Dekker et al. (2009) Ugarriza (2002) Wilby (2008)
Financial	• Financial difficulties • Poverty	Black et al. (2007) Dekker et al. (2009) Proctor et al. (2008) Wilby (2008)
Relationship issues	• Family problems, specifically isolation (not being visited or called by children or grandchildren); caregiving responsibilities for spouse, children, and grandchildren; children who want money or have substance abuse issues • Poor relationships	Bayer (2007) Black et al. (2007) Dekker et al. (2009)
No cause	• Some participants did not know how depression was related to other aspects of their lives • They didn't see a cause behind the depression • Could not give reason for depression	Orr & O'Connor (2005) Proctor et al. (2008) Ugarriza (2002)
Trauma	• Depression was caused by specific life events or series of traumatic events • History of childhood abuse including sexual and physical	Hedelin & Strandmark (2001) Wilby (2008)
Loneliness	• Loneliness, not being around others	Proctor et al. (2008) Wilby (2008)

CONCLUSION

Systematic review as its own methodology has developed recently and has burgeoned rapidly in the research literature as a way to accumulate knowledge in a particular topic area. Social workers should be conversant in locating and understanding systematic reviews, not only to know the practice approaches that have empirical support (evidence-based practice) but also so they can use the findings of systematic reviews in their own literature reviews. We have also described, in this chapter, how a particular form of systematic review, the meta-synthesis, can be undertaken as student research and the steps required to complete such a project. Because a meta-synthesis project is qualitative in nature, immersion in Chapter Ten on qualitative research will also be necessary. In the next section of this book, we start to develop the methodology for your study, reviewing material on research methods and applying these methods to student projects.

WEBSITES

http://www.cochrane.org
The website for the Cochrane Collaboration systematic reviews.
http://www.campbellcollaboration.org
The website for the Campbell Collaboration systematic reviews.
http://mason.gmu.edu/~dwilsonb/ma.html
David Wilson is the author, along with Mark Lipsey, of *Practical Meta-Analysis* (Sage, 2001), and provides resources for calculating effect sizes and doing meta-analysis on this site.

5

ETHICS AND VALUES RELATED TO RESEARCH

This chapter discusses the ethics involved with doing social work research. As a student, you're likely already familiar with the ethics and values that relate to practice behavior, such as the worth and dignity of the individual and commitment to social justice. The ethics and values that guide our practice also guide our research. In particular, you will recognize our commitment to client self-determination as one of the basic tenets that undergirds most of the universally agreed upon standards for ethical research adopted by all major organizations. The material in this chapter will help you to understand and apply ethical standards to your research projects.

The chapter is organized into three sections. First, we provide an overview of ethical considerations in social work research, illustrated by examples and some exercises. Next, we discuss the basic components and the review criteria of an Institutional Review Board (IRB) application. Third, we consider the extent to which student projects fall within the definition of "research" as guided by the U.S. Department of Health and Human Services Office of Human Research Protections (OHRP) and subsequent implications in regard to seeking university IRB approval.

ETHICAL CONSIDERATIONS IN SOCIAL WORK RESEARCH

Of course you know that ethical standards for research are not unique to the social work profession. Protection of human subjects and the ethical conduct of research is a standard practice in all professions and areas of scientific investigations. The federal government mandates policies and procedures related to research through the U.S. Department of Health and Human Services OHRP. These guidelines (2010) are found at http://www.hhs.gov/ohrp/humansubjects/guidance/45cfr46.html#46.110. Enacting the regulations of the federal government are IRBs, which are committees established at universities and organizations to do ethical reviews of proposed research in those institutions.

In addition to these federal mandates, ethical decision making in social work research is also mandated by the National Association of Social Workers *Code of Ethics* (2008). In fact, you will find that the core set of ethical practices required by the OHRP and those articulated by the National Association of Social Workers (NASW) *Code of Ethics* are almost identical. Although several references to the ethical research issues can be found throughout the *Code of Ethics* document, ethical standard 5.02 Evaluation and Research under 5 "Social Workers' Ethical Responsibilities to the Social Work Profession" specifically addresses the ethical responsibilities of social workers engaged in research (NASW, 2008). A summary of these ethical standards is presented in Summary Content 5.1.

Summary Content 5.1.

NASW CODE OF ETHICS, 5.02 EVALUATION AND RESEARCH

a. Monitor and evaluate policies, programs, and practice interventions.

b. Promote and facilitate evaluation and research to contribute to the development of knowledge.

c. Examine and keep current with emerging knowledge relevant to social work and fully use evaluation and research evidence in their professional practice.

d. Carefully consider possible consequences and should follow guidelines developed for the protection of evaluation and research participants. Appropriate institutional review boards should be consulted.

e. Obtain voluntary and written informed consent from participants without any implied or actual deprivation or penalty for refusal to participate; without undue inducement to participate; and with due regard for participants' well being, privacy, and dignity. Informed consent should include information about the nature, extent, and duration of the participation requested and disclosure of the risks and benefits of participation in the research.

f. When evaluation or research participants are incapable of giving informed consent, social workers should provide an appropriate explanation to the participants, obtain the participants' assent to the extent they are able, and obtain written consent from an appropriate proxy.

g. Never design or conduct evaluation or research that does not use consent procedures, such as certain forms of naturalistic observation and archival research, unless rigorous and responsible review of the research has found it to be justified.

h. Inform participants of their right to withdraw from evaluation and research at any time without penalty.

i. Take appropriate steps to ensure that participants in evaluation and research have access to appropriate supportive services.

j. Protect participants from unwarranted physical or mental distress, harm, danger, or deprivation.

k. Discuss collected information only for professional purposes and only with people professionally concerned with this information.

l. Ensure the anonymity or confidentiality of participants and of the data obtained from them.

m. Protect participants' confidentiality by omitting identifying information in reports unless proper consent has been obtained authorizing disclosure.

n. Report evaluation and research findings accurately.

o. Be alert to and avoid conflicts of interest and dual relationships with participants, should inform participants when a real or potential conflict of interest arises, and should take steps to resolve the issue in a manner that makes participants' interests primary.

p. Educate themselves, their students, and their colleagues about responsible research practices.

As you can see from standards a, b, c, and p above, the social work code of ethics mandates that social workers understand, utilize, and generate research and evaluation on behalf of clients ([NASW, 2008] available: http://www.naswdc.org/pubs/code/code.asp). This is the most straightforward justification for why research courses are part of the social work education curriculum.

In general, your research courses equip you with the knowledge and skills to carry out the basic research and evaluation to meet these overall ethical responsibilities. Also, please note the reference to risk and benefits in standard e. This means that, ultimately, the outcomes of your research efforts need to benefit the populations that are being studied. Because many of our studies are with people from historically (and currently) oppressed populations, it is essential that you keep the interests of the populations that we serve foremost in any research project.

When conducting research, the ethical guidelines stipulate the behaviors and practices that social work researchers must follow to protect the rights of human subjects. One of the first and most basic human subjects' rights is for potential study participants to decide freely and without consequence to become involved with the study and to be so informed of this right. Letters of informed consent are developed by the researcher to inform potential study participants about all aspects of the study. Following from standards e, h, and i above, the basic elements of an informed consent letter includes statements about: the voluntary nature of the research participation; information about the nature, extent, and duration of the participation requested; and disclosure of the risks and benefits of participation in the research; information about participants' right to withdraw from the study at any time without penalty; assurance of the anonymity or confidentiality of participants and of the data obtained from them; and assurance that participants in evaluation and research have access to appropriate supportive services. The letter should also provide the name of a specific office or person and the telephone number or e-mail address to contact if the research subject has any concerns about the ethics of the project. Example 5.1 is an example of a letter of consent for a research evaluation of a program. There are many ways to write a letter of Informed Consent. See Appendix 5.2 for more examples of Letters of Informed Consent.

Example 5.1.

SAMPLE LETTER OF INFORMED CONSENT

PARENTING PROGRAM EVALUATION

INFORMED CONSENT FORM

1. WHY AM I BEING INVITED TO TAKE PART IN THIS RESEARCH?

You are being invited to take part in a research evaluation of the Children's Health Maintenance Program (CHAMP). You are being invited to participate in this research because you and your child are now in the CHAMP program. If you take part in this study, you will be one of about 225 people to do so in the next 3 years.

2. WHO IS DOING THE STUDY?

The person in charge of this research is Dr. XXX XXXXXX, Professor from the College of Social Work at the University of Petersburg. There will be other people on the research team assisting at different times during the study. The research evaluation Project Director, Alexander Christophe, will be the person you will see most frequently.

3. WHAT IS THE PURPOSE OF THIS STUDY?

By doing this study, we hope to find out how well the CHAMP program meets its goals and to learn more about what will help primary caregivers teach good health and nutrition practices to their children.

4. WHERE IS THE STUDY GOING TO TAKE PLACE, HOW LONG WILL IT LAST, AND WHAT WILL I BE ASKED TO DO?

If you take part in this study, there are six different parts to this evaluation that may involve you. These are listed below and discussed separately:

A. EVALUATION SURVEY: You will be asked to answer written survey questions at the Petersburg County Health Department (PCCC) on two occasions, before starting AND after completing the CHAMP program. Each survey will take about 30 minutes to do. The survey questions will be about your background, your relationship with your children, and your feelings and attitudes about health and nutrition. The survey questions may be read to you or you may read the survey questions yourself. You will answer the questions in writing in a way that no one else in the room will be able to see your answers. You do not have to answer all the questions if you do not want to, and you can stop doing the survey at any time that you want. Staff from the CHAMP program and Petersburg County Health Department will not be in the same room when the survey is completed nor will they be given your individual answers when you have completed the survey.

B. CLASS SESSION REPORTS: Also, after each class session, you will be asked to answer a few written survey questions about what happened in the class that day. You will answer the questions in writing in a way that no one else in the room will be able to see your answers. You do not have to answer all the questions if you do not want to, and you can stop doing the survey at any time that you want. Staff from the CHAMP program and Petersburg County Health Department will not be in the same room when the survey is completed nor will they be given your individual answers when you have completed this short survey.

C. CLASS VIDEOTAPE: We will also videotape some class sessions (two for each 13-week CHAMP series). If you do not want to be videotaped during these particular class sessions, please let the researcher know and he will make sure you are not included on the video.

D. PARENT–CHILD VISIT OBSERVATIONS: We will also be present at parent–child special visits as observers.

E. CAREGIVER CONTACT: In some select situations, we will ask to contact (by phone) the primary caregiver of your children to ask her if she and your child have read their storybook. As always, this is optional and you can ask not to be included in this part of the evaluation.

F. FOLLOW-UP SURVEYS:—After your completion of the CHAMP program, we will contact you every 6 months or so to conduct a brief follow-up survey. This will be strictly voluntary, and you may ask to be dropped from our contact list at any time. In addition, you are not required to answer all the questions on the phone survey. This survey will be very brief and take no more than 10 minutes to complete. If you agree, then we will continue to contact you by phone after your release from prison into the community. Follow-up surveys will be conducted throughout the duration of the research project, ending in the fall of 2006.

5. WHAT ARE THE POSSIBLE RISKS AND DISCOMFORTS?

To the best of our knowledge, the things you will be doing during this study will not harm you more than anything you experience in everyday life. However, you may find some questions we ask you to be upsetting or stressful. If this is the case, we suggest that you ask Joe Smith to arrange for you to see Dr. Lucinda Jones, the staff psychologist.

6. WILL I BENEFIT FROM TAKING PART IN THIS STUDY?

There is no guarantee that you will get any personal benefit from taking part in this study. However, we are providing a small sum of money ($15) for answering the CHAMP Evaluation Survey after you have completed the health and nutrition education program. In addition, we will provide $15 each time you complete a follow-up survey (in person or by phone) after you have completed the CHAMP program.

7. DO I HAVE TO TAKE PART IN THIS STUDY?

Your participation is voluntary and is highly appreciated. If you decide to take part in the study, then it should be because you really want to volunteer. You will not lose any benefits or rights you would normally have if you choose not to volunteer. You can stop at any time during the study and still be a part of the CHAMP program. If you decide to take part in the study, you can still skip any questions you do not wish to answer.

8. WHAT WILL IT COST ME TO PARTICIPATE?

There are no costs associated with taking part in this study.

9. WILL I RECEIVE ANY PAYMENT OR REWARDS FOR TAKING PART IN THE STUDY?

As noted above, you will be provided a small sum of money ($15) for answering the CHAMP Outcome Survey, at the end of the health and nutrition education program during the last CHAMP session.

10. WHO WILL SEE THE INFORMATION I GIVE?

The answers you provide in this study are confidential. You will not put your name on this survey. We will make every effort to prevent anyone who is not on the research team from knowing that you gave us information or what that information is. For example, your name will be kept separate from the information you give, and these two pieces of information will be stored in different places under lock and key at the University of Petersburg.

Your information will be combined with information from other people taking part in the study. When we write up the study to share it with other researchers, we will write about this combined information. You will not be identified in these written materials.

However, you should be aware that there are some circumstances in which we may be required to show your information to other people. For example, the law may require us to tell authorities if we believe you are a danger to yourself or someone else. We may also be required to tell authorities if we suspect that child abuse might have occurred, either by you in the recent past or by someone else in a home in which you resided prior to your incarceration. Finally, we may be required to show information that identifies you to people who need to be sure we have done the research correctly; these would be people from organizations such as the University of Petersburg.

11. CAN MY TAKING PART IN THE STUDY END EARLY?

If you decide to take part in the study, then you still have the right to decide at any time that you no longer want to continue. You will not be treated differently if you decide to stop taking part in the study.

In addition, the individuals conducting the study may need to take you off of the study. They may do this if you are not able to follow the directions they give you, if they find that your being in the study is more risk than benefit to you, or if the agency funding the study decides to stop the study early for a variety of scientific reasons.

12. WHAT IF I HAVE QUESTIONS?

Before you decide whether to accept this invitation to take part in the study, please ask any questions that might come to mind now. Later, if you have questions about the study, you can call research team member Alexander Christophe toll free at 1-800-345-2483.

If you have any questions about your rights as a research volunteer, contact the staff in the Office of Research Integrity at the University of Petersburg at 456-355-8592 or toll free at 1-800-923-9428. We will give you a copy of this consent form to take with you.

13. WHAT ELSE DO I NEED TO KNOW?

This study has been funded through the Children's Fitness and Nutrition Bureau.

You will be told if any new information is learned that may affect your condition or influence your willingness to continue taking part in this study.

_____   _____
Signature of person agreeing to take part in the study   Date

_____   _____
Printed name of person agreeing to take part in the study   Date

_____   _____
Name of person providing information to subject   Date

OHRP (http://www.hhs.gov/ohrp/policy/consentckls.html) provides a checklist of the criteria required to be addressed in an informed consent letter and Project Development Worksheet 5.1 below will help you apply these criteria to your project.

Project Development Worksheet 5.1. DEVELOPING YOUR INFORMED CONSENT LETTER	
OHRP REQUIREMENT	**STATEMENT FOR YOUR RESEARCH PROJECT**
A statement that the study involves research	**Example** You are being invited to take part in a research study that will evaluate the XXX Parent Education program.
A statement that the study involves research	
An explanation of the purposes of the research	
The expected duration of the subject's participation	
A description of the procedures to be followed	
Identification of any procedures that are experimental	

OHRP REQUIREMENT	STATEMENT FOR YOUR RESEARCH PROJECT
A description of any reasonably foreseeable risks or discomforts to the subject	
A description of any benefits to the subject or to others that may reasonably be expected from the research	
A disclosure of appropriate alternative procedures or courses of treatment, if any, that might be advantageous to the subject	
A statement describing the extent, if any, to which confidentiality of records identifying the subject will be maintained	
For research involving more than minimal risk, an explanation as to whether any compensation, and an explanation as to whether any medical treatments are available, if injury occurs and, if so, what they consist of, or where further information may be obtained	
An explanation of whom to contact for answers to pertinent questions about the research and research subjects' rights, and whom to contact in the event of a research-related injury to the subject	
A statement that participation is voluntary, refusal to participate will involve no penalty or loss of benefits to which the subject is otherwise entitled, and the subject may discontinue participation at any time without penalty or loss of benefits, to which the subject is otherwise entitled	
A statement that the particular treatment or procedure may involve risks to the subject (or to the embryo or fetus, if the subject is or may become pregnant), which are currently unforeseeable	
The consequences of a subject's decision to withdraw from the research and procedures for orderly termination of participation by the subject	
A statement that significant new findings developed during the course of the research, which may relate to the subject's willingness to continue participation, will be provided to the subject	
The approximate number of subjects involved in the study	

Several examples of informed consent letters developed by students for their projects are found at the end of the chapter. Notice that many of these letters lack some of the detail in the sample CHAMP Program letter, the language is more general, and some do not have a place for the research participant signature. Social work students conducting research in community-based agencies must often modify the format and content of the informed consent letter to account for the low literacy levels of the vulnerable client populations in these agencies, for those for whom English is a new language, and for the feelings of intimidation and suspicion that formal and lengthy letters might generate in such populations. In addition, some of these student letters are associated with research projects that meet the criteria established by OHRP for a waiver of written consent or an exemption from federal regulations altogether. Information about written consent waivers can be found here at http://www.hhs.gov/ohrp/humansubjects/guidance/45cfr46.html#46.117. The reason that waivers are given is because the signature may be the only identifier revealing the participant in the study. By waiving the signature, the researcher can ensure that there is no way to identify a participant. On projects with a waiver of written consent, the potential research subjects are provided with a written statement regarding the research. Example 5.2 presents a sample that can be used for self-administered, mail, or Internet surveys.

Example 5.2.

SAMPLE WAIVER OF WRITTEN CONSENT

CHAMP SURVEY QUESTIONNAIRE

You are being asked to participate in this survey because you are the caregiver of a child and you and that child are enrolled in the CHAMP Program. This survey is being conducted by researchers at the University of Petersburg to help evaluate the CHAMP program.

Informed Consent:

Please let us know that you understand the nature of this survey and that your participation is entirely voluntary by checking the following items.

_____ I have read the Informed Consent Statement that came with this survey.

_____ I understand that the survey is about the CHAMP program at the Petersburg County Health Department.
_____ I am completing this study voluntarily.

Remember, the goal is to provide as much information to potential research participants as required in as easily accessible a manner as possible. To ensure this goal, researchers often repeat basic informed consent information on the questionnaire form itself. See Example 5.3 below.

> **Example 5.3.**
>
> BASIC INFORMED CONSENT ON QUESTIONNAIRE
>
> Date _____   Inmate number _____
>
> *CHAMP Program Survey*
> **As explained in the consent letter you just received, this study is being conducted by
> Dr. Mary Secret from the University of Petersburg. We hope that this study will make an
> important contribution to parent education programs everywhere. The information you
> provide is designed to be used when combined with the information collected from others
> completing the survey. No one will be able to identify you by the answers you give. Even
> though you volunteered to complete this survey, you may skip any questions that you wish
> or you can stop doing the survey at any time that you want.**

THE IRB APPLICATION

As noted above and discussed more thoroughly in your research methods text, the IRBs are committees established by universities and other organizations to ensure that research conducted with human subjects is done ethically. There are three levels of IRB review: *exempt*, *expedited*, or *full review*. Exempt and expedited reviews are allowed when the research activities present no more than minimal risk to human subjects. "Minimal risk means that the probability and magnitude of harm or discomfort anticipated in the research are not greater in and of themselves than those ordinarily encountered in daily life or during the performance of routine physical or psychological examinations or tests" (Protection of Human Subjects, 2009, §46.102). An expedited review is conducted by either the IRB chair or one other member of the University IRB committee—An exempt review means that the IRB authority has determined that the research activities are exempt from the requirements of Human Subjects Review. An example of a student project appropriate for IRB exempt status is a project using closed case files to determine whether there was a difference in treatment length based on demographic variables (e.g., race, age, marital status, etc.).

Full board review of research is required when the research does not meet the criteria for exempt or expedited review. The comprehensive research evaluation of a prison-based parenting education program required full IRB review because it involved prisoners. OHRP has identified several criteria that a research project must meet to qualify for either exempt or expedited review. See Appendix 5.1 for a full description of the categories exempt or expedited IRB and at the following URL: http://www.hhs.gov/ohrp/policy/expedited98.html.

Consider the following student projects in Test Your Skills Exercise 5.1. After you have studied the different IRB review categories in Appendix 5.1, try to determine which of the following projects should be considered for full, expedited, or exempt review. Two examples are provided to give you an idea of how to complete this exercise.

Test Your Skills Exercise 5.1.

DETERMINING THE TYPE OF IRB REVIEW

DESCRIPTION OF STUDENT RESEARCH PROJECT	TYPE OF REVIEW	REASON/CRITERIA
Example # 1 Nonexperimental: Secondary data analysis of closed cases in therapeutic foster care with client identifiers removed	EXEMPT	**Category 4 exempt:** Existing data, documents, records, specimens
Example # 2 Pre-experimental: Pre-/posttest interviews with middle school children in an afterschool art program	EXPEDITED	**Category 7 expedited**: Research on individual or group characteristics or behavior research employing survey, interview, oral history, focus group, program evaluation, human factors evaluation, or quality assurance methodologies.
Survey design: Administering the Alcohol and Substance Consumption questionnaires to a group of college-age students.		
True experimental: Testing the impact of a new intervention to work with adults with eating disorders; adults admitted to an outpatient program are randomly assigned to either the new intervention or to the regular intervention		
Survey research: Conducting focus groups with prisoners who completed a computer training program.		
Pre-experimental: Administering pre-/posttest surveys to children completing a self-esteem group.		

One of the first ethical decisions that you will make about your project is to determine which level of review your project requires. Use Project Development Worksheet 5.2 to document this information.

Project Development Worksheet 5.2.

IDENTIFYING THE TYPE OF IRB REVIEW FOR YOUR RESEARCH

Type of review that your project requires:

Based on what category:

Although IRB committees in all organizations follow the same federal regulations to protect human research subjects, the actual IRB process and IRB forms vary from institution to institution and are often modified on a regular basis. Most likely, the institution-specific forms and procedures can be found online on that institution's website. A few things to note as you begin the IRB application review:

- Be sure to read carefully the submission instructions at your institution; often there are different forms and procedures for each type of review.
- Some institutions require that researchers become certified to conduct ethical research through the Collaborative Institutional Training Initiative (CITI), a web-based training program in human subjects' protections as part of the IRB application process.
- In most cases, your instructor will be listed as the principle investigator on the project; you will list yourself as trainee or student.
- Special populations such as prisoners, pregnant women, and children often require additional forms and procedures.
- You will need to describe the basic elements of your project, including statement of the research question or hypothesis, rationale for the study, and type of research design. The recruitment and sampling plan will need to be discussed in detail; your Informed Consent Form will be included with your application. Remember, the procedures that you submit in your IRB application are the procedures that you must follow. If you decide to make changes, then you must go back to the IRB, submit the proposed changes, and wait for them to approve your changes.
- Conflict of interest or self-disclosure forms are often required.
- Most applications need the signature of your instructor and a representative from your program.
- Most IRBs publish the dates for their scheduled meetings and specify due dates for IRB applications for the different reviews.
- If your project involves collaboration with additional agencies, then you will have to submit copies of any collaborative agreements. Also, you will have to address how any third-party agency will adhere to human subject protections.

IS IRB REVIEW ALWAYS REQUIRED?

Federal regulation defines research as any 'systematic investigation, including research development, testing, and evaluation, designed to develop or contribute to generalizable knowledge. Activities that meet this definition constitute research for purposes of the human subjects review policy (Code of Federal Regulation, Protection of Human Subjects, 2009). At many universities and colleges, including the one affiliated with the authors, student research projects—particularly those that are used as research class assignments—do not meet the federal definition of research and are not subject to IRB review. These classroom-based research projects are primary learning activities geared to help students apply and learn basic research concepts and methods. The projects are not developed for publication, not intended to contribute to generalizable knowledge, and thus do not fall under the research definition requiring formal review and approval by the university IRB. Look at the second line of the following decision tree chart developed by OHRP (see Figure 5.1

in Appendix). If you answer "no" to the question "Is the activity a **systematic** investigation **designed** to develop or contribute to **generalizable** knowledge?" then your project is not considered a research activity that requires IRB approval.

Despite the fact that some student research projects do not require university IRB approval, social work research students nevertheless need to learn the process and procedures about conducting ethical research. Social work instructors are responsible to monitor this learning and ensure that students adhere to ethical conduct in all research learning activities regardless of whether formal IRB approval is necessary. Thus, the authors recommend that all student research projects comply with all ethical standards in conducting research activities and at least complete an IRB application as part of their learning. In most cases at the program where the authors teach, the IRB application is not forwarded for formal IRB approval but, rather, reviewed and approved by the instructor. The letter presented in Example 5.4 was developed to help explain the IRB review process and implications to community agencies where students are conducting classroom-based research projects in agency settings.

Example 5.4.

COPY OF LETTER TO PROSPECTIVE AGENCIES WHERE STUDENT RESEARCH WILL BE CONDUCTED

To: Agencies and Organizations Involved With Social Work Student Research Project

From: Dr. XXXX
          Associate Professor
          XXXX School of Social Work

Re: Student research projects in SLWK 706 taught by Dr. XXXX
Date: XXXX

As part of requirements for SLWK 706 Research For Clinical Social Work Practice I course, MSW students at XXXX are expected to conduct a small research project. These projects are designed to help students understand the research process, learn how to conduct scientifically sound and socially relevant research, and use research knowledge to inform their practice. Ideally, the projects will provide useful information to the agency where they are implemented, but the findings are not intended to be published or publicized.

These research projects will be closely supervised by the professor and are expected to pose no more than minimal risk to clients. Students will adhere to all policies for the protection of human subjects in the design and implementation of their project. Because the projects are not intended to be published or to produce generalized knowledge, formal Institutional Review Board (IRB) review and approval is not required unless specified by the professor.

If you have any questions or concerns about any of these student research projects, please contact me: XXXX.

Thanks again for your support of our XXXX MSW students.

Project Development Worksheet 5.3 is an opportunity for you to "pull the pieces together" as you go about conducting ethical research. Please use this worksheet to help you think about your project and the guidelines that you must follow to engage in research. If you are engaging in qualitative research, then you may want to refer to Chapter Ten, which focuses on qualitative research to identify and think through some particular ethical challenges associated with this method.

Project Development Worksheet 5.3.
ETHICS SUMMARY WORKSHEET

Project Description:	
Risks To Participants:	
Benefits to Participants, the Agency, and Field:	
How will you protect participants against risks?	
Do you need to complete an IRB? Why or why not?	

CONCLUSION

This chapter has introduced some key concepts related to conducting ethical research. As a student, you will be faced with determining how to implement a rigorous study, while protecting the rights of your participants. You will also be challenged with understanding your agency's processes within the context of what is permissible in ethical research.

Some students may initially believe that understanding OHRP guidelines introduces more "work" into the research project. However, it is important to underscore why we do this. As social workers, we are tasked with helping, rather than harming, clients. This includes engaging in research practices that will not intentionally harm clients. The OHRP guidelines are a "safeguard" for us. It is a way for us to engage in research while being attentive to the rights of our participants. Thus, these guidelines are critical for social work students conducting research.

Additionally, being attentive to conducting ethical research reflects on you and your potential as a professional social work practitioner. For example, a student who has a strong plan to protect the rights of human subjects demonstrates that he or she respects the field agency, clients, and the profession of social work. These are all qualities that agencies desire when evaluating the fit of potential employees or deciding whether to serve as an employment reference.

The next few chapters will discuss some methodological issues related to your student project. These chapters will help you to determine what information you will collect, how you will collect it, from whom you will collect data, and what you will do with the information after you collect it. As you read through these chapters and determine how you will develop your project, it is important that you make a mental note to refer back to the activities in this chapter. This technique will help ensure that you are developing and implementing your project while being attentive to the rights of your participants.

Test Your Skills Exercise 5.2.

TEST YOUR KNOWLEDGE OF ETHICAL STANDARDS RELATED TO HUMAN SUBJECTS RESEARCH

1. Which of the following is the best statement of "informed consent" in social work research? _____

   a. Potential research participants should be told about all similar prior studies.
   b. Potential research participants should be told what they will be asked to do in the research.
   c. Potential research participants should be told all aspects of the research in which they will participate except the research hypotheses.
   d. Potential research participants should be told about all aspects of the research that might reasonably influence their decision to participate.

2. The risk–benefit approach to requiring informed consent is that: _____
   a. Informed consent must always be followed.
   b. Informed consent should usually be followed, except when it is possible to ensure confidentiality.
   c. Questionable practices such as deception can be used if they are essential to the research and will bring no harm to participants.
   d. Questionable practices such as deception can be used because research findings generally outweigh the advantages of informed consent.

3. A social work student wants to collect data about attitudes toward "aging out of foster care" in the child protective services agency where she is employed. Informed Consent is not necessary if: _____
   a. The respondents are employees of the agency.
   b. The agency provides permission for the study.
   c. The researcher is an employee of the agency.
   d. None of the above.

4. Which of the following is not required information for a standard informed consent form? _____

   a. The purpose of the study.
   b. Who is conducting the study.
   c. The amount of time needed to complete the study.
   d. Assurance that research subjects will be provided with a copy of the study findings.
   e. All of the above are required in a standard informed consent form.

5. Review the following letter that is being sent to potential participants in a research study. Discuss which ethical issues that protect human subjects in research studies **are adequately** addressed in this letter and which **are not**?

Answer:

Consent to Participate in a Research Study
FACT Families Survey: Another Aspect of the XXX Program Evaluation

Dear Caregiver:

You are being invited to take part in a research study about the XXX parenting program that is offered at XXX Correctional Complex. You are being invited to participate in this research study because your child's father has completed the XXX parenting program while he was incarcerated at XXX Correctional Complex. If you take part in this study, you will be one of about 200 people to do so.

WHERE IS THE STUDY GOING TO TAKE PLACE AND HOW LONG WILL IT LAST?

This questionnaire that you have received has been mailed from the University of Someplace. We are mailing the questionnaires out to custodial parents from now until the end of the evaluation. It should take you between 15 to 30 minutes to complete this questionnaire and return it to the researcher at the University of Someplace.

WILL YOU BENEFIT FROM TAKING PART IN THIS STUDY?

There is no guarantee that you will get any direct benefit from taking part in this study. Your willingness to take part, however, may, in the future, help society as a whole better understand the experiences of families of incarcerated individuals and learn more about the types of programs and services should be provided to incarcerated fathers and their families.

WHAT WILL IT COST YOU TO PARTICIPATE?

There are no costs associated with taking part in this study.

CAN YOUR TAKING PART IN THE STUDY END EARLY?

If you decide to take part in the study, then you still have the right to decide at any time that you no longer want to continue. You will not be treated differently if you decide to stop taking part in the study.

WHAT IF YOU HAVE QUESTIONS?

If you have questions about the study, you can contact the investigator, Jane Doe, at XXX-XXX-XXXX. If you have any questions about your rights as a research volunteer, contact the staff in the Office of Research Integrity at the University of Someplace at XXX-XXX-XXXX or toll free at 1-800-XXX-XXXX. We will give you a copy of this consent form to take with you.

WHAT ELSE DO YOU NEED TO KNOW?

The U.S. Children's Bureau is providing financial support and/or materials for this study.

On the questionnaire itself, you will be asked if you have read the information on this form and that you are agreeing voluntarily to complete the questionnaire.

Please let me know if I can answer any questions for you concerning the survey. Thank you for your time.

Sincerely,

Jane Doe, PhD
University of Someplace
Email jane.doe@xxx.edu
Phone: XXX-XXX-XXXX

APPENDIX 5.1

IRB Exempt and Expedited Review Categories	
EXEMPT REVIEW CATEGORIES	**EXPEDITED REVIEW CATEGORIES**

1. Research conducted in established or commonly accepted educational settings, involving normal educational practices, such as (i) research on regular and special education instructional strategies, or (ii) research on the effectiveness of or the comparison among instructional techniques, curricula, or classroom management methods.
2. Research involving the use of educational tests (cognitive, diagnostic, aptitude, achievement), survey procedures, interview procedures or observation of public behavior, unless: (i) information obtained is recorded in such a manner that human subjects can be identified, directly or through identifiers linked to the subjects; and (ii) any disclosure of the human subjects' responses outside the research could reasonably place the subjects at risk of criminal or civil liability or be damaging to the subjects' financial standing, employability, or reputation.
3. Research involving the use of educational tests (cognitive, diagnostic, aptitude, achievement), survey procedures, interview procedures, or observation of public behavior that is not exempt under paragraph (b)(2) of this section, if: (i) the human subjects are elected or appointed public officials or candidates for public office; or (ii) Federal statute(s) require(s) without exception that the confidentiality of the personally identifiable information will be maintained throughout the research and thereafter.
4. Research involving the collection or study of existing data, documents, records, pathological specimens, or diagnostic specimens, if these sources are publicly available or if the information is recorded by the investigator in such a manner that subjects cannot be identified, directly or through identifiers linked to the subjects.
5. Research and demonstration projects that are conducted by or subject to the approval of Department or Agency heads and that are designed to study, evaluate, or otherwise examine: (i) Public benefit or service programs; (ii) procedures for obtaining benefits or services under those programs; (iii) possible changes in or alternatives to those programs or procedures; or (iv) possible changes in methods or levels of payment for benefits or services under those programs.
	1. Clinical studies of drugs and medical devices only when condition (a) or (b) is met.
	  a. Research on drugs for which an investigational new drug application (21 CFR Part 312) is not required. (*Note*: Research on marketed drugs that significantly increases the risks or decreases the acceptability of the risks associated with the use of the product is not eligible for expedited review.)
	  b. Research on medical devices for which (i) an investigational device exemption application (21 CFR Part 812) is not required; or (ii) the medical device is cleared/approved for marketing and the medical device is being used in accordance with its cleared/approved labeling.
	2. Collection of blood samples by finger stick, heel stick, ear stick, or venipuncture as follows:
	  a. from healthy, nonpregnant adults who weigh at least 110 pounds. For these subjects, the amounts drawn may not exceed 550 milliliters in an 8-week period and collection may not occur more frequently than two times per week; or
	  b. from other adults and children[2], considering the age, weight, and health of the subjects, the collection procedure, the amount of blood to be collected, and the frequency with which it will be collected. For these subjects, the amount drawn may not exceed the lesser of 50 milliliters or 3 milliliters per kilogram in an 8-week period and collection may not occur more frequently than two times per week.
	3. Prospective collection of biological specimens for research purposes by noninvasive means.
	Examples: (a) hair and nail clippings in a nondisfiguring manner; (b) deciduous teeth at time of exfoliation or if routine patient care indicates a need for extraction; (c) permanent teeth if routine patient care indicates a need for extraction; (d) excreta and external secretions (including sweat); (e) uncannulated saliva collected either in an unstimulated fashion or stimulated by chewing gumbase or wax or by applying a dilute citric solution to the tongue; (f) placenta removed at delivery; (g) amniotic fluid obtained at the time of rupture of the membrane prior to or during labor; (h) supra- and subgingival dental plaque and calculus, provided the collection procedure is not more invasive than routine prophylactic scaling of the teeth and the process is accomplished in accordance with accepted prophylactic techniques; (i) mucosal and skin cells collected by buccal scraping or swab, skin swab, or mouth washings; (j) sputum collected after saline mist nebulization.

EXEMPT REVIEW CATEGORIES	EXPEDITED REVIEW CATEGORIES
6. Taste and food quality evaluation and consumer acceptance studies, (i) if wholesome foods without additives are consumed or (ii) if a food is consumed that contains a food ingredient at or below the level and for a use found to be safe, or agricultural chemical or environmental contaminant at or below the level found to be safe by the Food and Drug Administration or approved by the Environmental Protection Agency or the Food Safety and Inspection Service of the U.S. Department of Agriculture	4. Collection of data through noninvasive procedures (not involving general anesthesia or sedation) routinely employed in clinical practice, excluding procedures involving X-rays or microwaves. Where medical devices are employed, they must be cleared/approved for marketing. (Studies intended to evaluate the safety and effectiveness of the medical device are not generally eligible for expedited review, including studies of cleared medical devices for new indications.) Examples: (a) physical sensors that are applied either to the surface of the body or at a distance and do not involve input of significant amounts of energy into the subject or an invasion of the subject = s privacy; (b) weighing or testing sensory acuity; (c) magnetic resonance imaging; (d) electrocardiography, electroencephalography, thermography, detection of naturally occurring radioactivity, electroretinography, ultrasound, diagnostic infrared imaging, doppler blood flow, and echocardiography; (e) moderate exercise, muscular strength testing, body composition assessment, and flexibility testing, where appropriate, given the age, weight, and health of the individual.
	5. Research involving materials (data, documents, records, or specimens) that have been collected or will be collected solely for nonresearch purposes (such as medical treatment or diagnosis). (*Note*: Some research in this category may be exempt from the HHS regulations for the protection of human subjects. 45 CFR 46.101(b)(4). This listing refers only to research that is not exempt.)
	6. Collection of data from voice, video, digital, or image recordings made for research purposes.
	7. Research on individual or group characteristics or behavior (including, but not limited to, research on perception, cognition, motivation, identity, language, communication, cultural beliefs or practices, and social behavior) or research employing survey, interview, oral history, focus group, program evaluation, human factors evaluation, or quality assurance methodologies. (*Note*: Some research in this category may be exempt from the HHS regulations for the protection of human subjects. 45 CFR 46.101(b)(2) and (b)(3). This listing refers only to research that is not exempt.)
	8. Continuing review of research previously approved by the convened IRB as follows: a. where (i) the research is permanently closed to the enrollment of new subjects; (ii) all subjects have completed all research-related interventions; and (iii) the research remains active only for long-term follow-up of subjects; or where no subjects have been enrolled and no additional risks have been identified; or b. where the remaining research activities are limited to data analysis.
	9. Continuing review of research, not conducted under an investigational new drug application or investigational device exemption where categories two (2) through eight (8) do not apply but the IRB has determined and documented at a convened meeting that the research involves no greater than minimal risk and no additional risks have been identified.

APPENDIX 5.2

Example 5.5.

SAMPLE INFORMED CONSENT LETTER

Date
Name of Bereaved
Street
City/State Zip

Dear (insert Name),

We hope that XXXX bereavement program has been of benefit to you over the course of the past year. We continue to be available to you at any time.

We would greatly appreciate your completion and return of the enclosed evaluation. Your feedback is very important and assists us with the continual improvement of our services. We ask you to focus on the role hospice played in the past year since the death of (insert name of deceased). We would like to know what you have to say, even if we played only a minor role in adjustment after your loss. Your participation in this effort is voluntary and will not affect any services you may receive from us in the future.

It should take about 10 minutes to answer the questions in the survey. Please return the survey in the enclosed postage-paid envelope. If you have any questions or desire additional information or support, please don't hesitate to contact me at (insert phone number).

Sincerely,

(Bereavement Coordinator or Social worker name and title)

Example 5.6.

SAMPLE INFORMED CONSENT LETTER

Date
Name of Potential Participant
Street
City/State Zip

Dear XXX Outpatient Client,

You are being asked to participate in this survey because you are currently receiving treatment at XXX Outpatient Services. We, as an agency, want to learn more about the factors that lead into relapse and what your opinions include about the topics presented in group sessions. This survey is being done by XXX STUDENT & XXX STUDENT, MSW students at XXX School of Social Work to gather information on this topic.

The following questions ask you about your past experiences in treatment, primary drug of choice, level of current satisfaction with treatment, and the importance level you place on specific topics addressed in treatment. It should take you approximately 15 minutes to answer the questions. If you don't understand any of the questions, please ask the administrator for helping in filling out this survey.

You are not required to put your name on the survey so your answers cannot be reconnected back to you. Information from everyone who participates in the survey will be added together to come to a conclusion on how we can improve treatment at XXX Outpatient Services.

If you decide to take part in this study, it should be because you want to provide information on this topic. You are not required to fill out this survey; however, your participation is greatly appreciated. Please answer the questions to the best of your ability. If at any point you do not feel comfortable answering a question, you may skip that question. However, 100% completion is greatly appreciated as it provides the researchers with the best possible survey results.

There are no reasons why you should not take part in this survey unless you do not want to provide information that is being asked. This research poses no harm to any individual participating.

Example 5.7.

RESEARCH SUBJECT INFORMATION AND CONSENT FORM

TITLE: Intimate Partner Violence and Hospital Policy Awareness Assessment

VCU IRB NO.:N/A student study

SPONSOR: XXXX School of Social Work

This consent form may contain words that you do not understand. Please ask the study staff to explain any words that you do not clearly understand. You may take home an unsigned copy of this consent form to think about or discuss with family or friends before making your decision.

PURPOSE OF THE STUDY
The purpose of this study is to measure hospital staff's knowledge of Intimate Partner Violence, IPV resources in the hospital, and the efficacy of the XXX Department of Health's Project RADAR IPV training for health-care professionals.

You are being asked to participate in this study because you are a current XXX employee who has direct content with patients.

DESCRIPTION OF THE STUDY AND YOUR INVOLVEMENT
If you decide to be in this research study, you will be asked to sign this consent form after you have had all your questions answered and understand what will happen to you.

In this study you will be asked to fill out a pretest at the beginning of an Intimate Partner Violence training module. At the end of the module you will be asked to fill out a posttest that is identical to the pretest. The whole process should take 1 hour. The educational module may include up to 15 people at a time. The education module will define Intimate Partner Violence and review screening procedures as well as hospital policies regarding Intimate Partner Violence.

The education module is considered an intervention and the pretest and posttest were developed to measure the effectiveness of the intervention as well your knowledge about Intimate Partner Violence, screening, and hospital policy.

Significant new findings developed during the course of the research that may relate to your willingness to continue participation will be provided to you.

RISKS AND DISCOMFORTS
The subject of Intimate Partner Violence can be upsetting to some people. The questions asked on the pretest and posttest are designed to be minimally invasive. However, the educational presentation does contain some graphic images. If you are upset by the pretest or posttest questions or by the presentation, please contact the help-line numbers that will be provided to you by the presenter.

BENEFITS TO YOU AND OTHERS
You may not get any direct benefit from this study, but the information we learn from the people in this study may help us develop a better educational IPV program for hospital staff and may assist in the development of an Intimate Partner Violence team here at XXX. You may experience some benefit from this study in the form of increase knowledge about IPV, screening, and hospital policy.

ALTERNATIVES
The alternative for this study is non-participation. If you choose, you do not have to participate in this study.

CONFIDENTIALITY

Potentially identifiable information about you will consist of your pretest and posttest. Data are being collected only for research purposes. Your data will be identified by a code consisting of the first three letters of your mother's maiden name and your mother's birth date. Your name will not be included on any form collected by the researcher. All pretests and posttests and consent forms will be stored in a locked filing cabinet in the researcher's office for the next 5 months and will be destroyed at the end of that time. Access to all data will be limited to study personnel only.

We will not tell anymore the answers you give us; however, information from the study and the consent form signed by you may be looked at or copied for research or legal purposes by the sponsor of the research, or by XXX. Personal information about you might be shared with or copied by authorized officials of the Federal Food and Drug Administration or the Department of Health and Human Services (if applicable).

What we find from this study may be presented at meetings or published in papers, but your name will not ever be used in these presentations or papers.

IF AN INJURY HAPPENS

XX University and the XXX do not have a plan to give long-term care or money if you are injured because you are in the study.

If you are injured because of being in this study, tell the study staff right away. The study staff will arrange for short-term emergency care or referred if it is needed.

Bills for treatment may be sent to you or your insurance. Your insurance may or may not pay for taking care of injuries that happen because of being in this study.

VOLUNTARY PARTICIPATION AND WITHDRAWAL

You do not have to participate in this study. If you choose to participate, you may stop at any time without any penalty. You may also choose not to answer particular questions that are asked in the study. Your decision to withdraw will have no consequences.

Your participation in this study may be stopped at any time by the study staff or the sponsor without your consent. The reasons might include:

- the study staff thinks it necessary for your health or safety
- you have not followed study instructions;
- the sponsor has stopped the study; or
- administrative reasons require your withdrawal.

If you leave the study before the posttest administered please let a staff member know.

QUESTIONS

In the future, you may have questions about your participation in this study. If you have any questions, complaints, or concerns about the research, contact:

Jane Doe
Jane.doe@web.edu

If you have any questions about your rights as a participant in this study, you may contact:

Dr. XXX, XXXX Professor of Social Work
XXXt@xxx.edu

You may also contact this person for general questions, concerns or complaints about the research. Please e-mail if you cannot reach the research team or wish to talk to someone else. Additional information about participation in research studies can be found at http://www. research.XXX.edu/irb/volunteers.htm.

CONSENT

I have been given the chance to read this consent form. I understand the information about this study. Questions that I wanted to ask about the study have been answered. My signature says that I am willing to participate in this study. I will receive a copy of the consent form once I have agreed to participate.

_____

Participant name printed   Participant signature   Date

_____

Name of Person Conducting Informed Consent Discussion/Witness
(Printed)

_____

Signature of Person Conducting Informed Consent   Date
Discussion/Witness

_____

Principal Investigator Signature (if different from above)   Date

---

Example 5.8.

SAMPLE INFORMED CONSENT FORM

FOCUS GROUP STUDY

**Latina Breast Cancer and Cervical Cancer Screening
Subject Consent for Participation in Consumer Focus Group**

We are asking you to be part of a study in an effort to discover the attitudes and beliefs of Latina women about breast and cervical cancer screenings. This study is being done by the XXXX.

If you agree to be part of the study, then you will be asked to come to what is called a focus group. A focus group is a meeting of people who are brought together to talk about topics that they may have in common. Group facilitators will ask questions of you and the other group members about breast and cancer screenings, and you will have time to discuss your responses. The focus group should take about two hours of your time and will be led by two Spanish-speaking, trained facilitators. The focus group study will be tape-recorded and detailed field notes will be taken by the co-facilitator. You will receive $35 for your participation in the focus group. This should compensate you for your time and effort in getting to the XXX location and being part of the focus group.

Your responses during the focus group will be kept private. Your name will not be put together with any of the information you give. When results of the research are published or discussed, no information will be included that will tell who you are.

There is little risk to being part of the focus group, in other words, nothing bad should happen. It is possible that some of the questions may make you feel uncomfortable or upset because they ask you to talk about cancer and your views on cancer screenings. However, you can choose not to answer any question for any reason and you can stop being part of the study at any time. If you get upset, you can tell the people leading the group, and they will be able to assist you. You might benefit from the study by learning more about cancer and cancer screening. You will also be helping the XXX better able to serve Latina consumers. Finally, you will be helping us learn about how Latina women think and feel toward breast and cervical cancer screenings.

Being in this study is totally up to you and you can change your mind at any time. Nothing will happen if you decide you don't want to be in the study. If you decide to be in the study you can drop out at any time for any reason.

You can ask questions about the study now or later. If you have a question at any time, you can call Jane Doe, Social Worker, XXX Network, at XXX-XXX-XXXX. She will be very happy to talk to you.

You may also feel free to contact the Office for Research Subjects Protection at the address and phone number below:

Office of Research Subjects Protection
XXX University
123 Main Street
Telephone: XXX-XXX-XXXX

Example 5.9.

SAMPLE INFORMED CONSENT FORM

Strengths- and Skill-Building Group for Adolescent Girls
Student Assent for Participation

We are asking you to be in a research study to help learn more about ways to help adolescent girls gain better coping skills. This means managing stress and dealing with others better so you feel like you can handle what comes your way in terms of life's challenges. The study is being done together by your school and XXXX University. As part one of this study, we asked you to fill out a survey on handling stress. The results of that survey show that you may benefit from joining a group, along with other teen girls, that will help you with handling stress. About (number will depend on the numbers of ninth to 12th-grade girls in the particular school who scored in a problematic range on the coping inventory) are being asked to participate.

Here is what we will do if you decide to participate:

You will be asked to join a group, along with other teen girls, that will help you handle stress better. The group will be held for 40–45 minutes for 8 weeks. What you talk about in group will remain confidential unless you say that you are a danger to yourself or others. In that event, we are required by law to break confidentiality.

During the first session of the group, you will be asked to complete a brief demographic form, which asks your age, race, and the number of parents and siblings living in your home. This should take about 3 minutes to complete. On the last day of group, you will be asked to complete the survey on how you handle once more. Six weeks after the group, you will again be asked to complete the survey. Your answers on the surveys will be kept private. All information you provide will be coded with an identification number. Your name will not be put together with any of the information you give. When results of the research are published or discussed, no information will be included that will reveal your identity.

If you want to participate in the group, you will get an opportunity to do so. However, part of the study is to find out how effective the group is compared to not getting the group. Therefore, initially you will be chosen randomly as to whether you will attend the group right away or at a later date.

We want to thank students who both fill out the assent form and have their parents complete the consent form by giving them a gift certificate valued at $5.00 for returning the two forms by (date). You will also receive a small free gift when you complete the surveys again after you finish the group.

There is little risk to filling out the surveys or being part of the group; in other words, nothing bad should happen. It is possible that some of the questions on the survey or discussions in group may make you feel uncomfortable or upset. You can choose not to answer any question for any reason and you can stop being part of the study at any time. You can talk to the person leading the group or the person leading the study, Dr. XXX, if you should get upset during group. Although we cannot promise that you will benefit from being in the study, we believe that joining the group will be helpful for handling stress, and it will help us learn how to assist other teenage girls with handling stress.

Please talk this over with your parents and show them the parental consent form. In that form, we explain to your parents the study and ask them if it is all right for you to be in the study. Being in this study is totally up to you and your parents. You can change your mind at any time. Nothing will happen if you or your parents decide you don't want to be in the study. If you decide to be in the study you can drop out at any time for any reason.

You can ask questions about the study now or later. If you have a question at any time, you can call Dr. XXX at XX University, School of Social Work, at XXX-XXX-XXXX. She will be very happy to talk to you.

Please return this form and the form for your parents to let us know whether you do or do not agree to be in this study. You will receive a gift certificate valued at $5.00 for completion of the assent and your parent's consent whether or not you decide to join the group. We are giving you two copies of this form. One is for you to keep and the other is for you to return.

Check the appropriate box below to indicate whether you have decided to be in the study or not, and then print and sign your name. Make sure you also have a witness sign.

If there is any part of the form that is unclear to you, be sure to ask questions about it. Do not sign the form until you get answers to all of your questions. Remember, being in this study is up to you and your parents.

_____ I agree to be in the study.

_____ I do not agree to be in the study.

_____

Youth name printed   *Youth signature*   *Date*

_____

*Witness Signature (**Required**)*   *Date*

_____

Signature of person conducting informed consent   *Date*

_____

Investigator signature (if different from above)   *Date*

Example 5.10.

SAMPLE INFORMED CONSENT FORM

Parent Consent for Participation
Strengths- and Skills-Based Group Intervention for Adolescent Girls

Dear Parent,

This letter is to ask permission for your child to take part in a research study designed to learn more about ways to help adolescent girls handle stress better. This study is a joint effort between XX University and your child's school. XX Public Schools, including your child's, are participating in collaboration with a researcher from XX to help girls handle stress better.

Why am I being asked?

You have been asked to give your consent because your child's score on the survey on handling stress shows that she may benefit from joining a group, along with other teen girls, to learn how to handle stress. We ask that you read this form and ask any questions you may have before allowing your child to be in the research.

What am I being asked to do?

You are being asked to allow your child, along with other teen girls, to participate in a group to learn how to handle stress. The group will be held for 40–45 minutes for 8 weeks during school hours at no cost to you.

During the first session of the group, your child will be asked to complete a brief demographic form, which asks your age, race, and the number of parents and siblings living in your home. This form will take about 3 minutes to complete. On the last day of group and 6 weeks after group, your child will be asked to complete the survey on handling stress that was used for the screening.

If your child chooses to participate in the group, she will get an opportunity to do so. However, part of the study is to find out how effective the group is compared to not getting the group. Therefore, initially she will be selected randomly to either attend the group right away or at a later date.

What are the potential risks and benefits of taking part in this research?

There is little risk to filling out the survey on handling stress or attending the group, although it is possible that your child could become uncomfortable or upset by some of the questions on the survey or discussions in group. However, she can talk to the person leading the group or the person leading the study, Dr. XXXX, if your child should get upset.

Although we cannot promise that your child will benefit from being in the study, we believe that joining the group will be helpful for handling stress. It will also help us learn how to assist other teenage girls to handle stress better.

What will my child and I receive for participating?

We want to thank students who fill out the assent form and have their parents read and sign the consent form. Therefore, your child will receive a gift certificate valued at $5.00 for returning these two forms signed by (date), even if she or you decide that she will not be part of the research. Your child will also receive a small gift each time she completes the survey (on the last day of group and 6 weeks after the group is finished).

<u>What about privacy and confidentiality?</u>

What your child talks about in group will remain confidential unless she reveals that she is a danger to herself or others, or if she reveals that she is the victim of abuse. In those events, we are required by law to break confidentiality. In addition, your child's answers on the surveys will be kept private. All information she provides will be coded with an identification number. Therefore, her name will not be put together with any of the information she gives. Furthermore, when results of the research are published or discussed, no information will be included that will reveal her identity.

<u>Voluntary participation/withdrawal</u>

You and your child can choose whether she is in this study or not. If you decide to allow your child to be in the study, you or your child may withdraw at any time with no consequences of any kind.

<u>Who should I contact if I have questions?</u>

If you have a question at any time, please call Dr. XXX at XXX University, School of Social Work, at XXX-XXX-XXXX.

You may also feel free to contact the Office for Research Subjects Protection at the address and phone number below:

XXX University
XXX St., Room 1-023
P.O. Box XXXXX
Somewhere, USA XXXXX
Telephone: XXX-XXX-XXXX

<u>Consent</u>
I have read this consent form and understand the information about the study. All my questions about the study and my participation in it have been answered. Below I have checked the appropriate box, whether or not I have decided to allow my child to be part of the study. I have also gotten a witness signature to my own.

We are giving you two copies of this form. One is for you to keep and the other is for you to return.

_____

Name of child (print)

_____ I agree to allow my child be in the study.

_____ I do not agree for my child to be in the study.

_____

Parent name printed   *Parent signature*   *Date*

_____

*Witness Signature (**Required**)*   *Date*

_____

Signature of person conducting informed consent   *Date*

_____

Investigator signature (if different from above)   *Date*

Is an Activity Research Involving Human Subjects
Covered by 45 CFR part 46?

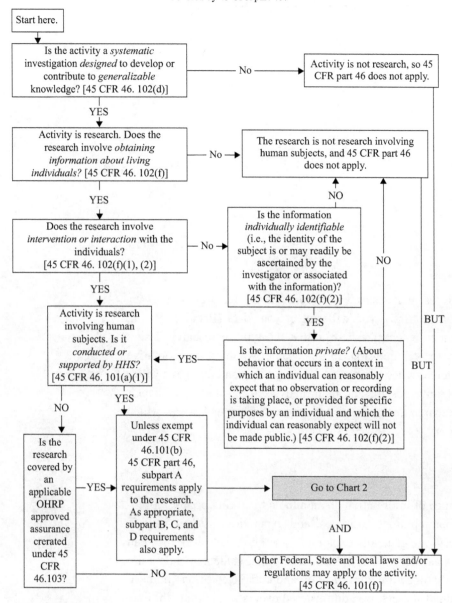

FIGURE 5.1 OHRP Decision Tree

WEBSITES

Five Principles for Research Ethics from the American Psychological Association

    http://www.apa.org/monitor/jan03/principles.aspx

Collaborative Institutional Training Initiative

    https://www.citiprogram.org/default.asp

Council on Social Work Education- National Statement on Research Integrity in Social Work

    http://www.cswe.org/cms/17157.aspx

Stanford Prison Experiment

    http://www.prisonexp.org/

Office of Research Integrity

    http://ori.dhhs.gov/

6 QUANTITATIVE: RESEARCH DESIGNS

The focus of this chapter is research designs, which provide the blueprint for answering your research questions and how you will collect your data (Brink & Wood, 1998). An important point to emphasize here is that the type of research design you use is based on your research question. In this chapter we discuss quantitative designs—surveys and different types of intervention research—and threats to validity to these designs. Qualitative designs and their analysis are explored in Chapter Ten. You will also see research designs revisited again in Chapter Eleven, which involves evaluation research.

SURVEYS

Surveys gather a broad range of information about a topic by asking people closed-ended questions about their opinions, attitudes, and experiences. When little is known about a topic, surveys are generally exploratory in nature. However, they can also be descriptive and explanatory. Most of the surveys that students conduct are cross-sectional, meaning that they are administered and completed at one point in time. In contrast, longitudinal surveys are administered over several points in time. Gathering data over time allows researchers to argue that events in the past, such as lack of education or SES, predict outcomes in the future, such as pregnancy or criminal offending.

Surveys are often used in macro social work projects (Tripodi & Bender, 2010). For example, a student research team studied the provision of information of the Earned Income Tax Credit to clients among child welfare workers, surveying all the workers in the students' field placement building. One excellent reason for surveying at the macro level is to conduct a needs assessment, "a form of research conducted to gather information about the needs of a population or group in a community" (Tutty & Rothery, 2010, p. 149). Students often conduct needs assessments when they are working with particular ethnic populations such as Asian or immigrant groups who do not typically access traditional social services. Needs assessment research is critical to determine not only what the service needs are in these communities but also to discern how services and interventions can be delivered in the most appealing and accessible way. For example, one social work student surveyed ministers associated with churches in Latino neighborhoods to explore ways to reach victims of intimate partner violence in families where women may be reluctant to seek outside help for personal problems.

Example 6.1 provides some other examples of surveys from student research projects.

Example 6.1.

EXAMPLES OF SURVEYS FROM STUDENT PROJECTS

Example #1: A student interested in health literacy (defined as the degree to which individuals have the capacity to obtain, process, and understand basic health information) wanted to research social workers' knowledge of their clients' health literacy and ways they could enhance health literacy. For this project, she designed a survey on client health literacy and mailed it to members of the state NASW organization.

Example #2: Given data about the need to prepare MSW students to work in interdisciplinary teams in their employment settings, a student research team surveyed field instructors about the use of interdisciplinary teams in their agencies, the role of social workers on these teams, and the preparedness of MSW students to participate.

Example #3: Two research students in school settings were curious about the wide range of duties that school social workers performed across the county. They surveyed school social workers in the twelfth largest county in the United States about their roles and responsibilities.

Creation of Surveys

Many research texts already cover the construction of surveys in great detail, so we will not go into detail other than to present some guidelines in Summary Content 6.1 here. Note that this information also overlaps with material in Chapter Eight, which involves questionnaires, their validation, and their creation.

Summary Content 6.1.

Tips on Constructing Surveys

1. Try to keep your survey brief. People get disheartened when they face a long survey.
2. Try to keep the formatting easy to read.
3. Write the survey using simple wording.
4. Pose only one question at a time.
5. Consider the response set you want. Too many choices (i.e., strongly agree, somewhat agree, slightly agree, neither agree or disagree, slightly disagree, somewhat disagree, strongly disagree) may frustrate a respondent, but too few choices (i.e., agree, disagree) may not capture the respondent's opinions on a topic.
6. When you have prepared an instrument, bring in copies for all your class members and instructors, asking them to provide feedback. Having feedback from a large number of people will be helpful in improving your survey and giving it face validity. Face validity means that the survey appears to assess what it is supposed to tap into. (Measurement validity will be covered further in Chapter Eight).

Response Rate and Administration. One major aspect of surveys to consider is how they will be administered to get the response rate you need. Response rates vary based on the population that your are surveying. A response rate of at least 50% is generally believed to be acceptable (Drake & Jonson-Reid, 2008; Monette, Sullivan, & DeJong, 2011; Rubin & Babbie, 2011). If you don't think you can get that return, then the survey may not be worth doing. There is a generally accepted method to improve response rate (Dillman, 1992), but it requires sending out reminders with the survey a second and then a third time. This process requires resources that are generally not available in terms of cost and time for a student budget, although it is expected of funded research surveys.

When considering the way in which the survey is delivered, mail surveys are usually too expensive for students' projects given the cost of envelopes and postage. Telephone interviews are also challenging given the preponderance of mobile cell telephones and the resources involved in doing probability sampling (*see* Chapter Seven). E-mail surveying has increased in popularity and is a less expensive method than using mailed surveys.

Most online survey software systems provide several questionnaire formats for you to use in creating your own questionnaire, link to designated respondents to collect data electronically, manage the responses, and return both the raw data and some preliminary data analysis. Survey Monkey is one of the more commonly used free online survey software systems that students have successfully used and in Example 6.2, we have provided some of the student projects we have supervised that relied on Survey Monkey.

Example 6.2.

EXAMPLES OF STUDENTS USING SURVEY MONKEY

Our students, for example, have used Survey Monkey to:
1. Survey social work graduates to explore the use of spirituality in social work practice.
2. Investigate the relationship between stress and burnout in work with clients diagnosed with Post-Traumatic Stress Disorder among a sample of hospital social workers.
3. Survey members of a child developmental disabilities advocacy group to assess their attitudes and experiences with animal-assisted interventions.

One of the biggest barriers to overcome in online surveying is gaining access to the appropriate listservs. Organizations are proprietary with this information, and some are not allowed to share e-mail addresses without permission of the e-mail holder. In the student project noted above on the use of spirituality in social work practice, the social work program administration queried alumni listserv and shared only those e-mail addresses that were explicitly approved by the individual alumnae to the student research group. For the survey of hospital social workers, approval from the hospital administrator had to be obtained to use the social worker listserv.

One way to guarantee a high response rate for your survey is to administer it in-person at a time when your potential respondents are gathered together in a group (e.g., staff meeting or training). For example, students who were placed at a county school system attended all four mandatory trainings with county social workers to ensure that they accessed all potential respondents for their survey on school social work functions and duties. Similarly, a student group interested in testing the association between family and peer relationships and sexually transmitted infections in adolescents planned to administer their survey with high school students immediately after they were screened for infections by a mobile unit of the health department.

Another example is a survey that was done of field instructors to discover their opinion of the need for graduate-level curriculum on preparation of MSW students on interdisciplinary teams. Field instructors were mandated to attend a training at the school of social work where the surveys were then administered.

INTERVENTION RESEARCH

Intervention research allows the researcher to measure the amount of change that occurs as a result of the introduction of an intervention. In such experiments, the ability to infer causality to the intervention itself rather than to other factors is called *internal validity*. External validity involves the extent to which one can apply the findings to a larger population beyond only the people who took part in the study. These factors will be elaborated on after we cover the different types of intervention research that students will typically carry out.

Single-System Designs

You likely are already interested in discovering the effect of your interventions on your clients. You probably ask them about the helpfulness of services and obtain an update on their status in your contacts. In this way, you are trying to understand whether your efforts are beneficial to your clients. The single-system design is an extension of this natural tendency, but with a more systematic method of collecting data and assessing the impact of our work by repeatedly tracking an outcome (e.g., temper tantrums, ability to sleep through the night, arguments, positive thoughts) to determine whether—and how—we are helping clients achieve their goals.

Single-system designs (also called single-case or single-subject designs) involve the social worker or student collecting data over time for a single client system on a certain outcome. A *client system* can refer to an individual client, but it could also mean a larger set of clients, such as a family or a classroom. Example 6.3 gives illustrations of student projects using single system designs, and Summary Content 6.2 provides the basic procedures for doing a single-system design.

Example 6.3.

EXAMPLES OF STUDENT PROJECTS INVOLVING SINGLE-SYSTEM DESIGNS

Example # 1: The implementation of a social skills training program in a classroom of an alternative school for adolescents with emotional and behavioral disturbances. The outcome tracked was a teacher report standardized measure on child behaviors called The Behavior Rating Index for Children (BRIC) (Stiffman, Orme, Evans, Feldman, & Keeney, 1984). The client system comprised the adolescents with emotional and behavioral disturbances. The baseline was established by teacher report on the BRIC for each student once a week for five weeks. After the introduction of the intervention (the social skills training), the teacher continued to complete the BRIC for each student weekly until the training was complete.

Example #2: The relationship of parental involvement through promoting family activities in attendance for low SES kindergarteners to attendance. Six kindergarten classrooms in a school located in a low SES neighborhood participated in the intervention. Attendance data from the school was collected for five weeks prior to the intervention. Each classroom represented its own system, and attendance was averaged for students in each classroom. After the 5 weeks, monthly parent activities were introduced as the intervention with attendance continuing to be tracked on a weekly basis for each classroom.

Example #3: The effectiveness of a school social skills group intervention on disciplinary referrals. A group of 10 students identified by teachers as being discipline problems in the classroom were assigned to a social skills group implemented by the social work intern. Data on school disciplinary referrals were gathered for 5 weeks, and then the intervention was administered for 10 weeks, with disciplinary referrals continuing to be tracked on a weekly basis for each student.

Summary Content 6.2.

PROCEDURES FOR SINGLE-SUBJECT DESIGNS

1. Assess the client and determine a target outcome (what does the client want to improve or reduce?). *See* Chapter Eight for further information on measurement.
2. Gather and graph baseline information.

    Baseline data act as the subject's "control" for internal validity threats. Baseline data-gathering involves obtaining at least 5 data-points (and hopefully closer to 10) *before* intervention begins. This can often be a stumbling block for the implementation of a single-subject design. Usually, when you first see clients, you immediately begin your intervention. You would rarely want to hold off on doing anything to help your client for 5 weeks (if your client would eventually be seen on a weekly basis) to first collect baseline data. This might pose an ethical problem in which you are withholding services to clients in need.

    However, there may be a way to ethically collect such data. For example, many agencies complain of long waiting lists. One option is to collect baseline data from clients at regular intervals. Another way to get baseline data is from administrative records. For example, in a single-subject design on kindergarten attendance among at-risk children, attendance was already being tracked by the school, and the student researchers accessed these data and used them to establish their baseline before implementing parenting workshops to improve classroom attendance of kindergarteners.

    Baseline data are put on a graph with the target behavior on the vertical axis and time as the horizontal axis. *See* Figure 6.1.

3. Begin intervention and track the same target outcome over the same time-interval (e.g, "weeks," if you collected baseline data on a weekly basis) on the graph. *See* Figure 6.2.
4. After the intervention is complete, perform data analysis. The particular analysis you use will depend on the visual array of the data and can be found in Rubin (2010) or Rubin and Babbie (2011).

When considering whether a single-system design would work for your intervention research, consider the following advantages and disadvantages:

Advantages:

1. Can carry out with few numbers of people (less than 10 and as few as 3 clients)
2. Because you are collecting data at each point of contact, you may be able to pinpoint what was particularly helpful (or unhelpful) about the impact of your intervention. You can also track life events other than the intervention that may have altered the functioning of the system.

Disadvantages:

1. Lack of generalizability to other people
2. Figuring out how to build in data collection at regular and frequent intervals
3. Establishing baseline data that matches the frequency intervals of your intervention

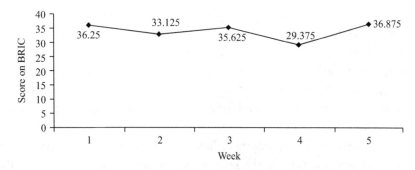

FIGURE 6.1 **Baseline Data for Single-Subject Design: Effectiveness of "Strong Kids" Curriculum**

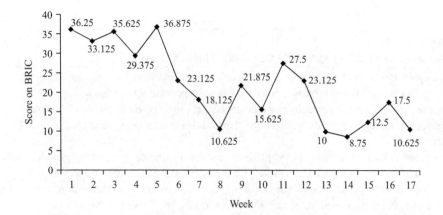

FIGURE 6.2 **Intervention Data for Single-Subject Design: Effectiveness of "Strong Kids" Curriculum**

Pre-Experimental Designs

Pre-experimental designs are characterized by the fact that they do not have a control group to assess change against. Therefore, they are subject to many threats of internal validity; in other words, you could attribute change not to the intervention itself but many other factors. Despite these weaknesses, posttest only and pre-/posttest studies, which comprise what we call pre-experimental designs, can often be feasibly enacted by students and can give us some information about the effect of an intervention; therefore, they are often a good choice for projects. Indeed, in the social work academic literature, these pre-experimental designs are the most frequently used as well (82% of studies) (Holosko, 2010).

POSTTEST-ONLY DESIGN

In a *posttest-only* design, the researcher assesses the impact of an intervention at posttest (or when the intervention is complete). The posttest design is commonly used to assess client satisfaction. For example, social workers may want to know whether child abuse victims and their families are satisfied with counseling designed to reduce their symptoms related to the abuse (Corcoran, 1995). As we will emphasize, however, client satisfaction in itself is not a sufficient outcome for student research projects, although agencies are often interested in this.

One main disadvantage of posttest designs is that baseline information is not collected in a posttest-only experiment, and therefore comparisons before and after intervention cannot be made. For example, if we collect information on client adjustment after our intervention, and we obtain the average score for our group of participants, then what is our basis of comparison? If we don't have pretest scores to compare the scores after the intervention or a control group, then we cannot say that participants improved.

Posttest-only designs are appropriate, however, if there is no opportunity to measure a certain outcome prior to the intervention because it has yet to occur. Put another way, you would use this design if measurement is only possible *after* a subject has undergone an intervention. Examples of student research projects using posttest-only designs are displayed here (*see* Example 6.4).

Example 6.4.

EXAMPLES OF STUDENT PROJECTS USING POSTTEST DESIGNS

Example # 1: A team of three research students did a study on a Work Empowerment Program to help people with criminal offenses find employment. A posttest-only design was appropriate because the participants entered the program immediately after incarceration (they could not be employed during incarceration). Therefore, they could only achieve employment after the intervention.

Example # 2: Two researchers in a public foster care agency studied permanency planning. As children in care were supposed to achieve what is known as a "permanency placement plan" (reunification with their biological parents or adoption proceedings by a relative or nonrelative) 14 months after they entered foster care, the student researchers looked at the outcome in terms of placement at the 14-month period. There was no opportunity to collect pretest information because all the children in the study had newly entered foster care. Without any pretest information, the posttest only design was appropriate.

ONE GROUP PRETEST/POSTTEST DESIGN

Pretest/posttest designs are one of the most basic of the intervention research designs in which a group of participants are assessed before the intervention is introduced and then after it is complete, using the same instrument. Pretest/posttest designs are often chosen by students; they are often feasible because such data are already being collected by agencies or they can be gathered by students within a semester. The pretest/posttest design can also be less disruptive to services than designs that demand a control group. After all, if you are interested in seeing the influence of an already-established group intervention to improve parenting skills, then you can just administer a standardized instrument at the beginning of the group (provided it begins when you are starting the implementation of your study) and then after the group is complete (provided that it finishes before your semester is over and that there are at least 10 participants to the group).

The advantage of a *pretest/posttest design* is that baseline information is known before the intervention begins. This allows the researcher to more confidently attribute observable changes to the intervention. However, many other reasons unrelated to the intervention could explain these changes, as well. Without a control group, you cannot necessarily claim that the changes were a result of the intervention. Pretest/posttest designs used in student projects are presented in Example 6.5.

Example 6.5.

EXAMPLES OF STUDENT PROJECTS USING PRETEST/POSTTEST DESIGNS

Example #1: Social work students delivered a 3-hour intervention on end-of-life care in graduate school masters classes. The participants filled out an instrument on end-of-life care knowledge and one on death anxiety prior to the class and then at the end of the class on end-of-life care.

Example #2: A dyad of researchers placed in a child welfare setting studied the impact of the Parent Nurturing Program, which is a group intervention to help parents gain greater understanding of child development and positive parenting practices (http://www.nurturing parenting.com/about.html). Part of the evaluation of the Parenting Nurturing Program is a self-report instrument completed by parents both at the beginning of the intervention and at its conclusion. Because the program structure already contained both tests, the students naturally described their study as a pretest/posttest design.

Example #3: Two student researchers assessed a family preservation program to determine whether families improved on the risk and safety assessment that was completed before intervention and then at 6 months.

Experimental and Quasi-Experimental Designs

The experiment is considered the strongest type of design in terms of inferring causality (i.e., the independent variable caused the dependent variable). In the experiment, there are two conditions (an experimental group and a control group), *and* participants are randomly assigned to one or the other condition. Hence, participants are selected into a group for no reason other than mathematical probability, which assures that the groups are comparable in their characteristics. The advantage to having a control group with randomly assigned participants is that we can assume that differences in outcome between the two groups are the result of the intervention. In other words, experimental designs control for all internal validity threats, except in some cases (Monette et al., 2011). However, we will not explore these further, although they are considered the "gold standard" of intervention research, because in student projects at community agencies during the time frame of a semester, experimental designs cannot typically be carried out because of feasibility. Indeed, experimental designs are rarely published in the social work literature. Holosko (2010) found, in a content analysis of social work journals, that experimental designs were only used in 2.3% of the studies published.

An optimal alternative is to conduct a quasi-experimental design. These are similar to experimental designs in that they use two groups, comparing an intervention to a control condition (or more typically a comparison condition). However, quasi-experimental designs do not randomize participants into groups. Instead, participants are assigned to conditions based, usually, on some kind of convenience factor, such as the classroom a child attends, the county in which one resides, or the people that obtain services at a particular point in time. Although quasi-experimental designs still retain control over many threats to internal validity, selection bias looms as a central issue (Monette et al., 2011).

When considering whether to use a quasi-experimental design, think about naturally occurring treatment and control groups that will take part in an intervention that will be completed within the semester you are collecting data. Another option is to look at already-collected data from your agencies and compare two groups retrospectively. Example 6.6 below shows the use of quasi-experimental designs in student research projects.

Example 6.6.

EXAMPLES OF STUDENT PROJECTS USING QUASI-EXPERIMENTAL DESIGNS

Example #1: In a sexual assault response center, group treatment was a mandatory modality for all women who were interested in receiving counseling after having experienced a sexual assault. Women could also elect to have individual counseling as long as they attended group sessions. A team of two student researchers decided to conduct a quasi-experimental design, comparing women who only received group treatment versus those who received group and individual.

Example #2: In a child welfare setting, a team of three students decided to evaluate the family group conferencing program. (Family group conferencing brings together a child's extended family to figure out a placement plan for the child. This can be preferable to relying on the child welfare system to determine placement of a child, especially when maltreatment exists within the immediate family). Family Group Conferencing (FGC) was a relatively new intervention offered at the agency, and therefore only 15 families had undergone FGC and been tracked to determine its impact. The students matched the FGC treatment participants with cases that had not gone through FGC in terms of ethnicity, region, risk level, and whether the case was categorized as a child protective services or a foster care case.

Example #3: In a child welfare setting, the quality assurance department wanted to know if protective supervision guidelines introduced 2 years prior were being implemented county-wide for the family preservation program. The control group therefore involved cases prior to the introduction of the guidelines, and the experimental group comprises cases after administration of the protective services guidelines.

DECISION-MAKING FOR INTERVENTION RESEARCH

1. Best alternative: quasi-experimental design taking advantage of naturally occurring groups.
2. Next best: pretest/posttest design.
3. Choose a posttest-only design when it is either not feasible or it is impossible to collect pretest data.
4. If there are fewer than 10 people in your intervention and you can figure out a way to collect baseline data: use a single-subject design.

Now that you have been given information on the various designs, Test Your Skills Exercise 6.1 requires you to apply your knowledge to scenarios that our research students have faced in considering their agency projects. Project Development Worksheet 6.1 asks you consider the designs you could use for data collection in your own research study.

Test Your Skills Exercise 6.1.

RESEARCH DESIGNS

1. A military outpatient mental health clinic wanted to determine the effectiveness of its counseling services of adults—service members, veterans, and their dependents—as determined by the change scores on the QR-40. The student researchers placed there also wanted to see whether people with various DSM mental health diagnoses—mood disorders, anxiety disorders, and adjustment disorders—improved on the QR-40. What is the appropriate design in this case?

2. A battered women's shelter has court accompaniment as one of the services they offer. The shelter contacts every woman who has a court date for family violence and offers to accompany her. Most women, however, do not want the services. Of those that do choose are asked to fill out a client satisfaction survey after their court hearing is over. The women's shelter also could collect data on disposition of the court hearing. The battered women's shelter wants to conduct an evaluation of the court accompaniment program. What additional information would you want to know? What type of design would you advise?

3. A team of two researchers was interested in examining the effectiveness of support groups for breast cancer survivors. Because they didn't have access to a breast cancer support group at either of their agency field placement settings, they planned to contact different hospitals in the area that conducted breast cancer support groups. If they collected baseline data for groups in which they received permission, they would get clients at different points in the group process. For example, on the day they turned up to collect baseline data, some participants would have been attending the group for a long period of time, whereas other participants might have just started. In light of this pattern, what design might be feasible?

4. A team of student researchers was interested in evaluating the effectiveness of a new foster parent training introduced into the county's system. The members of the team compared foster care cases before the implementation of Parents' Resources for Information Development Education (PRIDE) and then after PRIDE had been implemented by the agency. What kind of design is this?

5. A team of two researchers in a child welfare setting wanted to examine the effect of structured decision making (SDM). SDM was designed to improve the decision-making capabilities of caseworkers through the completion of a risk-assessment tool within 30 days of a child's entry into foster care. Responses to the risk assessment tool were used to create a targeted service plan for the child's reunification with the family. The tool is completed at regular intervals after that. The researchers wanted to look at how effective SDM was on the outcome measure "length of stay in foster care." Only 50 cases had gone through the child welfare system since the implementation of SDM. In this type of situation, at what points can the outcome data be collected?

6. What kind of designs are possible in #5 above? What are the limitations of each kind of design and which one would you ultimately choose?

Project Development Worksheet 6.1.

RESEARCH DESIGN

Considering your research topic, discuss two alternatives for the kind of design you may implement for your research project.

Alternative #1

What type of research design would be optimal?

Describe it briefly here:

What are its advantages?

What are its disadvantages?

Alternative #2

Type of research design:

Describe it briefly here:

What are its advantages?

What are its disadvantages?

Threats to Internal Validity

Threats to internal validity make it unclear that the change in the dependent variable was caused by the independent variable and not by other factors. Without strong internal validity, the cause of the change cannot be confidently identified. Because most foundation research methods texts cover internal validity in great deal, we will only offer examples of the most common kinds that you will encounter in Test Your Skills Exercise 6.2. We then ask you to consider ways to resolve problems in internal validity in a study you plan to implement in your setting or one that could hypothetically be of value to your agency. In Test Your Skills Exercise 6.3, you will take scenarios derived from student agency settings and figure out how to face internal validity issues.

Test Your Skills Exercise 6.2.

THREATS TO INTERNAL VALIDITY

THREAT	EXAMPLE	HOW TO SOLVE	EXERCISE
			Will this be an issue in your intervention research? Why or why not?
Maturation—When people change over time, the change may have nothing to do with the intervention (independent variable). Rather, the change may simply reflect skill, knowledge and experience acquisition, or symptom improvement that would have happened without the intervention.	Grief may naturally dissipate over time with or without attendance at a bereavement group. Well-designed research in this area would need to distinguish between natural dissipation of grief and the dissipation that occurs because of participation in a bereavement group.	Implement a control group.	
Testing—Filling out a pretest may impact study participants' performance on the posttest. For example, as a result of taking a pretest, people might experience less anxiety and/or become more comfortable with the material. Improved posttest scores may be related to the experience of the pretest and not the intervention.	Graduate students in a social work research class were given a "research diagnostic assessment" on the first day of class. They took the same test on the last day of class so that the instructor could tell how much they had learned over the course of the semester. Because the posttest included the same questions as the pretest, students who looked up the correct answers after the pretest were able to remember the test questions and respond correctly on the posttest as a result.	Tends to be an issue with knowledge (they may gain knowledge from taking the pretest) or attitudes (they may learn socially desirable attitudes) questionnaires, but not for adjustment/emotions/thoughts, which hopefully would change as a result of an intervention. Having a control group may help you disentangle the effect of testing (which may operate in both groups) or, in such a case with a control group, you could drop the pretest and only compare the experimental and control groups on posttest scores.	

THREAT	EXAMPLE	HOW TO SOLVE	EXERCISE
Selection Bias involves discrepancies in how people are assigned to treatment conditions. As a result, the different outcomes in the groups—experimental versus control/comparison—result not from the intervention but from the attributes of the people selected into each group.	In a sexual assault response center, group treatment was a mandatory modality for all women who were interested in receiving counseling after having experienced a sexual assault. Women could also elect to have individual counseling as long as they attended group sessions. It could be that women who elect to receive both individual and group treatment differ in some way from those who only receive group treatment; perhaps they feel more distress and have more problems recovering from the sexual assault. Therefore, any differences found between groups at the end of treatment might be due to these initial differences rather than the treatment received.	Randomization to treatment and control groups	
History—Changes in experimental subjects over time might not result from the intervention but instead from events that happened over the intervention period.	A team of student researchers was interested in evaluating the effectiveness of a new foster parent training introduced into the county's system. They compared foster care cases before the implementation of PRIDE and then after PRIDE had been implemented by the agency. But prior to the new foster care training, other practices and interventions in the foster care system might have contributed to any differences found between the groups (PRIDE and non-PRIDE).	Conduct experimental and control group interventions at the same period of time. If not possible, note in limitations section.	
Mortality (also known as *attrition*) involves loss of subjects over time.	If 100 people are pretested prior to the intervention but only 50 complete the intervention at posttest, not much can be concluded based on the remaining 50% of the sample. Subjects may be less motivated to continue if they are dissatisfied with the intervention. On the other hand, participants may believe they have gotten what they needed as a result of an intervention and may discontinue as a result. Whatever its basis, there may be differences between dropouts and study participants who complete the posttest.	Among the various ways to overcome this barrier, incentives may offer a way to ensure participant retention. For example, a $5 telephone card can be provided to study participants who complete the study. As a general rule, the incentive should commensurate with time and effort to complete measurement instruments, but not be so high as to be coercive. A too high monetary incentive is seen as coercive as participants might see the value as too high to resist, thus "making them" be part of an intervention they would not otherwise consider.	

THREAT	EXAMPLE	HOW TO SOLVE	EXERCISE
Mortality (also known as *attrition*) involves loss of subjects over time.		Another way to address problems with study retention is to employ an "intent to treat" statistical analysis that essentially attributes zero change from pretest to posttest for dropouts. Score differences between dropouts and those participants completing the study at posttest may also be compared using statistical analysis (*see* Chapter Nine). If differences between the two groups are not statistically significant, then one can make the case that groups are sufficiently similar, enabling the researcher to draw conclusions about those who stayed in the study.	

Test Your Skills Exercise 6.3.

THREATS TO INTERVAL VALIDITY

Example #1: When comparing the studies of group-versus-individual treatment at the sexual assault response center and the child welfare agency's family group conferencing, which design is more methodologically rigorous in terms of controlling for threats to internal validity?

Example #2: A team of student researchers was interested in evaluating the effectiveness of a new foster parent training introduced into the county's system. They compared foster care cases before the implementation of PRIDE and then after PRIDE had been implemented by the agency. What are the chief limitations of this design?

CONCLUSION

Research designs are an important initial consideration for a research project because they provide the blueprint for how your data will be collected. This chapter provides descriptions and examples of the main quantitative research designs and discusses threats to internal validity. The illustrations and exercises should help you conceptualize your own research design and be more able to understand the research you read and the choices that authors make in their studies. We will return to the topic of research designs in Chapter Eleven, where you will see how they dovetail into program evaluation. The next chapter turns to the "who"—the people who will participate in your study—and how you will select them to be part of your design.

WEBSITES

http://www.socialresearchmethods.net/kb/design.php
Research Methods Knowledge Base Research Design webpage, with more detail on the various types of research designs, with accompanying graphics.
http://www.statpac.com/surveys/index.htm#toc
Survey Design Tutorial, with more information about constructing your survey.
http://www.surveymonkey.com/
The website to access SurveyMonkey.

SAMPLING

7

Samples allow us to study something on a small scale and to then apply those findings on a larger scale. Although research sampling can be very technical in practice, the basic idea of sampling is quite simple. In fact, we frequently make use of sampling strategies in our daily lives. Tasting food samples at the grocery store is a common example. If we like the small piece of cheese or cake on display, we are more inclined to buy the whole item. Reading a few pages of a new book before buying it is another example of everyday sampling. We might read a few pages to see whether the story appeals to us. If they are enjoyable, then we may decide that the book may be equally enjoyable and we buy it.

This chapter will address the questions of sample size and participant selection. In research terms, the "sample" refers to the *participants* in your study. By observing a small group of participants, we are hoping to learn something about the larger group to which they belong. A study with too few participants will be of limited use. This would be akin to reading only one or two sentences of a book before buying it. We might not learn enough from those sentences to know much about the rest of the book. To be a good researcher, we also need to think about how we choose participants. This is akin to thinking about what books to sample in the bookstore. If we only pick up books with bright covers or that sit at eye level, then we introduce a bias against books with plain covers or books that happen to be on the bottom shelf. Indeed, it is a fact that authors with last names beginning with the last letters of the alphabet do not get as much exposure to readers as authors with last names beginning with letters at the start of the alphabet. An appropriate sampling strategy allows us to pick books regardless of their location and cover design.

Learning about *sampling* can be confusing because instructors and textbooks often use different terminology to describe the same concepts. For example, some writers refer to a *study population*, whereas others talk about a *sampling frame*. Similarly, *convenience sample* and *availability sample* have the same meaning, as do the terms *representative sampling* and *probability sampling*. It is no wonder that students become confused when a multitude of terms are used to describe similar entities. This chapter will familiarize you with sampling terms so that you feel more comfortable with the language of research. As you read through the chapter, make sure you identify the important sample terms to include in the Terminology Worksheet that you began earlier.

REPRESENTATIVE AND NONREPRESENTATIVE SAMPLING

Ideally, the sample you choose for your project will accurately *represent* your population. To the extent that it is *representative*, it can be described in one of three ways:

1. *Representative sample*—this sample looks like the actual population. There are equal proportions of units (males, females, African-Americans, Muslims, those living in poverty, etc.) to that of the actual population.
2. *Unrepresentative sample*—a sample in which some characteristics are overrepresented or underrepresented relative to the total population. For example, more females are in your sample than there are in the population. Often, when we study vulnerable populations, there is no way to obtain a representative sample because we don't know what this population looks like. We may have no way of knowing how many homeless people there are living in a city, for example, to conduct an assessment of their needs. In this situation, the best we can do is survey the people that are available and find out from them where other homeless people may congregate so we can contact them.
3. *Population sample*—a study of the entire population. Surveying an entire population of, say, a city, may be too expensive and time-consuming to be practical. However, if your population is a manageable size and/or you have access to everyone in it, then it might make sense (and might even be easier) to use the whole population. For example, two research students wanted to survey the whole population of school social workers in a single county regarding the kinds of work they did and how long they spent on their tasks. The students knew that attendance at social work trainings were mandatory in that county, and they requested permission to appear at the trainings and distribute the survey. This granted the students access to the entire population.

POPULATIONS AND SAMPLING FRAMES

To obtain a sample you must first consider your *population*. The *population* is the entire set of individuals or other entities to which you want to generalize your study findings. The population may be the foster care families that are involved with your agency, the clients with severe mental illness that come to a clubhouse setting, or the school in which you work as a school social worker. This brings up an important distinction. The population you hope to generalize the results to may be different from the *universal population*. *The universal population* usually involves the national population, such as all foster care families or every school in the country. Usually, student research projects will attempt to obtain a representative sample to be able to generalize their results to their agency only.

How does the *sample* fit into all this? Remember that the *sample* (the people who will actually take part in your study) is a smaller representation of your population. For example, if you wanted to study the student body at your school, then you could take a random sample of 10% of the students. This would be much easier than trying to interview each and every student. After surveying 10% of students (the *sample*), you may be able to generalize the results to the entire student body (the *population*).

Before selecting a sample, you first have to figure out the *sampling frame* from which to draw your sample. A sampling frame is a list of all the people or cases (called *elements* or *units* in sampling terms). Understand that the sampling frame may be similar, but not always identical, to your population, and we will go into these differences in the next paragraph. We just want to make clear this distinction because you will be using the sampling frame and not necessarily the entire population when you select your sample. Notably, you don't necessarily need to identify your sampling frame—and it may be impossible to do so—when you are using a nonrepresentative sampling method (as discussed earlier).

One way that the sampling frame can be different from the population is the time frame that it involves. The population may involve all cases that a program has served, but to create a sampling frame that covers the entire existence of the program might encompass so many cases as to be burdensome. It would be prudent for you (in tandem with your agency) to address the time frame that will be used. Here are some considerations:

- Did the program go through an overhaul or critical change at some point in the recent past? If so, you might want to look at cases from that point forward for your sampling frame.
- Did the program or agency go through a change of administration or ownership? If so, a particular administrator or director may only want to know how the program has been operating since she took the helm.
- Did the program start adapting the use of a particular measurement tool at some recent point? If so, then it would be logical to only include cases that have this information collected. Similarly, was certain information, such as recidivism of offenders, only collected from a certain point in time?

Another point to consider is that you may only want to include closed rather than open agency cases in your sampling frame. It is only with closed cases that you can determine certain outcomes or results in which you are interested. For example, reducing the length of services is often a goal of child welfare agencies, but cases have to be closed to know how long services have lasted. As you consider these sampling time frame options, however, you need to remember that whatever decision you make about sampling frames, the sample must enable you to answer your research question.

Example 7.1 illustrates the differences between the *population*, the universal population, the *sampling frame*, and the *sample*, and Project Development Worksheet 7.1 and Test Your Skills 7.1 asks you to apply these terms to the development of your projects and other agency research scenarios, respectively. Note that although we touch on sampling methods here, they will be discussed in more detail later in the chapter.

Example 7.1.

ILLUSTRATIONS OF SAMPLING TERMS

Example #1: Three students wanted to evaluate the effectiveness of services in an outpatient clinic that served active duty military, their dependents, and veterans. The *population* is all the people (active duty military, their dependents, and veterans) that the outpatient clinic served. The *universal population* would be all U.S. military personnel, veterans, and their dependents seeking psychological assistance on an outpatient basis. The *sampling frame* involved all cases that were closed at this particular outpatient clinic in the last 5 years. The recent 5-year period was chosen because a self-report measure had been required of all clinicians to implement with their clients during this time. Although the researchers had planned to use a random sampling method to select their cases, there were so few clinicians who had used the standardized instrument that was supposed to be administered at pre- and posttest, the team had to be content with an availability sample.

Example #2: A study measured the effectiveness of an employment program for people who had been convicted of crimes. In this study, the *population* was ex-offenders taking part in a Work Empowerment Program. The *universal population* was ex-offenders who are interested in obtaining employment. The *sampling frame* included every person who has participated in the program a year from the outset of the research project and whose case was closed. This time frame was chosen because the current administrator had assumed the position at that time, and she wanted to know how well the program was being utilized and how effective it was in facilitating employment since she had taken charge of the program.

Example #3: A student research group wanted to know whether a new foster parent training had an impact on length of time children were in foster care. The study population in this case was children in foster care in a certain Northern Virginia county. The universal population was children in foster care throughout the United States. The sampling frame was 155 children placed in foster care over the previous 5-year period. The sample involved randomly selecting cases of foster care children whose foster parents had undergone the new foster care training, and randomly selecting cases of foster care children who were being take care of by parents who had been trained using the old foster care training.

Example #4: A student research group was interested in the life satisfaction of parents of children with Down Syndrome compared to parents of children without Downs Syndrome. The universal population was parents of dependent children. The study population was parents of dependent children in a municipal locality. An online survey was sent to a convenience sample drawn from two sources: a list of parents affiliated with the local Down Syndrome Association where one of the students was placed and the parents of children in a local suburban public elementary school where the other student was placed.

Example #5: In one qualitative project, a student was concerned about the cultural competency of staff working with unaccompanied refugee and immigrant minors. The student asked all staff members at a residential setting for unaccompanied minors to share their experiences and insights about working with this group of children in an interview with the student researcher. Nine staff members agreed to be interviewed. In this study, the universal population would be staff members working with refugee minors, and the sampling frame could be a list of all employees at this particular agency. However, because the respondents volunteered to be interviewed and were not randomly selected from the list of employees, the nine respondents constituted an availability sample.

Project Development Worksheet 7.1.

POPULATION AND SAMPLING FRAME

Think about the project you are developing. What is the universal population, the population, and the sampling frame? Or do you have a convincing rationale for why you are unable to get a sampling frame?

SAMPLING METHODS

One of several different methods may be used to obtain your sample. The method you select is based on three factors:

1. the representativeness of the population
2. convenience and time constraints
3. access to the population

Ideally you want to have a large sample that is representative of the population. Summary Content 7.1 demonstrates both representative and nonrepresentative sampling methods. Note that this is not an exhaustive list; we have selected only those that student projects have used in our courses. You will need to consult your main research text to get more detail on all the different sampling methods that are potentially available.

Summary Content 7.1. SAMPLING METHODS			
REPRESENTATIVE SAMPLING			
TYPE OF METHOD	DESCRIPTION	PROCEDURE	EXAMPLE
Simple random sampling	Each member of the population gets an equal chance at being selected.	By using a random procedure (table of random numbers, coin toss, computer program, or drawing names out of a hat).	In the Workforce Empowerment Program, to assess the impact on employment, the researchers randomly select 40 out of 200 closed cases.
Systematic random sampling	A variant of simple random sampling.	A first element is selected at random from a list (or from sequential files). Then, every nth element is selected.	In an evaluation of structured decision making in a child welfare agency, the research students took every third case of closed cases for the last 2 years.
Stratified random sampling	The percentage that you need from each group, category, or *strata* so that your overall sample is a small replica of the actual population.	Break up a population into categories that are important (such as intervention and control group) and then take random sampling from each category.	In the military outpatient clinic, researchers wanted to assess the impact of services on depression, PTSD, other anxiety disorders, and marital problems. The researchers broke up the sampling frame into these DSM categories and sampled a certain percentage so they were both guaranteed of getting these types of cases and that they were represented in the sample as they were in the sampling frame.

Cluster sampling	Use naturally formed clusters or groupings within the population and then sample from these groups.		Let's take a look at the foster care example again. You may not have a listing of every family in foster care. Therefore, you may select a natural cluster of cases—say, within an agency—and then sample from that group.
NONREPRESENTATIVE SAMPLING			
Purposive sampling	Used in qualitative research; based on your knowledge or judgment, you find a sample that will best apply to your research aims.	Hand-selecting those that you believe will have valuable information for your study.	A student interested in the civil commitment and detainment process developed a purposive sample by asking clinicians in area to nominate clients who had experienced civil commitment and who agreed to be contacted to participate in the study.
Convenience	Using a sample that is readily available; is used in both quantitative and qualitative research.	Various procedures but basically involves sampling only those who are available or convenient (e.g., only surveying people in classes you have access to; asking people on street corners to complete your survey).	Posting a link to a survey on gay adoption on a GLBT website and see who responds.
Snowball sampling	Typically used for qualitative studies on sensitive topics about which little is known, such as teenage sex workers, when the population is not very visible or accessible.	Once you find a member of the population, you ask them to serve as an informant for your study and let other people who have the same characteristics know about the research.[1]	A student group studying access to services in the Hispanic community talked first with one of the religious leaders in the community who provided the names of two church members who were Hispanic for the researcher to contact; each of these individuals provided the name of one of his/her Hispanic neighbors to contact and each of the neighbors provided names of subsequent Hispanic neighbors or friends.

1 Typically, snowball sampling is described as the member of the population providing you with names and you contact these people, but this doesn't seem to preserve people's confidentiality; therefore, a more ethical arrangement is to ask people to let other people in their population know about the study and how to contact you.

Project Development Worksheet 7.2.	
SAMPLING METHODS	
1. One type of sampling procedure you envision using for your research project: Strengths: Weaknesses: 2. Name an alternative sampling procedure: Strengths: Weaknesses:	

RESEARCH DESIGNS AND SAMPLING: HOW THEY WORK TOGETHER

This section will outline some of the more common pairings of research design and sampling strategy. Most research textbooks fail to discuss sampling from the standpoint of different research designs. This is unfortunate because there are some sampling procedures that are often used in conjunction with certain research designs. For example, if you are conducting a survey ideally, then you should use a method that relies on random sampling; however, this is difficult to do when you are limited in terms of time and resources (sending reminders to get people to participate, offering incentives so that people will participate, and doing replacement sampling when people do not want to participate). One alternative so that rigor is not replaced is to survey the whole population (if it's not too large and you have access to the whole population). Most of the time, student surveys end up being based on availability sampling, which limits generalization to the population being studied. For example, in course evaluations, people who end up replying to an online survey method may be the ones that are most dissatisfied with the class, rather than being truly representative of all members of a class.

If you are doing intervention research *prospectively* (meaning that you recruit participants to be part of an intervention and collect the data during your research project), then chances are you will be relying on a *convenience sample*. In other words, when doing intervention research, we are usually happy to get enough people to participate in the study. With such few participants, we don't worry about creating a random selection of the population unless you have the opportunity of working with a potentially large group, all of whom may be fitting for your intervention (i.e., students in a school).

However, if you are conducting retrospective research on an intervention (i.e., collecting data from cases that have already been worked and may be closed), then you should use one of the statistically random methods (such as *simple random sampling*) or study the whole population. If your study design is quasi-experimental and has two groups (an experimental and control group), then you can use a *stratified sample*. Recall again the example of the study on Parents' Resources for Information Development Education (PRIDE), the foster care parent training. The experimental group involved the foster care cases after the new foster care parent training, and the control group was the cases prior to the new foster care parenting training. After putting these cases into their separate groups, you can then take a simple random sample from each group. Test Your Skills Exercise 7.1 and Project Development Worksheet 7.3 give you opportunities to consider the sampling methods you might use in real-life practice situations and your project.

Test Your Skills Exercise 7.1.

SAMPLING METHODS

1. A student was interested in social workers' knowledge of health literacy. She obtained the NASW list of members for her state, which comprised 2000 names. She planned on surveying all 2000 members. What kind of sampling technique was used here? What other kind of sampling technique can she use?

2. In the research project on structured decision making discussed under the systematic sampling example, what other kind of sampling technique(s) could be used?

Morgan and Aaron are social work students. As part of their course requirements, they must work collaboratively to develop, implement, and present the results from an original research project.

Morgan and Aaron have decided to investigate the impact of employment on African-American mothers living in an area housing project who neglect their children. Both students work in a field agency that provides services to neglectful parents across the city. Many, but not all, of their clients come from the housing project. The students are excited about the project but they cannot agree on key elements of the research design.

Morgan does not think that their question is refined, and she wants to see how other researchers have conceptualized and conducted studies on this population. She believes that she and Aaron should randomly select participants from a list of current clients who have been employed within the past year. Morgan believes that results gained from the mailed questionnaires should be generalizable to the larger population of neglectful African-American mothers living in the housing project.

Aaron disagrees with Morgan's thoughts. He is frustrated because of the lack of established studies on interventions for neglecting mothers. He believes that it is important to understand each person's experience and that they must seek to uncover "hidden knowledge." Furthermore, he does not believe that the mothers will be receptive to a mailed questionnaire. Rather, Aaron wants to work with agency personnel who are already working with clients and have them locate at least on prospective respondent. He believes that the first respondent will lead to others.

Consider the ways the students can obtain a sample for their study and match the correct sampling strategy with the appropriate description.

a. **A cluster or area sample**
b. **A snowball sample**
c. **A stratified sample**
d. **An availability or convenience sample**
e. **A systematic random sample**

_____ Contact the housing project office and ask for a list of clients who live in the housing project. Randomly select every fifth person on the list and mail them a questionnaire.

_____ Visit a group parenting session at the agency and ask if anyone would be willing to answer your questions.

_____ Ask agency personnel who are already working with neglecting African-American mothers for the name of one client to interview and then ask that client for the names of other neglecting African-American mothers who might be willing to participate in the study.

Project Development Worksheet 7.3.

SAMPLING METHOD

Based on your research design, what kind of sampling method will you use?

SAMPLE SIZE

Finding an adequate number of participants for your study can be challenging and sometimes dooms student projects to noncompletion or less than satisfying results. As you plan out your student projects, be sure to consider the feasibility of your study with regard to the number of participants with whom you will have access. Getting enough people to participate in your study is important because to perform statistical analysis, you have to have what is called *group data*—data on a certain number of people. We will be talking in more depth in Chapter Nine about statistical significance. But one fact to keep in mind for now is that to detect statistically significant results (referred to as statistical power), you need enough people to study. Further, the number of cases needed for statistically significant results often depends on the type of statistical test you use. Your main research text will detail further statistical power, its computation, and its implications for sample size, but here in Summary Content 7.2 are provided some basic go-to's so you have a rough idea of what you will need. In Project Development Worksheet 7.4 you will consider what sample size is required for your project.

Summary Content 7.2.

SAMPLE SIZE GUIDELINES

1. *Intervention Research*: Should have at least 10 cases in each condition. If you have an experimental and control group, then you would have a minimum of 20 total cases. If you have a pretest/posttest design, then you will have 10 total cases. The rationale for this is that you cannot perform statistical data analysis on any fewer than these. Twenty-five to 30 per group (50–60 for the total sample for an experimental or quasi-experimental design) is an even better number to reach because such numbers are better able to detect statistically significant results if they exist (i.e., they have better statistical power).
2. *Prediction Research* (*see* Chapter Eleven): Needs to have 10 cases for each independent variable that predicts the dependent variable. For example, a student research group was interested in the factors associated with post partum depression in Latinas. For each factor (the independent variables)—culture of origin, social work involvement, domestic violence, marital status, number of children—10 cases are required. Therefore, the students' sample size needs to be at least 50 cases.
3. *Qualitative Research*: For student projects (as opposed to those that will be submitted to professional journals), you should have at least 5 cases for in-depth interviews; focus groups should ideally have been between 8 to 12 participants.

Project Development Worksheet 7.4.

SAMPLE SIZE

What sample size will you need for your study? How will you ensure that you can attain that size sample? If you are not able to do so, what is your plan instead?

CONCLUSION

This chapter has described and attempted to clarify the terminology associated with sampling, the part of the research project where you decide what people or cases will be involved in your study. We discussed the differences between representative and nonrepresentative sampling and the types of methods under each that are relevant to student research projects. We have also explored sampling methods relevant to both quantitative and qualitative research. We concluded with an essential aspect of sampling, which involves how many people to involve in your research design. In the next chapter, we move to measurement that will involve the type of data that you collect from your sample.

WEBSITES

http://www.socialresearchmethods.net/kb/sampling.php
Research Methods Knowledge Base on Sampling webpage with detailed descriptions, accompanied by graphics, of sampling terms and methods.
http://www.psycho.uni-duesseldorf.de/aap/projects/gpower/
A power analysis calculator.

MEASUREMENT

8

This chapter discusses the tools by which you collect data for your research project if you are using a quantitative research method. As researchers, we gather data by systematically measuring something in a structured way. Thus, understanding the *language* of measurement—how and why we use scales and various other tools to measure behaviors—is an important aspect of becoming conversant in research. After a discussion of important measurement terms, we discuss the assessment of your independent variable (for intervention research) and how to select standardized measures for your dependent variables. Finally, we end with tips on developing your own measures. Again, there are many more terms in this chapter for the Terminology Worksheet that you've been developing since Chapter One.

OPERATIONALIZATION: HOW TO MEASURE YOUR IDEA

To perform quantitative research on these topics, the topics have to be defined concretely so that you can quantify their existence. In other words, the research process requires you to translate your ideas and concepts (which we usually describe in words) into numerical quantities. This process is called *operationalization* of your concepts. Once a concept is operationalized, it is referred to as a *variable*.

Let's examine how topic areas (your concepts or ideas) can be translated into numerical terms, or *operationalized*. A simple way to quantify a concept is to count whether the problem exists or not. For example, we might quantify depression by having subjects undergo a diagnostic interview to discover whether they meet DSM criteria for having a depressive disorder. The presence of a DSM-defined depressive disorder is counted as a "yes." If the DSM criteria is not met, then the case is counted as a "no." A more sophisticated way to translate depression into a numerical phenomenon is to use a standardized instrument, such as the "Beck Depression Scale" (Beck, Ward, Mendelson, Mock, & Erbaugh, 1961). The Beck Scale defines the degree to which the individual is depressed, which is represented by a total score on the scale.

Use Test Your Skills Exercise 8.1 to begin thinking about conceptualizing and operationalizing variables.

Test Your Skills Exercise 8.1.

DEFINING VARIABLES

The following are a few of the student research questions introduced in Chapter Two. Look at the underlined variables. How you would measure or "operationalize" these variables?

1. Does participation in an *afterschool art program* increase a participant's *level of hope*?

2. Is there a correlation between *body size*, *body perception*, and *body satisfaction*?

3. Will individuals with developmental disabilities increase *communication ability* and *empathy* more so than clients coping with other disabilities after participation in a *6-week therapeutic riding program*?

4. Do women with more progressive *gender role attitudes* report higher levels of *binge-drinking behavior*?

USING STANDARDIZED MEASURES

Many times when students approach their research project, they are eager to come up with their own instrument. The problem with such an approach is that these instruments have not been *standardized*. A standardized instrument has been "normed" (tested) on a large number of people and the results have been statistically analyzed to determine reliability and validity of the instrument (more on this in a later section). We recommend that whenever possible, you use a measurement instrument that has already been developed and standardized. There are several reasons for this position:

1. Researchers who have developed existing measures have already put considerable effort into formulating them. They have normed their instruments by gathering data on numerous participants and calculating its reliability and validity (these terms will be discussed in more detail below). If you create a new measure, then you will not be able to establish this level of standardization.

2. This process of instrument development and norming also involves developing a way to score the instrument and to figure out what these scores mean. If you make up your own instrument, then it will be difficult to know how score it. Additionally, arriving at some kind of meaningful summary score (adding items up with a very basic scale) is difficult. This becomes vitally important for the statistical analysis of your findings. If you are only able to work with the items that make up the scale (rather than total scores), then you must run countless individual data analysis tests. If you run this many tests, then you are bound to find some findings that are statistically significant, and in doing so, you violate the principle of statistical probability. The latter means that if you run a large number of tests, then you are bound to find some that are significant based on the laws of probability. You will not know what your scale taps into as a whole if you are only reduced to examining the findings on an item-by-item basis.

3. Students sometimes argue that no one has created an instrument that represents what they wish to measure in their study. In truth, there are hundreds

of standardized measures available on an amazing array of even the most obscure and topics. It may be that the student has not searched thoroughly enough for a measure that fits his or her research needs.

4. By using standardized measures, you are not "re-inventing the wheel" in your research project; rather, you are building on an existing knowledge base.

One problem with using standardized measures, however, is that they can be expensive. For example, the Beck Depression Inventory is as expensive as $3 per person.[1] Most professors at the undergraduate and graduate levels are not interested in having their students incur expenses as they conduct required research projects. Therefore, it is important to select measures for which you will not have to pay. There are several ways you can do this:

1. Find out if your agency has purchased a measure for its use. Even if you see no evidence of data collection using a standardized measure, it is worth asking the person who evaluates services or the executive director about whether a measure has been purchased for agency use.

2. Contact the creator of a measure (if the author's affiliation is not listed in source material you find on a particular measure, then run a Google search on his or her name to locate current contact information) and request permission to use the measure for educational purposes. Note that if your project will benefit the agency in any way, then the agency should purchase it. Be sure when you locate the developer that you ask for scoring information and clinical cut-off scores, as these become important for data entry and statistical analysis later.

3. When you are doing your literature review, you will come across studies that have been published and may point to instruments that have been used in your area. You may contact the researcher of the particular study if the bibliographic reference to the measure doesn't provide enough information on how to find the instrument.

4. Fischer and Corcoran (2007a, 2007b) are social work academics who have written two volumes of compilations of instruments. The benefit of their books is that they include the instruments themselves. Most articles and books will not supply these, but without being able to see the measure, sometimes it is difficult to know whether you would like to use it or not.

5. Corcoran and Hozack (2010) have an exhaustive list of other books and Internet resources that may help you find measures.

6. For strengths-based measures and how to access them, see Early and Newsome (2004).

Now that we have talked about sources for finding standardized instruments, we turn to a more detailed discussion of reliability and validity of measures.

Reliability and Validity. When conducting research, we want to know that our results are trustworthy and are a close approximation of what we want to observe. The terms *reliability* and *validity* are used to describe many aspects of research

---

1 http://www.musc.edu/dfm/RCMAR/Beck.html

methodology. In this chapter, the terms refer to measurement reliability and measurement validity. Be sure to add these terms to your Terminology Worksheet. *Reliability* refers to the consistency of your measurement instrument. If you were to repeat your measure over and over again with the same sample, you will always get the same results. For example, if you measure the length of an Olympic running track 100 times with a long tape measure, will you find that it is exactly 100 meters every time? If my tape measure gives you different lengths, possibly because of how you hold it or stretch it, then it has weaker reliability as a measuring instrument. The different types of reliability are listed in Example 8.1.

Example 8.1.
TYPES OF RELIABILITY

TYPE OF RELIABILITY	DESCRIPTION	EXAMPLE
Internal consistency	Extent to which items are inter-correlated. You can use multiple questions that are supposed to measure the same thing and test them out on a sample of people. If all the items consistently measure the same thing, then you have internal consistency.	Center for Epidemiologic Studies Depression Scale (Radloff, 1977) Internal consistency in the general population was 0.85 and 0.90 in the psychiatric population.
Split-half reliability	After having your sample complete the instrument, divide the test into two parts. If the scores on both halves are correlated together and have consistent results, then you have demonstrated split-half reliability.	The Wender Utah Rating Scale (Ward, Wender, & Reimherr, 1993) Split-half reliability correlations comparing odd/even items were satisfactory
Test–retest reliability	Have your participants take the instrument at two different times. If the scores stay constant both times, then you have test–retest reliability.	Attention Deficit Disorder Evaluation Scale—Second Edition (McCarney, 1995) Excellent 30-day test–retest reliabilities
Interrater reliability	Two different raters complete the instrument and see how these raters correlate with each other.	Attention Deficit Disorder Evaluation Scale—Second Edition (McCarney, 1995) Interrater agreement is good between teachers and between parents.

Validity indicates how well your instrument is measuring what it is supposed to be measuring. In the example of a running track, you would want a tape measure designed to measure a long distance in meters. A stopwatch and a wind-speed meter are important measuring tools for the 100-meter dash, but they are not valid for measuring length. Example 8.2 indicates the different types of validity that you have learned from your research methods classes with examples, followed by Project Development Worksheet 8.1 to apply your knowledge to your own project.

Example 8.2.

TYPES OF VALIDITY

TYPES OF VALIDITY	DESCRIPTION		EXAMPLE	EXAMPLE FROM STUDIES
Criterion (gold standard)	Establishing validity by showing a correlation between a measurement device and some other criterion or standard that we believe accurately measures the variable under consideration.	*Concurrent*—comparing the measure to a criterion (diagnosis, indicator) when both measures are taken at the same time.	To test if GRE scores are an accurate measurement of grades, correlate both GRE scores and undergraduate grades (the criterion in this case) and see how they correlate.	PTSD Symptom Scale-Self Report (PSS-SR) (Foa, Riggs, Dancu & Rothbaum, 1993) Concurrent validity was supported by the correlation between the PSS-SR and similar measures.
		Predictive—an instrument is used to predict a future state of affairs.	Use the GRE to see whether it predicts a graduate students' future grades.	Self-Report Delinquency Scale (Elliott, Huizinga, & Ageton, 1985) good predictive validity with chronic offenders (Dunford & Elliott, 1984) and serious offenders (Elliott et al., 1985)
Construct	The extent to which the measure in question taps into the theoretical construct that it was designed to measure.	*Convergent*—like other measures that are theoretically linked to our construct	(Beck, Ward, Mendelson, Mock, & Erbaugh, 1961) and (Zung, 1965).	Davidson Trauma Scale (Davidson, 1996) Good convergent validity, correlating strongly with other trauma measures.
		Divergent— unlike other measures that are theoretically different.	An instrument aimed to measure anger is not correlated with an instrument assessing passivity.	Brown Attention-Deficit Disorder Scales for Children and Adolescents (Brown, 2001) Divergent validity is shown by lower correlations between BADDS and reduced correlations with internalizing measures.

Project Development Worksheet 8.1.

INSTRUMENTS

Find an instrument that might fit your research project needs. Name here. _____

What are its advantages? _____

What are its disadvantages? _____

What is the information provided on reliability? _____

What is the information provided on validity? _____

Has it been standardized on a population similar to your sample in terms of diversity (age, ethnicity, SES)? _____

How do you score the instrument? _____

How do you interpret the scores? _____

How realistic is it for you to use this instrument in your project in terms of the following:

  Access to instrument? _____
  Length and language of instrument? _____
  Congruence with the variable you are measuring? _____

ADAPTING AND CREATING INSTRUMENTS

If, after extensive research, you decide that no instrument taps into what you want to study, then first consider adapting an existing instrument. If a search of the literature turns up an instrument that has some elements of what you are looking for, then you may write to the authors and ask permission to adapt their measure, assuring them that you will properly cite their work. For example, in a focus group study of Latina attitudes and perceptions of breast and cervical cancer screening, a literature reviewed turned up similar studies. A semi-structured interview created by Borrayo, Buki, and Feigal (2005) and Borrayo and Jenkins (2001) tapped into a lot of the same information we were interested in. When contacted, the lead author was amenable to sending on the instrument and allowing us to adapt it to our needs. She was, of course, cited in the final write-up of our results.

It must be recognized that if a scale has been standardized, then adding, deleting, or changing the items in any way will mean that it no longer has the reliability and validity on which it was tested. The testing process involved the exact items that are part of the scale. Therefore, you will lose the psychometric properties with which it came. The advantage of adapting an existing measure, however, is that at least you aren't "starting from scratch" and "pulling items out of thin air." There is at least some foundation to your work that draws on the knowledge that other researchers have developed.

If there is no work from which to draw and you are certain that you have exhausted all resources for finding an existing scale, you may decide to develop your own instrument. Draw on your literature review to ensure that you are tapping into the relevant constructs of your topic. Another guideline is to be sure to get input into your scale. We advise that you not only share it with relevant agency personnel to get their thoughts on its face validity and its ease of administration, but also bring it into your research class for distribution and feedback. Your fellow classmates, as well as your instructor, will have valuable input that you can incorporate as you finalize your instrument. Example 8.3 discusses one of the author's process of developing a scale, and Test Your Skills Exercise 8.3 asks you to apply information you have learned about reliability and validity to this instrument.

Example 8.3.

DEVELOPMENT OF AN INSTRUMENT TO MEASURE POSITIVE GROUP BEHAVIOR

One of the authors of this workbook uses collaborative learning groups extensively in her courses and wanted a way to measure "positive group behavior" of the students working in groups. After a review of the literature on group dynamics, task groups, and constructivist pedagogy, she identified several concepts that were indicators of positive group behavior: *Regular attendance at meetings; Contributing of ideas to the group task; Researching, analyzing, and preparing material for the group task; Contributing to the cooperative group process;* and *Supporting and encouraging group members.*

The next step was to define each of these concepts:

Regular attendance at meetings was defined as group member attended all meetings, stayed to agreed end, worked within time-scale, and was active and attentive during the meeting.

Contribution of ideas to the group task was defined as group member thought about the topic in advance of the meeting, provided workable ideas that were taken up by the group, built on others' suggestions, and was prepared to test out ideas on the group rather than keep quiet.

Researching, analyzing, and preparing material for the task was defined as the group member fulfilled promises to the group in terms of outside activities and bringing materials to the group meetings, did an equal share of the research, and helped to analyze and evaluate the material.

Contributing to the cooperative group process meant that the group member left personal differences outside the group, was willing to review group progress and tackle conflict in the group, took on different roles as needed, and kept group on track, willing, and flexible but focused on the task.

Supporting and encouraging group members was the group member's ability and willingness to listen to others, encouragement of participation of all group members, sensitivity to issues affecting group members, and support of group members with special needs.

The next step was to "operationalize" these concepts, to turn each of the concepts into specific and concrete variables that could be measured on a questionnaire.

	STRONGLY AGREE 4	AGREE 3	DISAGREE 2	STRONGLY DISAGREE 1
Regular attendance at meetings Attended all meetings, stayed to agreed end, worked within time-scale, active and attentive.				
Contribution of ideas for the task Thought about the topic in advance of the meeting, provided workable ideas that were taken up by the group, built on others' suggestions, and were prepared to test out ideas on the group rather than keep quiet.				
Researching, analyzing, and preparing material for the task Did what you said you would, brought materials, did an equal share of the research, and helped to analyze and evaluate the material.				

Contribution to the cooperative group process Left personal differences outside the group, willing to review group progress and tackle conflict in the group, took on different roles as needed, and kept group on track, willing, and flexible but focused on the task.			
Supporting and encouraging group members Keen to listen to others, encouraged participation, enabled a collaborative learning environment, sensitive to issues affecting group members, and supported group members with special needs.			

Note that the categories 4 through 1 are values. The values represent how each variable "varies"—how one person completing the questionnaire differs from another person on that specific variable. As you can see, positive group behavior is a complex construct with many different dimensions.

Instead of analyzing and reporting each of the variables separately, a better measure of positive group behavior would be to combine the variables into one score that represents overall positive group behavior. A scale is created by adding or averaging the values of several variables, each of which is an indicator of a complex construct, and using that one number as a measure of the construct. Thus, one student's positive group behavior score would be the sum of the values of each variable. The scores could range from 20 (4s on all 5 items) to 5 (1s on all items). A person who scored 20 on the scale would have more positive group behavior than someone who scored 10. Scale is another word for your Terminology Worksheet.

Test Your Skills Exercise 8.2.

MEASUREMENT AND VALIDITY

Take a few minutes now to think about this questionnaire in terms of measurement reliability and validity that was discussed above.

- Do the variables measure what they are intended to measure?
- Are the questionnaire items good indicators of positive group behavior?
- How similar are the conceptual definitions and the operational definitions?
- Would a student respond the same way each time he/she was asked any of the questions?
- How would you, as a student, assess the validity of this instrument?
- How would you assess the reliability?

DATA COLLECTION INSTRUMENTS FROM AGENCY RECORDS

We have already discussed some of the challenges associated with agency-based research, such as getting personnel to agree to collect data on a consistent basis in the way you have planned and the time limits involved in data collection for student projects (usually only a semester long). Therefore, one alternative is to design your study so that you can include data that are already being collected. In other words, you can rely on agency records and administrative data. When you rely on agency records, you typically create your own instrument to do so. In Example 8.4 we have listed various settings in which social workers are employed and the outcomes that are often available at such agencies. Consider using these as part of your research as they involve key variables that are important for program and policy formation.

Example 8.4.

KEY OUTCOMES AT AGENCY SETTINGS

SETTINGS	COMMON OUTCOMES
Child welfare	• Length of time case is open • Re-occurrence of maltreatment • Safety/risk assessment • Length of foster care stay • Number of foster care placements
Criminal justice	• Recidivism (arrests or convictions) • Domestic violence police calls
Schools	• Academic performance (grades) • Attendance • Discipline referrals
Mental health	• Hospitalization • Volunteer work/employment • Medication compliance • Diagnosis • Length of treatment
Health	• Hospitalization • Compliance with treatment • Diagnosis • Length of treatment

Agency records have the advantage that you do not have to wait for "live" clients to go through an intervention or program in which case they may not fit the time frame for completion of your research project. A disadvantage is that record keeping is not always consistent between different agency personnel. For example, in a research project evaluating the effectiveness of mental health services with active duty military, veterans, and their dependents, the students found that very few of the therapists actually administered the QR-40 as planned. Therefore, the number of cases from which they could draw data was severely restricted. Because there is not always consistency in agency records and your data collection instrument will not have been standardized, your study will be limited by the lack of *reliability* and *validity*.

To conclude this section, we have put in a sample data collection instrument that involved agency records (*see* Figure 8.1). This project involved an evaluation of a foster care training program (PRIDE) and its influence on foster care outcomes. Feel free to use this example as a starting point for an instrument to collect data from your own agency records.

LEVELS OF MEASUREMENT

Now that we have talked about different types of instruments that you can find, adapt, and create, we turn to a more detailed discussion of how to translate data into numbers so it can be analyzed. There are basically four ways that variables can be translated into numerical terms. In order of sophistication, they are nominal measurement (the most basic), followed by ordinal, interval, and ratio (the most precise and highest level of measurement). The level of measurement you choose determines the type of data analysis you can later perform (*see* Chapter Nine). Using more precise measurements increases your options for statistical analysis and the depth of your findings.

Figure 8.1.

DATA COLLECTION INSTRUMENT (FOSTER CARE TRAINING PROJECT)

CLIENT ID:_____

Demographic Information:

Birth Date: _____   Gender: Male   Female

Race: Caucasian   African-American   Latino   Asian   Other: _____

Research Project Information:

Date the Child Entered Custody: _____

Primary Reason for Entering Custody:

    1. Physical Abuse

    2. Sexual Abuse

    3. Physical Neglect

    4. Child In Need of Supervision/Services (CHINS)

    5. Relief of Custody

    6. Other _____

Date the Child Left Custody: _____

Reason for Leaving Custody:
    1. Reunification
    2. Placement with Relatives
    3. Adoption
    4. Reached age of majority

Placement in Foster Home #1

Foster Parent Training: PRIDE   Other

Date of Placement: _____

Date of Termination of Placement: _____

Reason for Termination of Placement:
    1. Reunification
    2. Placement with Relatives
    3. Adoption
    4. Provider Request (cannot meet child's needs)
    5. Provider Closed

Placement in Foster Home #2

Foster Parent Training: PRIDE   Other

Date of Placement: _____

Date of Termination of Placement: _____

Reason for Termination of Placement:
    1. Reunification
    2. Placement with Relatives
    3. Adoption
    4. Provider Request (cannot meet child's needs)
    5. Provider Closed

<u>Placement in Foster Home #3</u>

Foster Parent Training: PRIDE   Other

Date of Placement: _____

Date of Termination of Placement: _____

Reason for Termination of Placement:
  1. Reunification
  2. Placement with Relatives
  3. Adoption
  4. Provider Request (cannot meet child's needs)
  5. Provider Closed

<u>Placement in Foster Home #4</u>

Foster Parent Training: PRIDE   Other

Date of Placement: _____

Date of Termination of Placement: _____

Reason for Termination of Placement:
  1. Reunification
  2. Placement with Relatives
  3. Adoption
  4. Provider Request (cannot meet child's needs)
  5. Provider Closed

Comments about this record: _____

_____

_____

Although it is good practice to define your variables at the highest level possible, it is also important to be sensitive to your participants. For example, many people are uncomfortable revealing their exact income (or they do not know it), but they will agree to report the range of income in which they fall. Similarly, with age, adults—especially older adults—might think it rude to have to report their exact age but will report their age more generally in category form. In Example 8.5, you will see the levels of measurement, their definitions, and some common examples of these levels from student research projects.

Example 8.5.

LEVELS OF MEASUREMENT

LEVEL OF MEASUREMENT	DESCRIPTION	EXAMPLE	QUESTION TO ASK ABOUT HOW TO QUANTIFY DATA
Nominal	Categories that are exhaustive and mutually exclusive	• Gender • Major in college • Ethnicity • Diagnosis • Region	Does this fall into a category? What category does this fall into?

LEVEL OF MEASUREMENT	DESCRIPTION	EXAMPLE	QUESTION TO ASK ABOUT HOW TO QUANTIFY DATA
Ordinal	Can be logically rank-ordered, but the differences between ranks can't be quantified.	• Level of education (high school, college, graduate degree) • Income (when divided into categories, such as $0–$30,000; $31,000–$50,000; $51,000–$75,000; $76,000–$100,000; >$101,000) • Likert scale item: strongly disagree, agree, disagree, and strongly disagree	Can I place these items in an approximate order?
Interval	The distance separating attributes has meaning but no real zero or absolute (zero in temperature does not mean a complete lack of temperature).	• Scores on a standardized test • Age	Can I place this on a scale that is very exact and precise?
Ratio	Categories have a true zero, known as an absolute value, and differences can be quantified.	• Number of children • Number of out-of-home placements • Number of hospitalizations • Income, when defined as a specific number	Can I place this on a scale that is very exact and precise AND has an *absolute* value?

Test Your Skills Exercise 8.3.

LEVELS OF MEASUREMENT

1. To ensure that you are clear on different levels of measurement, answer the following questions below.

   Which of the following variable is most clearly NOT a ratio level variable?
   a. income
   b. ethnicity
   c. number or prior arrests
   d. number of magazines subscribed to

2. The variable "number of persons in household" would be considered a _____ variable?
   a. nominal
   b. discrete
   c. ratio
   d. reliable

3. An ordinal variable has all of the following characteristics EXCEPT:
   a. mutually exclusive categories
   b. an order to the categories
   c. equal spacing between the categories
   d. ordinal variables have all of the above

Project Development Worksheet 8.2.

RESEARCH CONCEPTS

What are the concepts you are interested in exploring in your research? Take one of the concepts and operationalize it by defining it at each of the different levels of measurement:

Concept: _____

1. Nominal:
2. Ordinal:
3. Interval:
4. Ratio:

ASSIGNING VALUES

The next part of defining your variables involves assigning values to these variables so they are represented as numbers. We introduced the assignment of numbers to variables in Chapter One. In the case of nominal variables, numerical values are assigned arbitrarily. In the nominal variable of gender, the values assigned can be "male" = 1 and "female" = 2, but there is no meaning to the number 1 or 2 here in terms of ranking or mathematical properties.

At the ordinal level of measurement, we use the numbers that symbolize the levels. Using the above example of income, a "1" could be assigned to represent $0–$30,000; a "2" can indicate $31,000–$50,000; a "3" for $51,000–$75,000; "4" for $100,000; and "5" for $101,000 and greater. One tip for assigning values: For the interval and ratio levels of measurement, you can use the actual value. For example, at the interval level, you can use the score on a standardized test; at the ratio level, you actually count the number of children a household has and use that number as your value. You will get practice applying this information in Test Your Skills Exercise 8.4 and Project Development Worksheet 8.3.

Test Your Skills Exercise 8.4.

IDENTIFY THE VARIABLE AND THE VALUE IN EACH BELOW

Age _____

Are you currently: (*Check one*)

a. ☐ Married
b. ☐ Separated
c. ☐ Divorced
d. ☐ Widowed
e. ☐ Never married

In the month before your present prison term, were you: (*Check one*)

a. ☐ Unemployed
b. ☐ Employed: (**If employed**, please check one)
    ☐ Part-Time ☐ Full-Time ☐ Worked on and off

With whom do these children live? CHECK ALL THAT APPLY

a. ☐ Child's Mother
b. ☐ Child's Grandparent(s)
c. ☐ Other Relative
d. ☐ Foster home/agency
e. ☐ Friends/other

Please list the charges for which you are currently serving time:

_____

_____

_____

Project Development Worksheet 8.3.

VARIABLE AND VALUE

Take each of the levels of measurement you jotted down in the previous exercise. Name the values that you will use to further define each level.

1. Nominal variable;
    Values;

2. Ordinal variable;
    Values;

3. Interval variable;
    Value;

4. Ratio variable;
    Value;

To pull all the information on defining your variables together, now you can prepare Project Development Worksheet 8.4 that contains the variables you will be studying in your research project. By spending time now on carefully defining your variables and values and how they will be measured, you are setting up how you will handle the management of your data once it has been collected. At that point, you will simply be able to enter it into the database as you have collected it, rather than translating the data into a form at that point that can be used in a database. A sample worksheet from the Family Group Conferencing student project has been provided in Example 8.6, along with a blank sheet.

Example 8.6.

STUDENT PROJECT: "COMPARING THE EFFECTIVENESS OF FAMILY GROUP CONFERENCING WITH TRADITIONAL SERVICES IN A CHILD WELFARE SETTING"

1. SHORT-TERM OUTCOME MEASURES

VARIABLES	HOW MEASURED	INDEPENDENT/ DEPENDENT OR CONTROL	LEVEL OF MEASURE-MENT	VALUES OF THE VARIABLE
1. Purpose of the FGC according to participants	Self-report (in-house survey)	Dependent	Open-ended	N/A
2. Participants level of preparedness	Self-report (in-house survey)	Dependent/ Independent	Ordinal	1 = very prepared 2 = somewhat prepared 3 = not at all prepared

3. Overall participant satisfaction with the FGC process	Self-report (in-house survey)	Dependent/ Independent	Ordinal; Likert	1 = Strongly Disagree 2 = Disagree 3 = Neutral 4 = Agree 5 = Strongly Agree
4. Participant satisfaction with the FGC Coordinator	Self-report (in-house survey)	Dependent/ Independent	Ordinal	1 = Very Satisfied 2 = Somewhat Satisfied 3 = Not at all Satisfied
5. Satisfaction with family plan	Self-report (in-house survey)	Dependent/ Independent	Ordinal	1 = Very Satisfied 2 = Somewhat Satisfied 3 = Not at all Satisfied
6. As a result of the FGC, participants family feels understood by DFS	Self-report (in-house survey)	Dependent/ Independent	Nominal	1 = Yes; 2 = No
7. Participants have better understanding of DFS's concerns	Self-report (in-house survey)	Dependent/ Independent	Nominal	1 = Yes; 2 = No
8. Overall helpfulness of the FGC process	Self-report (in-house survey)	Dependent/ Independent	Ordinal	1 = Very Helpful 2 = Somewhat helpful 3 = Not at all Helpful
2. INTERMEDIATE AND LONG-TERM OUTCOME MEASURES				
1. a. Re-referred for maltreatment? b. Allegation in re-referral c. Date of re-referral d. Length of time between FGC and re-referral e. Referring party f. Case track (investigation or assessment) g. If investigation, was there a finding?	a. DFS Records Database b. DFS Records Database c. DFS Records Database d. DFS Records Database e. DFS Records Database f. DFS Records Database g. DFS Records Database	a. Dependent b. Dependent c. Dependent d. Dependent e. Dependent f. Dependent g. Dependent	a. Nominal b. Interval c. Open-ended d. Ratio e. Open-ended f. Nominal g. Nominal	a. 1 = Yes; 2 = No b. 1 = Physical abuse; 2 = Sexual abuse; 3 = Neglect; 4 = Medical Neglect; 5 = Emotional abuse c. N/A d. N/A e. N/A f. 1 = Assessment; 2 = Investigation g. 1 = Yes; 2 = No

2. Number of FGC's held	DFS Records Database	Independent/ Dependent	Ratio	

3.
  a. Did out-of-home place-ment occur?
  b. Where was out-of-home placement?
  c. Was out-of-home place-ment part of FGC plan?
  d. Length of time out-of-home?
  e. Reunification with family?
	a. DFS Records Database
	b. DFS Records Database
	c. DFS Records Database
	d. DFS Records Database
	e. DFS Records Database
		a. Dependent
		b. Dependent
		c. Independent/ Dependent
		d. Dependent
		e. Dependent
			a. Nominal
			b. Interval
			c. Nominal
			d. Ratio
			e. Nominal
				a. 1 = Yes; 2 = No
				b. 1 = Relative 2 = Fictive kin 3 = Foster home 4 = Residential setting 5 = Institu-tional care
				c. 1 = Yes; 2 = No
				d. N/A
				e. 1 = Yes; 2 = No

4.
  a. Number of FGC par-ticipants that are relatives/ fictive kin
  b. Number of FGC par-ticipants that are professionals
	a. DFS Records Database
	b. DFS Records Database
		a. Independent/ Dependent
		b. Independent/ Dependent
			a. Ratio
			b. Ratio
				N/A

5. Is the case currently closed?	DFS Records Database	Dependent	Nominal	1 = Yes; 2 = No
6. Length of time case was opened	DFS Records Database	Dependent	Ratio	N/A

Project Development Worksheet 8.4.

MEASUREMENT TABLE

Fill in these variables you will be studying in your research project in the box on the following page

Name of variable:

How measured:

Used as independent/dependent/control/other:

Level of measurement:

Value of the variable:

Name of variable:	
How measured:	
Used as independent/dependent/control/other:	
Level of measurement:	
Value of the variable:	

INDEPENDENT VARIABLE: TREATMENT FIDELITY

Up until now, our discussion has mainly centered on our dependent variables, but now we turn to measurement of our independent variable. *Treatment fidelity* refers to how faithfully we have implemented the intervention in our research. For intervention research to be reliable and replicable, it is important that we implement the intervention as it was designed. If the intervention (independent variable) is implemented consistently, we will know that our results really tell us something about that intervention—namely, that it is the reason for the change in the dependent variable. If the intervention is altered or inconsistently implemented, referred to as *treatment drift,* then we muddy the waters about the true impact of the intervention.

Maintaining optimal treatment fidelity involves many things. It includes proper training and supervision of the people who administer an intervention. This includes an examination of their work in sessions to ascertain that it sufficiently meets the standards and tenants of that particular treatment as it was designed. Although it may sound relatively easy to stick to an established protocol, it is often difficult to do when you are facing people with individualized needs. *Manualized treatment* (treatment that follows a strict protocol) has been criticized on these grounds—namely, that it does not meet the needs of clients or match the expertise of a clinician who is allowed to choose the best technique in the moment to best help clients. However, for research to be successful, some degree of treatment fidelity is important. If we are to say with any certainty that the independent variable was responsible for change in the dependent variable, then an organized and repeated process must be in place.

In experimental designs, treatment fidelity is often assessed very systematically. More so than the solution-focused therapy example, some researchers will review video- or audiotaped sessions in great detail as well as use several measurement instruments. An extensive treatment fidelity protocol was implemented by Secret in her comprehensive evaluation of a prison-based parent education program (Secret, Berlin, Huebner, & Werner, 2007). A major component of the program consisted of parent education classes delivered by paid and volunteer professionals to groups of fathers in 2-hour segments, one segment per week, over the course of 10 weeks. Focusing on issues such as "Dealing with Anger and Other Emotions," "Understanding Children's Behavior," and "Parental Substance Abuse on Children," the parent education curriculum identified specific content, materials, and experiential learning activities and interaction discussions for each segment. Now that you know a little about the program, Test Your Skills Exercise 8.5 prompts you to think of the questions you would need answered to assess treatment fidelity. After you consider these elements, look at Example 8.7, which shows how fidelity was evaluated in this study. Test Your Skills Exercise 8.6 asks you to apply your knowledge gained of treatment fidelity to a study conducted by one of the authors.

Test Your Skills Exercise 8.5.

TREATMENT FIDELITY

- On what parts of program delivery would you collect data?

- Would you need to know whether one or both staff members were present to deliver the curriculum?

- How would you know how many fathers attended the classes?

- How would you know what content was covered … what topics discussed … and what exercises were involved?

- Would you collect data from the staff members or from the participants? Or, would you observe the sessions directly? If you observed the sessions, then would your presence impact the class?

- Would you need to collect these data for every segment and for the entire 2 hours or would a sample of segments or weeks be sufficient?

- Would you collect data by questionnaire, observation, records, and interviews?

Example 8.7.

TREATMENT FIDELITY PROTOCOL

INSTRUMENT	HOW ADMINISTERED	WHAT IT MEASURES
Parent Participation Index (PPI)	An inmate sign-in sheet was maintained by the program staff and used by each program participant to indicate his attendance at any of the program activities.	The number of classes, visits, storybooks etc attended by each individual inmate
Class Session Report (CSR)	A self-report brief survey was completed by each program participant at the end of each class session. There are 12 separate CSR survey forms, customized to correspond with each week's prespecified curriculum topic.	The participants' ratings of whether or not key concepts and topics specified for each particular week were talked about in class, whether or not participant increased understanding of the topic

Cost Analysis Data Form	Detailed records were kept by the program and prison staff of resources used by the program for one "typical" week of the program every other series. The weekly expenses are extrapolated to all weeks in the series to obtain an estimate of program costs.	Fiscal resources expended for staff time, volunteer time, space, equipment, supplies, and so forth, used by the different components of the program.
Videotapes	The program project director videotaped the entire 2-hour class meeting for two randomly sampled classes per session. The tapes were viewed and scored according to how well the three major key points of the curriculum topics specified for that class were actually covered.	Project director's objective assessment of the program's adherence to the curriculum

Test Your Skills Exercise 8.6.

TREATMENT FIDELITY

Review the following report of treatment fidelity that one of the authors described in her study. Considering the type of questions asked in Test Your Skills Exercise 8.5, discuss how reliable this plan was to collect information about treatment fidelity? Are there other aspects of the program that you think should be measured to determine whether the program is being delivered as intended? In which ways?

Corcoran (2006) conducted a study on the use of solution-focused therapy with children with behavior problems. Treatment fidelity was described as follows: "Twenty student interns were trained in solution-focused therapy by the author using videotaped demonstrations by Insoo Kim Berg, lecture, discussion, and role-plays on the following interventions, which were also used in the sessions by the students: (1) joining; (2) how to assess and intervene with different client types; (3) the phrasing of solution-focused questioning; (4) exception-finding; (5) externalizing the problem; (6) the miracle question; (7) goal-setting and scaling questions; (8) the pessimistic sequence; and (9) termination. Students were requested to video- or audiotape each of their sessions with clients. Supervision comprised weekly individual meetings with students in which discussion revolved around listening/viewing of taped sessions." Taping the student sessions helped students learn how to apply the therapy properly and identified sessions in which students were not maintaining treatment fidelity.

For a student intervention project, the following data need to be collected and reported for treatment fidelity:

1. How many sessions did each client attend/how many contacts did you have with each client in your intervention?
   This number may be correlated with treatment outcome later to tell us whether the number of contacts or sessions was associated with the dependent variable.

2. How well did sessions follow the planned intervention?
    In high-quality, published studies, sessions are audio- or videotaped, and a randomized selection of them are transcribed. Another person on the research team (not the person delivering the intervention) can then listen to these tapes to assess fidelity with an assessment tool. Because students will not have the time or resources for transcription services, what accommodations can be made for a student research project? The following exercise will get you to consider the aspects of treatment fidelity reasonable for student projects.

Project Development Worksheet 8.5.
EVALUATING TREATMENT FIDELITY

If you are doing intervention research, use the plan outline below to develop an ideal approach to evaluating treatment fidelity for your program and then to decide what aspects of the plan are realistic for your project.

TREATMENT FIDELITY WORKSHEET			
DATA COLLECTION INSTRUMENT	HOW ADMINISTERED	WHAT IT MEASURES	REASONABLE TO IMPLEMENT FOR YOUR PROJECT? WHY OR WHY NOT

CONCLUSION

This chapter has centered on the data collection tools for research with a special consideration for how these relate to student research projects. We started with how you can conceptualize and operationalize variables, along with what characterizes standardized measures—reliability and validity. Although you should rely on standardized measures whenever possible in your own research, we also discussed how to adapt and create measures, when necessary, and the use of agency records. Next, we talked about how to define your variables at the various levels of measurement, as well as how to assign values of these variables. Finally, we explored the importance of treatment fidelity to ensure that the independent variable, in intervention research, is being implemented the manner it was designed. Along the way, we have led you through a series of examples and exercises, which should result in your increased understanding of measurement and the instruments that you will use in your own project.

WEBSITES

http://www.socialresearchmethods.net/kb/measure.php
The Research Methods Knowledge Base webpage for measurement offers more detail on the concepts in this chapter, along with graphics accompanying explanations.

http://www.scalesandmeasures.net/search.php
A registry of over 1,200 scales searchable by topic area.

http://www.ull.ac.uk/subjects/psychology/psycscales.shtml
Psychological scales, alphabetized with their supporting references.

http://www.ppc.sas.upenn.edu/ppquestionnaires.htm
A list of strengths-based questionnaires with supporting references and with downloadable links, from the Positive Psychology Center website at the University of Pennsylvania.

9

QUANTITATIVE DATA ANALYSIS

Data analysis is the process of making sense or giving meaning to the numbers. Statistics are the tools that we use to make sense of the data or to do data analysis. Data analysis is usually the most intimidating part of the research process for students. A couple of points may ease some of the anxiety associated with data analysis. First, data analysis is a logical extension of the research you have already planned. The questions you have asked, the hypotheses you have set, the variables you have selected, and how they have been defined will act to determine the method of data analysis. Second, this chapter will not require you to perform any mathematical computations. Statistical computing packages, such as Statistical Package for the Social Sciences (SPSS), will typically do the computations for you. In this chapter, you will only be asked to understand the purpose behind each statistical test, how to make decisions about the statistical tests for your project, and how to interpret the results—all topics of this chapter. In the next section, we will further attempt to demystify the origins of the numbers that we ultimately use for data analysis.

WHERE DO THE NUMBERS COME FROM?

Recall from Chapter One that statistics are numerical representations of the characteristics, behaviors, attitudes, and so forth of the people and organizations that we are studying. In quantitative research, the numbers we use in statistics can be traced back to the information that is provided on our data collection instruments. Let's take a look at this process in detail. Our "numbers trail" begins with the responses that are reported or recorded or observed on data collection instruments (*see* Example 9.1a). The responses are either numerical in nature (i.e., **20** years old) or the responses are assigned a number by the researcher (i.e., **1** if a respondent indicates he/she is married/partnered, **2**, if separated, **3** if divorced, etc.). Each of these numbers from the data collection instrument is entered—by the researcher or a data entry person—into a SPSS spreadsheet (*see* Examples 9.1a and b). Exercise 9.1 will help you apply this understanding.

Example 9.1a.

CONNECTING QUESTIONNAIRE DATA TO DATA ANALYSIS

Date _____

Inmate number

[_____]

XXXX Program Survey

As explained in the consent letter you just received, this study is being conducted by Dr. XXXX XXXX the University of XXXXX. We hope that this study will make an impportant contribution to parent education programs everywhere. The information you provide is designed to be used when combined with the information collected form others completing the survey. No one will be able to identify you by the ansers you give. Even though you volunteered to complete this survey, you may skip any questions that you wish or you can stop doing the survey at any time that you want.

Sectin ONE: Demographic Questions

1. How do you describe yourself (*Check one*)

1__ African-American/Black	3__ American Indian	5__ Asian or Asian American
2__ White	4__ Mexican American/Latino	6__ Other _____

2. Age _____

3. Are you currently: (*Check one*)

1__ Married	3__ Divorced	5__ Never married
2__ Separated	4__ Widowed	

4. How much education have you completed? (*Check one*)

1__ 8th grade or less	3__ GED	5__ Some college or more
2__ Some high school	4__ High school diploma	

5. In the month before your present prison term, were you: (*Check one*)

1__ Unemployed

2__ Employed: (If employed, please check one >) □ Part Time   □ Full Time   □ Worked on and off

prison experience variable

6. Have you served time for any prior convictions? (*Check one*)   1. □ Yes   2. □ No

---

Example 9.1b.

CONNECTING QUESTIONNAIRE DATA TO DATA ANALYSIS

Can you see how each case has a number (i.e., 101, 102, 103) and each of the responses to each question has a "number" value (i.e., 1 for African-American, 2 for White, 3 for American Indian, etc.)? Now look at the following instrument next to the SPSS spreadsheet. Can you see how responses from the completed surveys can be "transferred" to the spread sheet? For example, case number 101 is one of the respondents who completed the survey answering that he was African-American, 41 years old, and divorced.

Example 9.1c.
CONNECTING QUESTIONNAIRE DATA TO DATA ANALYSIS

Data Collection Instrument

Date _____

XXXX PROGRAM SURVEY   Inmate number [ ]

As explained in the consent letter you just received, this study is being conducted by Dr. XXXX XXXX the University of XXXXX. We hope that this study will make an important contribution to parent education programs everywhere. The information you provide is designed to be used when combined with the information collected from others completing the survey. No one will be able to identify you by the answers you give. Even though you volunteered to complete this survey, you may skip any questions that you wish or you can stop doing the survey at any time that you want.

Section ONE: Demographic Questions

1. How do you describe yourself (Check one)

   1. [ ] African American/Black   3. [ ] American Indian   5. [ ] Asian or Asian American
   2. [ ] White   4. [ ] Mexican/American/Latino   6. [ ] Other

2. Age _____

3. Are you currently: (Check one)

   1 [ ] Married   3 [ ] Divorced   5 [ ] Never married
   2 [ ] Separated   4 [ ] Widowed

4. How much education have you completed? (Check one)

   1 [ ] 8th grade or less   3 [ ] GED   5 [ ] Some college or more
   2 [ ] Some high school   4 [ ] High school diploma

5. In the month before your present prison term, were you: (Check one)

   1 [ ] Unemployed
   2 [ ] Employed: (If employed, please check one =>) [ ] Part Time [ ] Full Time [ ] Worked on and off

   prison experience variable

6. Have you served time for any prior convictions? (Check one)   1 [ ] Yes ⇓   2. No

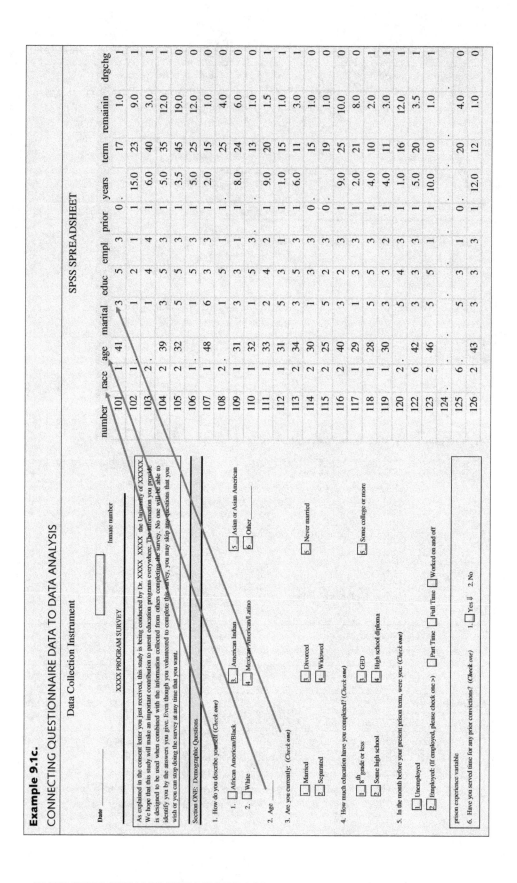

SPSS SPREADSHEET

number	race	age	marital	educ	empl	prior	years	term	remainin	drgchg
101	1	41	3	3	5	0	.	17	1.0	1
102	1	.	1	1	1	1	15.0	23	9.0	1
103	2	.	1	4	4	1	6.0	40	3.0	1
104	2	39	3	5	3	1	5.0	35	12.0	1
105	2	32	5	5	3	1	3.5	45	19.0	0
106	1	.	1	5	3	1	5.0	25	12.0	0
107	1	48	6	3	3	1	2.0	15	1.0	0
108	2	.	1	5	1	1	.	25	4.0	0
109	1	31	3	3	1	1	8.0	24	6.0	0
110	1	32	1	5	3	.	.	13	1.0	1
111	1	33	2	4	2	1	9.0	20	1.5	1
112	1	31	5	3	1	1	1.0	15	1.0	1
113	2	34	3	5	3	1	6.0	11	3.0	1
114	2	30	1	1	3	0	.	15	1.0	0
115	2	25	5	2	3	0	.	19	1.0	0
116	2	40	3	2	3	1	9.0	25	10.0	0
117	1	29	1	1	3	1	2.0	21	8.0	0
118	1	28	5	5	3	1	4.0	10	2.0	1
119	1	30	3	3	2	1	4.0	11	3.0	1
120	2	.	5	4	3	1	1.0	16	12.0	1
122	6	42	3	3	3	1	5.0	20	3.5	1
123	2	46	5	5	1	1	10.0	10	1.0	1
124	.									
125	6	.	5	3	1	0	.	20	4.0	0
126	2	43	3	3	3	1	12.0	12	1.0	0

Exercise 9.1.

SPSS DATA

Refer to the Example 9.1c and answer the following questions.
1. How old is respondent 109? _____
2. What is the educational level of response 105? _____
3. Provide the demographic characteristics of respondent 123? _____

HOW MANY VARIABLES?

Data analysis is also much less daunting when you tie the terminology with language with which you are already familiar. You will discover this to be the case when you consider the number of variables you examine at a time. We will look at analyses at the following levels. Remember that you were introduced to these terms in Chapter Two on Research Fundamentals.

- Univariate
- Bivariate
- Multivariate

Univariate

The analysis of one variable at a time uses statistics referred to as *univariate statistics*. As noted in Chapter Two, the "uni" in the word univariate means "one," and the "variate" means "variable." Thus, univariate statistics are used to analyze one variable at a time. Univariate statistics are also called descriptive statistics and are used to summarize and organize data. Some examples are provided in Example 9.2 below, but descriptives are usually performed on demographic variables we collect. The following are all descriptive statistics with examples from the project involving a social skills intervention for people diagnosed with schizophrenia and depression:

- Frequencies: counts of the values of the variables, usually presented for ordinal- or nominal-level data. The N is the total count for the study. For example, the intervention study had an $N = 10$. There were five males and five females.
- Percentages: accompany the counts of the values of the variables for ordinal- or nominal-level data. For example, 50% of the sample was male, and 50% was female.
- Measures of central tendency: an estimate of the center of a distribution of scores or values. For ratio- and interval-level data, we typically use the mean to describe the center. For example, the mean age of the sample for the social skills intervention with the inpatient hospital residents with schizophrenia and depression was 67.7 years. We might use the median value to describe ratio- and interval-level data when our numbers are skewed in some way; that is, you have outlier values that are pulling the mean up or down in an extreme fashion. This point is easily demonstrated if you conduct an informal classroom exercise on the number of cases (individuals or families) students see in their field placements. What typically happens is that most students have fairly few clients, but one or two will report a high number, usually because of the setting that they are in that lends themselves to brief, multiple contacts,

such as a hospital. If you take the mean of this sample (the class of students) on number of cases seen, this number will then be skewed upward by the fact that only one or two people will have seen many clients. Therefore, the median is a more precise estimate of the center of this sample. For nominal- and ordinal-level data, present the mode. For example, in the social skills intervention, there were two modes (bimodal); the most common diagnoses were either schizoaffective disorder (40%) or schizophrenia (40%).

- Measures of dispersion or variability: how far away the scores in the entire distribution are from each other and from the mean score. The standard deviation is the most commonly used. There will usually be no need to present the standard deviation for your descriptive variables, but note that variability plays a key role in many statistical formulas.

Example 9.2.

UNIVARIATE STATISTICS

Univariate statistics	One variable at a time	• Race • Gender • Self-esteem • Work states	• What percentage of sample is African-American? • What percentage of the sample is female or male? • What is the level of self-esteem in the sample? • How many people in the sample work full-or part-time?

Bivariate Analysis

For the relationship between two variable groups, you choose from a group of statistics referred to as bivariate statistics. Thinking back to Chapter Two and the different types of research, bivariate statistics can be either descriptive (*see* correlation and depending on its usage, chi-square below) or inferential (the other bivariate techniques discussed in this section). Example 9.3 provides illustrations of bivariate statistics and the types of questions related to them.

Example 9.3.

BIVARIATE STATISTICS

Bivariate statistics	Two variables at the same time	• Race and self-esteem • Race and work status • Gender and self-esteem • Gender and work status	• Do more African-American or non-African-Americans have higher levels of self-esteem? • Is there a difference between men and women in terms of work status? • Is work status related to self-esteem?

Summary Content 9.1 presents the bivariate statistics we will cover and their purpose. One column addresses the level of measurement required by the independent and dependent variables. We spent time in Chapter Eight talking about defining our variables and the values of those variables. These become vitally important in choosing a statistical test. We further provide the types of research designs that may use the particular statistical test. Bivariate analysis is the first time we encounter statistical testing, so we will describe that in the next section here before detailing the specific tests.

Summary Content 9.1.		
BIVARIATE ANALYSIS CHART		
STATISTICAL TECHNIQUE	**PURPOSE**	**LEVELS OF MEASUREMENT**
Correlation	To find out how two variables *associate* with each other	Interval/ratio
Chi-square	To find out the difference in frequencies of the various categories between variables	Nominal
Paired samples t-test (repeated measures, within subjects)	To find out the difference *between* the mean values of the posttest and the pretest scores	Independent variable: Nominal Dependent variable: Interval or ratio
Independent t-test (student)	To find out the difference *between* the mean values of two different samples	Independent variable: Nominal Dependent variable: Interval or ratio
ANOVA	To find out the difference *between* the mean values of three or more different samples	Independent variable: Nominal Dependent variable: Interval or ratio

STATISTICAL TESTING

All statistical analysis is based on one idea: Did our result happen because of chance (a random occurrence) or because we truly have found something that, at least statistically, is meaningful? When we do statistical testing, we want to set a significance level at the risk we are willing to take that our results did not occur by chance. The level at which we call a relationship or a difference in our data statistically significant or not is called the *p*-value, the *alpha level*, or the *significance level*. The value of a probability falls between 1 and 0. The convention in the sciences is to use a minimum *p*-value of 0.05. In other words, we have a less than a 5% probability (1 in 20) that the relationship occurred by chance.

The laws of probability are another reason why we don't run numerous statistical tests in hopes of discovering statistically significant findings. If you run a lot of tests, your chances of having significant results will increase. For example, just by chance, the odds of getting a pair of dice coming out the way you want will occur the more times you throw the die. Therefore, you are limited to statistical tests on variables you have specified beforehand.

Scientists worry about saying an event is statistically significant when it is not (referred to as a Type I error). To avoid a Type I error, the strict convention of a 0.05 probability level has developed. Scientists are not quite as worried about missing a potentially significant finding (called a Type II error), but this represents risk, too. With medical, as well as social science research, we want to be sure to capture a finding when it exists. Generally speaking, the way to do that is to increase sample size, but a power analysis will give you a more precise calculation of sample size, based on the *p*-value you use and your willingness to accept a Type II error.

When sample sizes are very small, it is difficult to attain statistical significance. For example, the social skills intervention for elderly African-Americans with schizophrenia found nonstatistically significant results for the 10 participants who underwent the intervention. At the same time, there was a trend in the data, detected by the mean scores on the Depression Anxiety Stress Scale at pretest and at posttest, for improvement to occur in terms of reduction in depression. With a larger sample size, it is possible that the results may have become statistically significant.

Speaking of sample size, sometimes students lose sight of the fact that statistical testing is done with a sample of at least 10 people or cases and hopefully more (*see* Chapter Seven). Therefore, the results might not be true of a particular person, but it seems to be true on average (according to mean scores) in this group of people we are testing. We now turn to the different bivariate tests and examples of each.

Correlations. Correlate is a word that we use in everyday language, so you are already familiar with the term. In statistics, it has the same meaning: "to associate" or "related to." You can also see it as the two variables "varying" together—that is, the variables are linked together in some way. In other words, as the values or numbers of one variable change, so do the values of another variable. Some common examples are the higher the self-esteem one has, the greater sense of happiness one has; the higher the intellectual capacity, the higher the educational attainment; and the higher the level of social support, the greater the resiliency. When we talk about correlation, we mean how do two variables associate with each other?[1] When one changes (increases or decreases), what does the other variable do?

In the Pearson *r*, the most common type of correlation, both variables have to be at the ratio or interval levels. There does not need to be an independent variable and a dependent variable specified; we can look at the relationship between any two variables that we identify in advance are important to each other in answering our research question. Examples are offered below.

EXAMPLE 9.4.

CORRELATIONS USED IN STUDENT RESEARCH PROJECTS

Example #1: In a project on attendance at breast cancer support groups, students looked at the correlation between number of sessions attended and the level of adjustment as measured by the Functional Assessment of Cancer Therapy-Breast (FACT-B) scale, version 4 (Brady, Cella, Mo et al., 1997).

Example #2: In the Work Empowerment Program project, students correlated number of workshops attended and the number of days it took program participants to find employment. They also correlated number of caseworker contacts.

Example #3: Students, as a replication of Secret, Rompf, and Ford's (2003) study with undergraduate students, surveyed fellow social work graduate students for their knowledge and attitudes toward research. Correlations were run on the Social Work Empowerment Scale, Research Course Appeal, Knowledge of Statistical Symbols, and Fear of Research scales.

---

1 There is also multiple correlation that uses three variables, but we will keep our attention to the most commonly used correlation, between two variables.

There are three ways to evaluate a correlation:

- whether it is statistically significant (i.e., Is the statistical significance less than 0.05?)
- whether it is positive or negative
- its strength

A positive correlation means that if one variable increases, the other variable increases. A common example is height and weight, which is usually positively correlated. A negative correlation means that as one variable increases, the other decreases (or vice versa). An example is the higher the fear of public speaking, the lower the level of confidence about public speaking.

Figure 9.1.

CONSIDER SCATTER DIAGRAM A

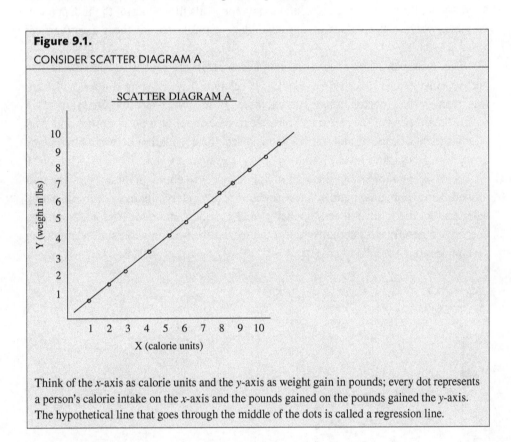

SCATTER DIAGRAM A

Think of the *x*-axis as calorie units and the *y*-axis as weight gain in pounds; every dot represents a person's calorie intake on the *x*-axis and the pounds gained on the pounds gained the *y*-axis. The hypothetical line that goes through the middle of the dots is called a regression line.

The more dots that a hypothetical line can go through, the more correlated the variables are. In the Scatter Diagram A in Figure 9.1, the correlation is +1.0, meaning that for every person who increases his/her calorie units by 1, there is an increase in 1 pound. Using the Scatter Diagram, answer Test Your Skills Exercise 9.2.

Test Your Skills Exercise 9.2.

UNDERSTANDING CORRELATION

See if you can answer the following questions:

If a person consumes 3 calories, how many pounds will he/she gain? _____

If someone consumes 8 calories, how many pounds will he/she gain? _____

If you answered 3 pounds for the first question and 8 pounds for the second, then you are correct. The strength of the correlation has to do with how close to one it is. The correlation ranges between a value of –1 and +1. A –1 or a +1 means that a perfect correlation exists (this never happens in the real world). A zero correlation means that the two variables really don't have any association with each other. In other words, when one goes up or down, the other one doesn't necessarily respond in a similar fashion. The closer to 1 a correlation is, the more strength the relationship between the two variables. How strong is strong? Different authors have a variety of ways to talk about what is weak, small, moderate, strong, very strong, and so forth, but one easy guideline is to see if it is 0.5 and over.

To get a bit more technical, a "regression" line, plotted on a scatter diagram, is often used to illustrate visually how two ratio- or interval-level variables are correlated. Typically, the *x*-axis (horizontal axis) represents the values of the independent variable, whereas the values of the dependent variable are on the *y*-axis (vertical axis).

This example, of course, represents an ideal; in the real world, there are few perfect correlations. More than likely, the relationships in your studies will have less than perfect correlations. For example, think about Scatter Diagram B in Figure 9.2 in terms of the relationship between attendance at support groups and level of adjustment of cancer patients. As you can see, the correlation between attendance at support groups and level of adjustment is 0.5, meaning that, in many—but NOT ALL—cases, an increase in one unit of attendance will equal an increase in one unit of well-being. For some people, a few sessions result in large increases in well-being, whereas for others, several sessions only yield a modest increase. And, there may be one or two people who actually report decreased well-being scores after attending several sessions.

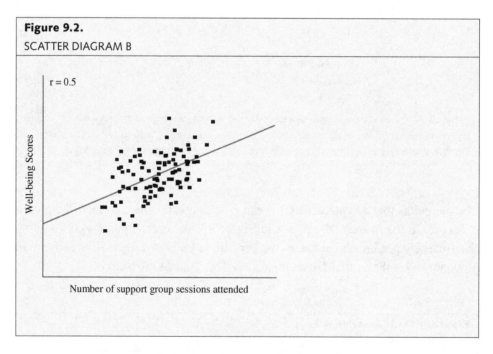

Figure 9.2.
SCATTER DIAGRAM B

$r = 0.5$

Well-being Scores

Number of support group sessions attended

It is important to consider what such a finding means in terms of both practice and research. You know from practice experience, observations of everyday life, and your readings of the scholarly literature that most outcomes are a result of several factors. In the above study of support group attendance and well-being of breast cancer patients, well-being likely depends on several additional factors, such as age, prognosis, family relationships, quality of health care, attitudes about death and dying, and so forth. Attendance at the support group is but one of these factors, yet it is the only independent variable examined by this correlation coefficient. We do not know, from this data analysis, what other variables might influence a breast cancer patient's well-being because the correlation coefficient, like other bivariate statistics, examines only two variables at a time. We will end our discussion of correlation by presenting Example 9.5 of a research project that relied heavily on correlation as its main type of data analysis.

Example 9.5.

CORRELATIONS IN A STUDENT RESEARCH PROJECT

GRADUATE STUDENTS IN SOCIAL WORK: KNOWLEDGE AND ATTITUDES TOWARD RESEARCH

This project was a replication of an earlier study conducted by Secret et al. (2003). Correlations were run on the Social Work Empowerment Scale, Research Course Appeal, and Fear of Research. There was a weak, negative, statistically significant correlation between fear of research courses and knowledge of statistical symbols ($r = -0.23$, $p = 0.00$). The negative sign tells you this is a negative correlation in that the more fear of research a person has, the less well people did on the knowledge test. The correlation, however, is quite weak at 0.23. A statically significant relationship between Fear of Research and RCAI score ($r = -0.21$, $p = 0.02$) was found. Similarly, a negative relationship was present here in that the more fear people had, the lower the level of research appeal. Again, however, the correlation, although statistically significant, was weak. Scores on the Social Work Empowerment Scale had a weak, nonsignificant correlation with scores on the Research Course Appeal Index ($r = 0.049$, $p = 0.60$). In other words, Research Course Appeal did not appear to relate well to the Social Work Empowerment Scale.

Chi-Square. Chi-square, χ^2, is used when analyzing the differences among frequencies in nominal-level data. Example 9.6 offers several examples of chi-square used in student research projects.

Example 9.6.

CHI-SQUARE ANALYSES USED IN STUDENT PROJECTS

Example #1: In the Work Empowerment Program, chi-square was used to examine the differences between those participants who had a felony conviction and those who had a misdemeanor on whether employment was obtained.

Example #2: In an inpatient mental health facility, a chi-square was used to determine the differences between men and women on the type of violent incident committed (against self, against others, or against objects).

Example #3: In the Family Group Conferencing program evaluation, students examined whether participation in Family Group Conferencing compared to usual casework services resulted in re-abuse or not.

The results are displayed in a cross-tabulation table to illustrate frequencies. The cross-tabulation table is also known as a chi-square table, cross-break table, or a contingency table. The independent variable is presented in the rows, whereas the dependent variable is displayed by the columns. It is also common to substitute percentages for frequencies to compensate for the differences in the number of cases. Figure 9.3 is an example of a cross-tabulation table generated from SPSS from the project researching the effectiveness of permanency planning in foster care. The independent variable here is the presence of mental illness in parents (yes or no), and the dependent variable was foster care outcomes.

Figure 9.3.

MENTAL ILLNESS OF PARENT * FOSTER CARE OUTCOMES CROSSTABULATION

Count

		Foster care outcomes				
		Return to parent	Child remains in FC	Parental rights terminated	Kinship care	Total
Mental illness of parent	No	27	34	34	13	108
	yes	36	49	17	15	117
Total		63	83	51	28	225

In the chi-square formula, our data (the observed data) are compared against the *expected frequencies*. These are hypothetical values that are derived from the marginal totals of the cross-tabulation table. Notably, an adequate number of frequencies need to be represented in the cells. If not, then the chi-square operation will flag an error. One option in such a case is to collapse cells so that frequencies become sufficiently large. For example, let's say an independent variable on mental health treatment is initially defined as: (1) therapy; (2) medication; and (3) combined medication and therapy. However, you find that few people received therapy alone, meaning you don't have enough cases in that one cell. To solve the problem, you can collapse the values of the independent variable. They can now be either: (1) a single treatment (medication or therapy) or (2) combined treatment.

When you run a chi-square, you will have the following results:

- a chi-square value that is determined by a formula along with its degrees of freedom (defined as the amount your data are free to vary)
- a level of statistical significance
- the frequencies of the occurrences of the nominal level variables

To evaluate chi-square results, first hone in on the level of statistical significance. If it is statistically significant, then look at the frequencies to determine the pattern of the relationship. You will see in Example 9.7 how one student research group analyzed the results of the chi-square test and then in Test Your Skills Exercise 9.3, you will be asked to do the same.

Example 9.7.

ANALYSIS OF CHI-SQUARE RESULTS: VIOLENT INCIDENTS AT AN INPATIENT MENTAL HEALTH FACILITY

A chi-square was performed on gender and the type of act committed. The chi-square value was 25.25, degrees of freedom were one, and the p-value was 0.000. The latter tells us that this finding was statistically significant at a high level. When looking at the pattern of frequencies in the cells, the students realized that men were more likely to commit acts against objects (92% of these incidents were by males), and women were more likely to commit acts against others (96% of the incidents by females involved those against other patients and staff members).

Test Your Skills Exercise 9.3.

CHI-SQUARE RESULTS FROM STUDENT PROJECTS

In a therapeutic foster care agency, students wanted to find out characteristics of the youth and their families to discover how these characteristics related to outcome. When they ran their chi-square analysis, the following results were found.
Which hypotheses were supported and which ones were not?

A. Child diagnosis and outcome: The hypothesis was that clients who had an externalizing disorder (e.g., ADHD, ODD, or CD) or developmental disorder (e.g., an Autism Spectrum Disorder) would be less likely to graduate from high school and to maintain part-time employment than clients who had internalizing disorders or PTSD. Results were: $\chi^2 = 1.924$, df = 2, $p = 0.382$ (for high school graduation) and $\chi^2 = 3.675$, df = 2, $p = 0.159$ (for part-time employment)

B. Biological family involvement: The hypothesis was that children with biological family involvement would be more likely to graduate from high school and maintain part-time employment than clients with no biological family involvement. Results were: $\chi^2 = 0.336$, df = 1, $p = 0.562$ (high school graduation) and $\chi^2 = 0.048$, df = 1, $p = 0.827$ (part-time employment)

C. Marital status of foster care parents: The hypothesis was that clients who lived in two-parent foster homes would be more likely to graduate from high school and maintain part-time employment than clients who lived in single-parent foster homes. Results: $\chi^2 = 0.205$, df = 1, $p = 0.651$ (high school graduation) and $\chi^2 = 1.047$, df = 1, $p = 0.306$ (part-time employment)

D. Number of foster care children in the home: They hypothesis was that placement in a foster home in which there were no other foster children would be associated with higher rates of high school graduation and part-time employment than placement in a foster home where there was one or more other foster child(ren). Results: $\chi^2 = 2.241$, df = 1, $p = 0.134$ (high school graduation) and $\chi^2 = 0.013$, df = 1, $p = 0.909$ (part-time employment).

t-Tests. The t-test examines whether there is a difference between means of a group (or groups) on a particular dependent variable. The most common types of t-tests used in student projects involve the dependent t-test (also called paired samples, pairwise) and the independent t-test. In t-tests, the independent variable is nominal, and the dependent variable is at the interval/ratio level. Supposedly, the data points of the dependent variable should also be normally distributed, but the t-test is sufficiently robust that we don't necessarily have to meet this assumption.

The dependent t-test involves the difference in the same sample's mean at two different time-periods. The dependent t-test is usually associated with pretest/posttest designs. See in Example 9.8 how dependent t-tests were used in student research projects.

Example 9.8.

DEPENDENT T-TESTS USED IN STUDENT RESEARCH PROJECTS

Example #1: Social work students delivered a 3-hour intervention on end-of-life care in graduate school masters classes. The participants filled out an instrument on end-of-life care knowledge and one on death anxiety prior to the class and then at the end of the class on end-of-life care. Two dependent t-tests were conducted: one for the pre- and posttest scores on end-of-life care knowledge and one on the pre- and posttest scores for death anxiety.

Example #2: A dyad of researchers placed in a child welfare setting studied the impact of the Parent Nurturing Program, which is a group intervention to help parents gain greater understanding of child development and positive parenting practices (http://www.nurturingparenting.com/about.html). The student looked at pretest scores on the Adult-Adolescent Parenting Inventory before the start of the program and then the posttest scores of participants after they had completed the program, using a dependent t-test.

Example #3: Two student researchers assessed a family preservation program to determine whether families improved on the risk and safety assessment that was completed before intervention and then at 6 months. A dependent t-test was carried out on the score on the risk and safety assessment at these two time-periods.

Independent t-tests are used when you have two different (or independent) groups, such as an experimental and control group, and are interested in comparing the average between these two groups on a dependent variable that is defined at the interval/ratio level. Independent t-tests can be used in intervention research to compare an experimental and control group, but they can also be used whenever an independent variable is dichotomous and the dependent variable is at the ratio or interval level. See in Example 9.9 how student research projects utilized independent t-tests.

Example 9.9.

INDEPENDENT T-TESTS IN STUDENT RESEARCH PROJECTS

Example #1: In a sexual assault response center, women who were interested in receiving counseling after having experienced a sexual assault could elect to have individual counseling as long as they attended group sessions. A team of two student researchers decided to conduct a quasi-experimental design, comparing women who only received group treatment versus those who received group and individual treatment. Their hypothesis was that those who attended group and individual therapy would reduce their level of shame compared to those who only participated in group therapy. They used an independent t-test to compare the differences between these modalities on a standardized scale on shame.

Example #2: In a child welfare setting, the quality assurance department wanted to know whether protective supervision guidelines introduced 2 years prior were being implemented county-wide for the family preservation program. The control group, therefore, involved cases prior to the introduction of the guidelines and the experimental group comprised cases after administration of the protective services guidelines.

Example #3: In a therapeutic foster agency, administrators were interested in finding out whether having a diagnosis of reactive attachment disorder compared to any other type of disorder would result in more foster care placements. An independent t-test was used to compare the average number of placements for each of these groups (reactive attachment disorder or not).

To analyze a t-test, you examine the following:

- the t-test value, which is generated by a formula
- the statistical significance of the test
- the average score
  - for dependent t-tests, at pre- and posttest
  - for independent t-tests, for each of the groups

An illustration of how students analyzed the results of a t-test is shown in Example 9.10 and then you are asked in Test Your Skills Exercise 9.4 to do the same.

Example 9.10.

T-TESTS: VIOLENT INCIDENTS AT AN INPATIENT MENTAL HEALTH FACILITY

As part of this research, the students wanted to explore whether males or females had a higher incidence of violent incidents. Their hypothesis was that males would commit more acts. The t-test score was 0.851, and the p-value was 0.514. This tells you there is no statistically significant difference between males and females on acts committed at the facility.

Test Your Skills Exercise 9.4.

EVALUATING RESULTS

When evaluating the effects of the Parenting Nurturing Program on the Adult-Adolescent Parenting Inventory, the research group found the following results on the subscales. The hypothesis was that the program would result in improved parenting.
Expectations subscale: ($t = -12.27$, $p = 0.000$)
Empathy ($t = -18.29$, $p = 0.000$)
Corporal punishment ($t = -17.58$, $p = 0.000$)
Role reversal ($t = -15.97$, $p = 0.000$)
Power and independence ($t = -11.48$, $p = 0.000$)
What do these results mean?

One-Way ANOVA. The purpose of a one-way (also called simple) Analysis of Variance (ANOVA) is very similar to the independent t-test. On an independent variable that is defined in nominal terms, you want to know the difference between mean scores on the dependent variable for each of the groups. But instead of two groups (or categories) being present in the independent variable, in an ANOVA you can have three or more groups. Example 9.11 illustrates the use of one-way ANOVAs in student research projects.

> **Example 9.11.**
>
> EXAMPLES OF ANOVA IN STUDENT RESEARCH PROJECTS
>
> **Example #1:** As part of the survey of social work graduate students' knowledge and attitudes toward research, one aspect of the project was to determine whether there were differences on people's undergraduate major and their fear or appeal of research. Undergraduate major was defined as social work, psychology, health sciences, or other. Therefore, the independent variable is undergraduate major, and the dependent variable involves scores on the Fear of Research test and the Research Course Appeal Index. In this case, because there were two dependent variables, you would have run two separate ANOVA's.
>
> **Example #2:** One aspect of the project involving violent incidents in the inpatient mental health facility was to determine whether legal status of the patients (voluntary, involuntary, or Not Guilty by Reason of Insanity) was related to acts committed. The hypothesis was that those who were involuntary would have the highest number of incidents. A one-way ANOVA was performed to test this hypothesis.
>
> **Example #3:** The evaluation of the Parent Nurturing Program examined whether participant ethnicity influences scores on the Adult-Adolescent Parenting Inventory. A one-way ANOVA was run to examine this question.

To evaluate findings for a one-way ANOVA, you are given:

- an F-value with its degrees of freedom. The F is the ratio of the differences among variances between the groups and the differences among variances within the groups.
- statistical significance for the test
- if it is statistically significant, then you look at a *post hoc* test, such as the Tukey's
- mean values of the independent variable

Multivariate Analysis

You are probably aware from your readings that many of the statistics presented in published articles are often much more complicated than what you will use in your student projects. These are called multivariate because they examine more than two variables at a time. Think of multivariate as "many variables" and add it to your Terminology Worksheet.

> **Example 9.12.**
>
> MULTIVARIATE STATISTICS CHART
>
> | Multivariate statistics | Three or more variables at the same time | Relationships between:
• Race and self-esteem and work status
• Gender and race and self-esteem and work status | • How do race and gender interact to influence level of self-esteem?
• Do women who work full-time have higher levels of self-esteem than men who work part-time? |
> |---|---|---|---|

Multivariate statistics are an attempt to capture the complexity of real-world conditions and relationships. It is important to remember that the bivariate statistics that most students use in their classroom research projects provide only a beginning understanding of the relationships that you will encounter in practice. You will need to consider what the other variables may be important when you write the discussion section of your report. Think about any of the bi-variate examples presented in this chapter. What other variables might be involved or influence the outcomes of these studies? Ask yourself similar questions as you analyze the data in your own research projects.

A couple of types of multivariate analysis that may be appropriate to your research projects with your instructor's guidance are briefly summarized in Summary Content 9.2.

Summary Content 9.2.

TYPES OF MULTIVARIATE ANALYSES

Multiple Analysis of Variance (MANOVA)	To find out the difference between the mean values of at least two different samples when there is more than one dependent variable	Independent variable: Nominal Dependent variable: Interval or ratio	Any time you have more than one dependent variable and either a one-group (posttest only or pretest/posttest design) or a two-group design (quasi-experimental or experimental)[2]
Logistic regression	To find out how various independent variables in combination predict the occurrence of the dependent variable	Independent variable: Ratio-, interval-, or nominal-level variables Dependent variable: Nominal with two or three values	Prediction models

Now that we have exposed you to different types of data analysis, it is time to put all the information together and apply it to your project as Project Development Worksheet 9.1, by using Example 9.13 as guide. Test Your Skills Exercise 9.5 further challenges your knowledge of material in this chapter.

Project Development Worksheet 9.1.

DATA ANALYSIS PLAN

NAME OF CON-STRUCT	HOW MEAS-URED	INDEP-ENDENT/ DEPENDENT/ CONTROL	VALUES OF THE VARIABLE	LEVEL OF MEAS-UREMENT	HOW USED IN ANALYSIS	UNIVAR-IATE STATISTIC	BIVARIATE STATISTIC	MULTIVARIATE STATISTIC
Ex: gender		Control	0 = male 1 = female	Nominal	To describe sample; to explore relationship with dependent variable; and, as a control in multivariate model	Mode	a. chi square b. t-test	Logistic regression

---

2 Although MANOVA is the most appropriate analysis when there is more than one dependent variable, we allow students to use multiple t-tests for this purpose. Note again that if you run multiple tests, then you may want to adjust your statistical significance level. A simple correction allows you to take the conventional level (0.05) and divide that by the number of tests you plan to run. Each test then has to meet this new standard to make it statistically significant.

NAME OF CON-STRUCT	HOW MEAS-URED	INDEP-ENDENT/ DEPENDENT/ CONTROL	VALUES OF THE VARIABLE	LEVEL OF MEAS-UREMENT	HOW USED IN ANALYSIS	UNIVAR-IATE STATISTIC	BIVARIATE STATISTIC	MULTIVARIATE STATISTIC

Example 9.13.

SAMPLE DATA ANALYSIS: POST PARTUM DEPRESSION IN LATINAS AT A HEALTH CLINIC

NAME OF CONSTRUCT	I.V./D.V./ CONTROL	VALUES OF THE VARIABLE	LEVEL OF MEASUREMENT	UNIVARIATE STATISTIC	BIVARIATE STATISTIC	MULTIVARIATE STATISTIC
Age	Independent variable		Ratio	Mean	Correlation with post partum depression	Regression (with marital status, region of origin, years of educa-tion, number of live births, abuse history as other independent variables and post partum depression and visits with social worker as dependent)
Marital status	Independent variable	1 = Married or with partner 2 = Single/ never married 3 = Divorce/ Separated/ Widow	Nominal	Frequency and percentage	ANOVA (with depend-ent variables as post partum depression and visits with social worker)	Regression (see above under age)
Region of origin	Independent variable	1 = North America/ Mexico 2 = Central America/ Caribbean 3 = South America	Nominal	Frequency and percentage	ANOVA (with depend-ent variables as post partum depression and visits with social worker)	Regression (see above)
Years of education	Independent variable		Ratio	Mean	Correlation (with depend-ent variables as post partum depression and visits with social worker)	Regression (see above)

Number of live births	Independent variable		Ratio	Mean	Correlation (with dependent variables as post partum depression and visits with social worker)	Regression (see above)
Abuse history	Independent variable	1 = Yes 2 = No	Nominal	Frequency and Percentage	Independent t-test (with dependent variables as post partum depression and visits with social worker)	Regression (see above)
Visits to social worker	Independent variable and dependent variable	1 = 1 2 = 2 3 = 3, so on.	Ratio	Mean	Correlation (with dependent variable post partum depression)	Regression (see above, dependent variable)
Post partum depression	Dependent variable	1 = 1 2 = 2 3 = 3, so on	Interval	Frequency and percentage		Regression (see above, dependent variable)

Test Your Skills Exercise 9.5.

DATA ANALYSIS

Based on knowledge gained in this chapter, apply the information to the following scenarios:

1. A student project, located in a child welfare agency, looked at the impact of Structured Decision Making (SDM) on the length of stay of foster children in care (defined in days). The hypothesis of these researchers was that SDM reduced the length of stay for children in foster care compared to usual casework. What analysis would you run in this situation?

2. This research team also looked at how diagnosis related to number of incidents. They compared (1) Axis I only and (2) Having a diagnosis of both Axis I and Axis II. Their hypothesis was that those with an additional diagnosis of Axis II would have more incidents. What analysis is appropriate to run here?

3. A research project involved finding out if the implementation of a different foster parent education program (PRIDE) made a difference on the length of placement of foster children compared to how it had been implemented (non-PRIDE). The results were as follows: t = 2.32, p = 0.022.

	What kind of training did foster parents receive?	N	Mean	Std. Deviation
Length of placement	Non-PRIDE	104	19.57	27.74238
	PRIDE	111	12.54	14.05553

What do these results mean?

CONCLUSION

This chapter has involved the analysis of quantitative data. The ways qualitative data are collected and analyzed are presented in Chapter Ten. Here, we have introduced statistical procedures, starting with univariate, then bivariate, with some beginning exposure to multivariate techniques. We have tried to stick with some of the main procedures that commonly arise, so that you do not become confused by all the choices. We have also demonstrated that data analysis is intimately related to the decisions you have already made about your research to reduce the intimidation students often feel about this part of the research process. Through the use of the examples and the exercises, hopefully you are in a place to plan for the analysis of the data you will collect for your research project.

WEBSITES

http://www.socialresearchmethods.net/selstat/ssstart.htm
A page that will help you figure out what statistical test to use for your data.
     http://www.socialresearchmethods.net/kb/analysis.php
An overview of data management and statistical analysis.
     [3] http://www.mhhe.com/socscience/intro/cafe/common/stat/intro.htm
Basic information on statistics compiled by The McGraw-Hill Companies.
     http://www.lyonsmorris.com/ma1/index.cfm
Effect size calculator

---

3 Grateful acknowledgement to Patrick Dattalo for these last three websites.

QUALITATIVE RESEARCH
METHODS AND DATA ANALYSIS

10

As you have learned, there are many types of research questions that may be appropriate for you to investigate at your agency. Qualitative research is used when a research question deals with exploring new topics and/or trying to understand the subjective meaning that individuals assign to situations, behaviors, or beliefs (Engel & Schutt, 2009). For example, if we want to know what it "means and feels like" to be a person who is homeless and with a disability, then qualitative methods would have several advantages over the quantitative methods that we've discussed in previous chapters. Qualitative data collection techniques such as in-depth interviewing or focus groups are better suited to groups of individuals who may struggle to understand or complete written questionnaires and thus be better able to communicate verbally. We may also have difficulty locating enough people who are homeless and who have a disability to develop a sample of sufficient size for survey research and quantitative data analysis. On the other hand, there are several qualitative research methods, such as phenomenology and case study, which are appropriate for fewer numbers of study participants. The material in this chapter will help you to further distinguish between quantitative and qualitative methods, decide which of the more common qualitative techniques might be most suitable for your project, think through the steps of the qualitative research process (including qualitative data analysis), and consider the specific ethical issues associated with qualitative designs.

UNDERSTANDING THE DIFFERENCES BETWEEN QUALITATIVE AND QUANTITATIVE METHODS

Historically, social work students become acquainted with qualitative research methods as something different from, in contrast to, or secondary to quantitative methods. It is important to recognize that neither method is better than the other. Rather, qualitative and quantitative research use different methods and techniques to answer different types of research questions. Use Test Your Skills Exercise 10.1

to see whether you know some of the important differences between qualitative and quantitative research.

Test Your Skills Exercise 10.1.

IDENTIFYING THE MAJOR DIFFERENCES BETWEEN QUANTITATIVE AND QUALITATIVE RESEARCH

Check whether the characteristic below is associated with qualitative or quantitative research methods.

	QUALITATIVE	QUANTITATIVE
is a deductive process	☐	☐
uses words and phrases to collect and analyze data	☐	☐
most often used for explanatory purposes	☐	☐
most often used for exploratory purpose	☐	☐
emphasizes precision and generalizable statistical findings	☐	☐
is theory-driven	☐	☐
tries to assess cause and effect	☐	☐
is an inductive process	☐	☐
uses numbers to collect and analyze data	☐	☐
emphasizes meanings and experiences	☐	☐
takes place in natural settings	☐	☐
tests hypotheses	☐	☐
avoids the artificiality of experiments and the structured questioning of surveys	☐	☐

Hopefully, the above exercise clarifies that, in contrast to quantitative research, qualitative research uses words and phrases; is used for exploratory purposes; is an inductive process; emphasizes meanings and experience; and, because it takes place in natural settings, avoids the artificiality of experiments and survey research (Holosko, 2006). It is especially important to be mindful that qualitative approaches seek to capture the richness and diversity of people's stories. Such information is often lost with quantitative methods that reduce information by forcing only one response on a questionnaire. Test Your Skills Exercise 10.2 will help you to practice identifying qualitative research questions and methods.

Test Your Skills Exercise 10.2.

IDENTIFYING QUALITATIVE AND QUANTITATIVE RESEARCH

Read each of the following projects and, in the appropriate space, state what you think may be the research question. Then, check whether the project is qualitative or quantitative research.

	QUALITATIVE	QUANTITATIVE
McKenzie held a focus group and asked six participants to discuss what it felt like to be a homeless woman with a disability. She used a digital recorder to record responses. **Research Question:** _____ _____	☐	☐
Peggy was interested in what "cutting" meant to preteen girls who had a history of being sexually assaulted. She conducted in-depth interviews with three girls. During the interviews, Peggy asked the girls to discuss the "meaning" of cutting to them. **Research Question:** _____ _____	☐	☐
Jasmine administered a standardized eating disorder scale to two groups of women: those with an eating disorder and those without an eating disorder. She wanted to determine whether the scale could successfully identify those with an eating disorder. **Research Question:** _____ _____	☐	☐
Lakeisha was curious about the relationship between type of attachment style and substance abuse relapse for those attending a substance abuse treatment center. She hypothesized that those with an avoidant attachment style would have a greater chance of relapse than those with other attachment styles. She administered an attachment index to 250 participants and then recorded the number of times that they relapsed during the 90-day program. **Research Question:** _____ _____	☐	☐

	QUALITATIVE	QUANTITATIVE
Sampson was asked to determine how new social work graduates felt about their career choice. He constructed a questionnaire and mailed it to 500 social work graduates who had completed their degree within the past 3 years. The questionnaire contained mostly closed-ended items. Once the questionnaires were returned, Sampson asked 10 of the graduates who completed the questionnaire to participate in a focus group. Sampson believed that the focus group could provide more in-depth information than just the questionnaire. **Research Question:** _____ _____	☐	☐

In the Test Your Skills Exercise 10.2, did you notice that Peggy and McKenzie conducted qualitative research while the others were quantitative? Also, did you notice that Sampson used both qualitative *and* quantitative methods to collect data? Increasingly, social work researchers use both qualitative and quantitative data approaches, known as mixed-methods designs, to explore complex social and behavioral issues.

QUALITATIVE RESEARCH DESIGNS

In this chapter, we use Strauss and Corbin's (1990) broad definition of qualitative research as "any kind of research that produces findings not arrived at by means of statistical procedures or other means of quantification" (p. 17). Furthermore, Holosko (2009) warns that it is important to know the difference between a research method and a research technique. As noted above, qualitative research methods study people in their natural environment and strive to understand the meaning that people attach to different aspects of their lives. (Tutty, Rothery, & Grinell Jr., 1996). Examples of qualitative methods are phenomenology, case study, ethnography, participant observation, and grounded theory. **Qualitative techniques** refer to the types of data collection strategies used in qualitative studies. The techniques that you are most likely to use in your student projects are observations, intensive interviewing, and focus groups, and those are the ones that we focus on in this chapter. We summarize Engle and Schutt's (2009) categorization of these techniques in Summary Content 10.1.

Summary Content 10.1.

TYPES OF QUALITATIVE METHODS

TYPE	CHARACTERISTICS	DATA COLLECTION ACTIVITIES	SAMPLING ISSUES
Observations (also termed field research)	Natural social processes studied as they happen *relatively undisturbed* in the field rather than in the laboratory Researchers enter into the natural fields of people whom they study	**Jottings:** brief notes taken in the field **Field notes:** written after observations, based on jottings **Daily log:** daily record of activities, sentiment, and perceptions	The researcher focuses investigation on particular processes that seem to be important and selects instances to allow comparisons or checks with which perceptions can be tested.
Intensive interviewing (individual)[1]	Develops a comprehensive picture of the interviewee's background, attitudes, and actions, in interviewee's own terms Seeks to describe and the meanings of central themes in the life world of the subjects. . . . to understand the meaning of what the interviewees say Seeks to cover both a factual and a meaning level Particularly useful for getting the story behind a participant's experiences Most utilized method of data collection Can be labor- and resource-intensive	**Informal, conversational interview:** no predetermined questions are asked, to remain as open and adaptable as possible to the interviewee's nature and priorities; the interviewer "goes with the flow" **General interview guide approach:** same general areas of information are collected from each interviewee; more focus than the conversational approach, but still allows some freedom and flexibility in getting the information from the interviewee **Standardized, open-ended interview:** the same open-ended questions are asked of all interviewees; facilitates faster interviews that can be more easily analyzed and compared **Closed, fixed-response interview:** interviewees are asked the same questions and asked to choose answers from among the same set of alternatives; useful for those not practiced in interviewing	The method used to select participants is important. The researcher must consider the following: • Are potential participants knowledgeable on the subject of interest? • Are potential participants willing to talk? • Do the potential participants represent a range of perspectives from within a group? Selection of new interviewees should continue until a *saturation point* is reached—that is, until new interviews yield little additional information
Focus groups	Groups of unrelated individuals that are formed by a researcher and then led in group discussion of a specific topic for 1 to 2 hours Focused discussion mimics the natural process of forming and expressing opinions—and may give some sense of validity Extensively used for identification of social service needs and utilization patterns The interactions between group members may reveal additional information regarding the topic	Open-ended questions are used to solicit answers from the group of respondents. Data can be captured by using a video or digital recording device or by writing copious notes.	A few individuals are recruited for the group who have: • time to participate • knowledge pertinent to the focus group topic • share key characteristics with the target population

Sources: Valenzuela & Shrivastava, 2002; Oka & Shaw, n.d. Neill, 2006.

Individual, face-to-face interviewing has been the primary data collection technique for most student qualitative projects. The examples provided in Example 10.1 illustrate various interviewing, data collection, and sampling approaches in qualitative projects designed by social work research students.

Example 10.1.
QUALITATIVE METHODS EXAMPLES

Example #1: Semi-Structured Interviews to Understand the Experiences of Students with Learning Disabilities

Two social work research students were interested in the experiences of learning-disabled young adults as they graduated high school and entered college. They contacted the university's Office of Disability Support Services for help in recruiting university freshmen to participate in the study. The Office solicited students with learning-disabilities from their list of students and provided the names and e-mail addresses for 10 freshman students who volunteered for the study. The researchers then contacted these individuals and scheduled interviews with each of them at different times at the university student center. One of the student researchers was responsible for guiding the interview process while the other sat quietly and took detailed handwritten notes. Because the published literature on this topic was quite limited and offered few specifics to guide questionnaire development, the student researchers developed a semi-structured interview format. They asked the same open-ended questions of each person about his/her high school academic history, motivations for and goals that prompted pursuit of a college degree, and his/her experiences with instructors and classmates in the class and on campus.

As you can imagine, the research students invested quite a bit of time preparing for and conducting this study but they obtained valuable in-depth, rich information helpful to both the Disability Office and to university professors in meeting the needs of this special group of college students. Researchers with more limited time could consider answering this question with a focus group study using the same participants and similar questions.

Example #2: Sampling in Underrepresented Populations

Sampling issues precluded substituting a focus group to answer the research question in another social work student project: "How knowledgeable are mental health agencies in the state about culturally competent practice and cultural barriers influencing Asian-Americans?" Similarly to Example #1, a qualitative research effort was chosen because the researcher was interested in the meanings ascribed to and experiences of cultural competence. Fortunately, the student was able to locate a semi-structured interview guide from a study on another ethnic group and adapt it to Asian-American population.

The most challenging issues centered on the study sample—who and how to select participants from the mental health agencies for the study. First, the student needed to decide which stakeholder group—administrators, clinicians, and/or clients—would be most appropriate. Although clients would be preferable, they were deemed inappropriate for this study because of confidentiality and access issues; administrators were excluded because their limited amount of direct client service time with clients made them unlikely respondents to discuss first-hand experiences about culturally competent clinical practice. The student decided to use clinicians as her study population and then had to consider how to capture the ethnic diversity that varied greatly across the state. The state provided mental health services through 40 comprehensive agencies located within four informally designated regions—north, south, eastern, west, and central. Because of her prior employment and current field placement in mental health settings, the student relied on personal contacts with mid-level agency administrators to obtain listservs of two to three agencies within each region. Referencing this midlevel administrator added credibility to her study. The student e-mailed the clinicians on the listservs and obtained the contact information from at least five individual clinicians from each region who were willing to participate in the study.

This student decided to do in-person interviews with agency employees in areas close to her and scheduled phone interviews with individuals in areas further away from her home. She audiotaped the in-person interviews but relied on extensive note-taking for the phone interviews. Although using two different interview approaches is not ideal, it was the most reasonable approach for the student to explore her research topic given the time and financial constraints.

Three points about this study are important for student researchers to consider. First, access to the study population was possible because this student social worker had personal contacts and legitimacy within this particular mental health system. It is difficult, if not impossible, to gain access to a study population through listservs without some prior relationship with and approval from the "gatekeepers" of these listservs. Second, despite the fact that qualitative studies are associated with natural settings, researchers have to be particularly sensitive to the context of the data collection setting to ensure that the interview occurs in a place that provides privacy for and free expression by the respondent. In this case, the social work student met with, or telephoned, the clinicians out of workplace premises during the lunch or immediately at the end of the work day. Third, trade-offs between design quality and implementation feasibility is especially challenging for qualitative researchers. Although audiotaping provided a more accurate data collection mechanism and allowed the research to be able to concentrate on the interview without note-taking distractions, transcription of the audiotapes for data analysis was more time-consuming than preparation of handwritten notes.

Example #3: Selecting a Qualitative Technique for Work With Immigrant Groups

Work with immigrant groups almost inevitably requires a qualitative approach. A student was interested in understanding how immigrants reconciled their home country's values with their new country's values. Specifically, the student wanted to know what happened when new immigrants had potentially competing value systems. She was placed at an agency that worked with immigrants and asked her field instructor if she could conduct intensive interviews with three immigrants. Her field instructor was hesitant; the process of immigrating to a new country was stressful and she did not want to interject any new stress into her clients' lives.

The student asked her field instructor whether she could ask a few clients if they thought the interviews would be acceptable. The field instructor agreed. The student asked a few clients and all indicated that they would like to talk about how "different" America was for them. An interesting finding was that the clients were more interested in talking in a group rather than one-on-one with an interviewer. One client even mentioned that she was having difficulty in this area but did not know how to bring it up with her counselor.

The student went back to the instructor and discussed the conversations that had occurred. Both the instructor and the student began to see this as an opportunity to bring people together to discuss this issue. The both acknowledged that it would be beneficial to conduct a focus group to collect data on this issue.

Qualitative Research Techniques As a "Default" Approach in Real-World Settings

Most researchers are intentional in their choice of a qualitative design, but there are a surprising number of quantitative studies that default to qualitative approaches in student projects because of unexpected barriers or last-minute problems within the agency setting. For example, one student doing her field placement in a residential setting for children and youth had received permission to administer a brief quantitative survey to the children ($n = 25$) about their eating preferences and nutritional knowledge to better explain and prevent childhood obesity. However, shortly thereafter, this residential placement organization encountered difficulties because of their Medicaid reimbursement contractand the majority of the children were abruptly moved to another facility, leaving the student researcher without a study population. Retaining her primary interest in the subject and most of her completed literature review, the student revised her research question and methodology and developed a qualitative study that interviewed the staff in the original residential setting concerning their perceptions about childhood obesity.

A default to qualitative methods is also an option for pre-experimental group designs that lose group members between pre- and posttest. Client attrition is not an unusual occurrence in short-term group interventions. When client participation in group interventions declines to the point that statistical analysis becomes meaningless, social work students can recoup some of their research efforts by revising the questionnaire into a structured interview guide and then conducting a follow-up focus group session for the remaining group members. Again, this is not an ideal situation but is sometimes the only option remaining for students to conduct research in real-world settings.

Now that you have had some exposure to qualitative methods, use the exercises in Test Your Skills Exercises 10.3 and 10.4 to apply some of the basic concepts and themes associated with various qualitative research techniques.

Test Your Skills Exercise 10.3.

QUALITATIVE METHODS AND STUDY PARTICIPANTS

Many military families must cope with deployment (when a military person is "called for military duty" and must leave his or her family). Think about the experience of deployment and redeployment in military families with young children. How would you explore this phenomenon using each of the qualitative approaches below? What questions would be of interest to you? How would you collect data for each of these approaches? Who would be your study participants for each approach?

	QUESTIONS OF INTEREST	STUDY PARTICIPANTS	DATA COLLECTION
Participant observation			
Focus groups			
Intensive interviewing			

Test Your Skills Exercise 10.4.

DEVELOPING A QUALITATIVE STUDY

One of your classmates is interested in health literacy (defined as the degree to which individuals have the capacity to obtain, process, and understand basic health information) and has designed a survey to research social workers' knowledge of their clients' health literacy. She plans to mail the survey to members of the state National Association of Social Workers (NASW) organization. You are also interested in health literacy and think a qualitative approach could greatly enhance understanding of health literacy in the field. You suggest partnering with your classmate to transform this study into a mixed-methods design.

- What types of research questions would be most appropriate for qualitative study?
- How would your sampling strategy differ from your classmate's?
- Who would you interview or gather for a focus group?
- What specific open-ended questions would you ask for individual sessions or the focus groups?

NOTE-TAKING AND RECORDING

Although often not addressed adequately in research methods texts, decisions about the type, content, and format of data-recording are critical to successful analysis of qualitative information. Capturing the words or narrative generated by your interviews or focus groups in either manual or electronic form and then transcribing or preparing the material for data analysis are the basic steps in this process. Given the current state of technological availabilities, the best way to capture the words or narrative verbatim is by either using an audio-recorder or by having an interview assistant who does nothing but take notes (we expect that technology will advance to the point where there will be new tools for recording interviews and focus groups). Collaborating with another classmate on your research project allows you to share this task. We suggest that you and your colleague take turns asking questions and recording in both interview and focus group efforts. If you are using an audiotape recorder, plan to have one person attend to the recorder while the other asks the questions and guides the interview or focus group. Many practice tips for recording interviews that are available online can be accessed at the following sites:

- Conducting E-Interviews—http://nbn-resolving.de/urn:nbn:de:0114-fqs020295
- Focus Groups—http://www.programevaluation.org/focusgroups.htm
- How and What to Code—http://onlineqda.hud.ac.uk/Intro_QDA/how_what_to_code.php
- Trochim (2006). Interviews. Retrieved from http://www.socialresearch methods.net/kb/intrview.php

This information is especially important if you are doing both the interviewing and the note-taking, and these same tips apply to transcribing the material from an audio-recorder to written notes. Although specialized equipment is available for transcribing, most social work students don't have access to such equipment and end up reviewing and replaying the audiotapes while making written notes. Another easier and more low-cost option, as long as you have another person present to act as recorder, is to is to ask that person to also write detailed notes of participants' responses during the interview or focus group. The person should type up their notes immediately after the interview/focus group, making sure that the notes are readable and as complete as possible, and indicate when there portions of the interview may be questionable because of lack of clarity. This method still requires that you listen to the audiotape but you do so as you compare it to the written notes, which entails filling in the gaps rather than direct transcription. This will save you a great deal of time in the transcription process, but, as noted, it means that a co-facilitator will have to be present. Overall, it is very difficult for one person to attend to the interview questions, formulate sensitive and appropriate responses, and probe when one is also writing detailed notes.

It is important to remember that the methods section in qualitative studies is similar to that in quantitative studies. Be sure to explain how you developed any precollection materials (e.g., interview schedule), how you chose and contacted your participants, who your participants were, and what instructions and information they were given. Give some indication of your participants' responses to the collection process (this may involve some reflective comment from you—were there any problems, unforeseen reactions, dilemmas for the researcher, etc.? This should lead you to discuss any relevant ethical issues, too) and give details of any processes of data treatment (note-taking, transcription, etc.). And, of course, you need to explain how you analyzed your data—give enough detail for the reader to understand how you developed your codes, themes, or interpretations (Woods, 1999).

QUALITATIVE DATA ANALYSIS

Similarly to quantitative analysis, qualitative analysis aims to make sense of and give meaning to the data collected. In general, the process of qualitative data analysis involves the identification and organization of themes or patterns from the words, text, and narratives obtained in the data collection (Rubin & Babbie, 2011). Researchers use a wide range of tools to accomplish this goal, including sophisticated computer software programs such as NUD*IST or NIVO (Gibbs, 2009, http://onlineqda.hud.ac.uk/Intro_QDA/index.php) and application of rigorous and labor-intensive activities such as peer debriefing and audit to ensure that the qualitative findings are trustworthy and authentic. For detailed information about the rigors of constructivist qualitative design and analysis, please *see* Rodwell (1998). However, for this workbook, we will focus on content analysis and some basic coding schemes associated with the type of intensive interviewing and focus group techniques primarily used in student social work research projects.

Although the terms content analysis and coding are sometimes used interchangeably, many researchers speak of content analysis as the method of systematically analyzing and making inferences from text (Engel & Schutt, 2009, p. 545; Rubin & Babbie, 2011) while coding refers to the primary tool used for doing content analysis (Busch, De Maret, Flynn, Kellum, Le, Meyers, Saunders et al., 2005). Coding means grouping key words or terms, phrases, sentences, topic items, and so forth garnered from your interview and focus group notes into a specific number of categories. The categories generally represent broader conceptual meanings or themes that describe or explain the entire meaning, experience or phenomena that you are studying.

For example, in a qualitative study on poverty, a student interviewed individuals in waiting rooms of social service agencies in both an urban and a rural county. Having first identified hunger as one of the concepts for his study, he then reviewed the notes from his interviews for the ways that the participants referenced hunger (i.e., he looked for words such as "famished," "starving," "not enough to eat,") and then counted the number of times that these hunger-related concepts were reported. The student summarized these findings in a paragraph or two on how respondents expressed hunger. This is one method of content analysis (known as conceptual analysis or first level coding) whereby the researcher identifies the existence and frequency of concepts.

Relational analysis, or second-level coding, is a type of content analysis that goes one step further (Tutty, Rothery, & Grinnell, 1996) than conceptual analysis. With this method, the student would examine the relationships among concepts, looking for the broader or entire or contextual meaning of the words or phrases. In the hunger example, the student would identify the words or phrases next to which the "hunger concepts" appeared and then identified the different meanings that emerged from these combinations of phrases. The results may be the situations that lead to hunger or the consequences of hunger (Busch et al., 2005).

As the researcher reads through his or her data set, codes will evolve and grow as more topics or themes become apparent. Summary Content 10.2 provides guidelines for conducting a content analysis of your qualitative project.

Summary Content 10.2.

GUIDELINES FOR CONDUCING A CONTENT ANALYSIS

- Decide the unit or element of meaning (i.e., word, phrase, sentence, topic item, etc.) for which you want to code. Usually the unit is passages of text that are coded but it can be sections of an audio or video recording or parts of images.
- Decide whether to code for existence or frequency of a unit of meaning.
- Systematically work through each transcript, marking similar passages of text using the coding scheme decided above. Any parts of the data that relate to a code topic are coded with the same label.
- This process of coding (associating labels with the text, images, etc.) involves close reading and repeated readings of the text.
- Review your coding topics to make sure that all passages and chunks that have been judged (by you) to be about the same topic, theme, concept, and so forth, are coded the same way— that is, given the same label.
- If a theme is identified from the data that does not quite fit the codes already existing, create a new code.
- Examine the units for similarities and differences and relationships among the units.
- Categorize the units by similarities, differences, and/or relationship and label the categories. The categories are given meaningful names that provide indications of the idea or concept that underpins a particular theme or category.
- Write one or two paragraphs summarizing each of the categories and identifying major themes; include some direct quotes to illustrate and highlight particular themes.

Source: Gibbs & Taylor (2010).

PUTTING IT ALL TOGETHER

After you have collected your data and analyzed it, you need to determine how to "put it all together" and report your results. Think about the questions in Summary Content 10.3 as you begin to write the findings section of your research project.

Summary Content 10.3.

QUESTIONS TO GUIDE THE FINDINGS SECTION

- What patterns and common themes emerge in responses dealing with specific items?
- How do these patterns (or lack thereof) answer the broader study question(s)?
- Are there any deviations from these patterns? If yes, are there any factors that might explain these atypical responses?
- Do any of these patterns or findings suggest that additional data may need to be collected?
- Do any of the study questions need to be revised?
- Do the patterns that emerge corroborate the findings of any corresponding qualitative analyses that have been conducted? If not, what might explain these discrepancies?

Source: Berkowitz (1997).

Many social work research students are intuitively attracted to qualitative research methods because the findings in qualitative studies are presented as narrative descriptions of people, interactions, and relationships in language familiar to and easily interpreted by social workers. You may find reading qualitative studies reminiscent of reading individual or family stories in case reports. Similarly, the absence of statistical data may have special appeal for you if you are one of those social work students who are "math-phobic." In other words, students who tend to "skip over" the statistical tables in quantitative studies are drawn to qualitative findings that provide rich glimpses into the lives of "real" people, unencumbered by numbers and statistics. For example, the excerpts in Example 10.2 from two published studies about work–family balance by one of the authors illustrate how compelling qualitative study findings can be in comparison to statistical tables.

Example 10.2.

QUALITATIVE STUDY FINDING EXAMPLES

Example #1: "I gave up a better paying job so that I could bring my granddaughter to work with me every day here. There were some special circumstances that meant that I had to keep a close eye on her all the time. She's two years old now and she's been with me at work every day since she was a baby. When she was younger she stayed near my desk in an infant seat or on a blanket. Now, because I'm a program director, I need to move around the building more and I have a stroller here so that she can come with me from place to place. The mornings at home are really hectic trying to get her and all her stuff collected and it's hard getting to work on time. Also, sometimes I get a little distracted at work because of her, but I just stay longer and put in more hours to make sure everything gets done. It's worth it because being able to bring her to work with me relieved an enormous amount of stress and conflict in our family without creating an additional financial burden that would have made matters worse."

Source: Secret, M. (2006).

Example #2: Similarly, elder care also frequently conflicted with employees' job responsibilities. Access to affordable quality elder care appeared limited; several focus group participants worried they would not be able to continue working if they were unable to find acceptable arrangements. Many reflected on the increased burden of elder care as compared to child care, including one employee who said, "The biggest difference between worrying about child care and elder care is that you know your children will eventually outgrow the need for child care. But, with aging parents and relatives, you know it's going to get worse."

Source: Secret, M. & Swanberg, J. (2008).

As you know, the findings section of a qualitative report is composed of text and narrative and is quite different from than statistical tables found in quantitative reports. In qualitative studies, findings are often organized and reported by the themes that emerged in the content analysis. For example, the subheadings of one of the work–family studies about parenting in the workplace noted above were followed by two to three paragraphs of text and direct quotes: *The power of trade-offs and pay-offs; The bottom line; Occasional and regular workplace parenting arrangements; Wish lists; Employee stories.* However, it is not unusual for a qualitative study to present findings in a text-based table format similar to Example 10.3.

Example 10.3.

USING A TABLE FORMAT TO REPORT QUALITATIVE RESULTS

Primary research questions	Focus group questions and interview guide	Key Findings
From the Spillover Model: 1. What are employees' personal circumstances and expectations related to work–life issues?	• Discuss the different types of work and family responsibilities that you "juggle." • Define what the terms "family-friendly" and "work–life issues" mean to you.	• Church, community volunteer work, child- and elder-care demands, second job or school, family crisis, household maintenance • Trusting, caring, family-like relationships with coworkers; Employers respect employees' life outside of work; "family-friendly" work environment benefits employees and employers
2. What is the nature of the work environment for employees; in particular, what are the demands and rewards of an individual's work situation?	• What are the day-to-day challenges that you find in your job? • What type of workplace supports have been helpful to you?	• Challenges from routine nature of the job = nontraditional work hours, on-call hours • Challenges exacerbated by problematic staffing patterns and poor personnel practices; negative attitudes of community and city council accusations • Rewards = sense of pride and commitment to the job; available leave time and benefits • Quality daycare and scheduling flexibility

Source: Secret, M. & Swanberg, J. (2008).

ETHICS IN QUALITATIVE STUDIES

Qualitative researchers need to be aware of specific ethical challenges that arise because of the level of direct involvement they have with study participants. For example, the sensitive and intense discussions that occur between researcher and participant in in-depth interviewing, often around painful life events such as divorce, death of a family member, and domestic abuse, can lead to a personal relationship and researcher involvement in a participant's life that extend beyond what is appropriate for a research setting. Social work research students in particular have to be cautious about study participants relating to them as "therapists" and sharing more intimate stories than they intended for their research study. Summary Content 10.4 provides some of the ethical issues about which research students should consider when conducting qualitative research and is followed by Test Your Skills Exercise 10.5 which helps you to apply these ethical considerations to your project.

Summary Content 10.4.

ETHICAL CONSIDERATIONS FOR QUALITATIVE RESEARCH

Voluntary participation: Sensitive topics should be not be introduced gratuitously; they should either be volunteered by the respondents or inquired about when they are the focus of the study

Subject well-being: Researcher needs to concerned about the feelings and reputation of informants

Identity disclosure: Researcher should endeavor to fully disclose his or her identity

Confidentiality: Researcher should make every effort to expunge all possible identifiers from published works

---

Test Your Skills Exercise 10.5.

UNDERSTANDING THE ETHICAL CONSIDERATIONS FOR QUALITATIVE RESEARCH

Think about how you would address the particular ethical considerations in the following study: Peggy was interested in what "cutting" means to pre-teen girls who have a history of being sexually assaulted. She asked three of her coworkers' clients to participate. She conducted in-depth interviews with three girls. During the interviews, Peggy asked the girls to discuss the "meaning" of cutting to them.

Voluntary participation: _____

Subject well-being: _____

Identity disclosure: _____

Confidentiality: _____

CONCLUSION

Qualitative efforts adhere to a defined step-by-step process that is just as systematic and rigorous as quantitative research. Let's return to our original question, understanding the meaning and feelings of being a person who is homeless and who also has a disability, and summarize this step-by-step process. First, we recognize that we are interested in learning information that cannot be found by using traditional quantitative methods and decide to pose a qualitative question. When thinking about this question, we could use snowball sampling to locate three to five homeless persons with disabilities to interview. We could record the interviews and then use content analysis to search for themes. The end result would be a deeper understanding of what being homeless and a person with a disability means to participants. This result can only be captured by a qualitative approach discussed above.

Students are sometimes surprised by how time and labor intensive a qualitative project can be. Use Project Development Worksheet 10.1 to help you think about the time commitment involved in your project. Use Project Development Worksheet 10.2 to sketch out preliminary plans for carrying out a qualitative study.

In summary, qualitative research provides an opportunity for social work students to gain in-depth knowledge, investigate "hidden" populations, and gain greater insight into work with client populations. Data collected from qualitative methods can enhance our understanding while giving those in minority populations a chance to have their voices heard. Further, qualitative and quantitative research are both valuable, and findings from one type of research can supplement and enrich the findings from the other type.

We have not finished discussing qualitative research. In Chapter Eleven, we will discuss how to use research methods to evaluate social work programs and interventions. Qualitative, quantitative, or a mixture of both may be used in evaluation studies. As you will read in the following chapter, it is important to remember that whatever method or methods are used, evaluation studies are intended to help us to understand some aspect of an intervention's functioning or outcome.

Project Development Worksheet 10.1.
ESTIMATING THE TIME COMMITMENT

Individual Interview(s)
How many researchers will be conducting individual interviews?

How many people will be interviewed ?

How long do you think it will take you to find each participant?

How long will each interview last?

How long will it take to analyze data from one person? Remember, if you have to transcribe data, this process may be longer than anticipated.

Focus Group(s)

How many researchers will facilitate focus groups?

How many focus groups will be conducted?

How many people will be in each focus group?

How long do you think it will take to recruit enough people for one focus group?

How long will each focus group last?

How long will it take to analyze data from one focus group? Remember, if you have to transcribe data, this process may be longer than anticipated

Project Development Worksheet 10.2.
WORKSHEET FOR DEVELOPING QUALITATIVE RESEARCH PROJECT
OVERVIEW OF PROJECT:

		IMPORTANT CONSIDERATIONS/QUESTIONS
Research question:		Is your question one that can be answered by using qualitative methods?
Target population:		How will you decide who is a member of your target population? Do you have access to members in your population of interest?
Concept(s) that need to be defined for the study:		Are there concepts that you need to define? How will you define it/them?
Ethical considerations:		How will you ensure that your participants are protected?
Barriers:		What are potential barriers that you may face? Have you thought about strategies to help you overcome these challenges?
Estimated time of project:		How much time do you anticipate this study will take?

AGENCY CONSIDERATIONS:

Resources needed from the agency (e.g., access to data, space for interviews, etc.):		Is your agency supportive of this project? What type of resources do you need?
Permission secured from the following person/people:		From whom do you need to secure permission? Do you need written permission? Think about your data collection method(s)—Does the agency need to do anything to support your data collection method(s)?
Benefits to the agency and or clients:		What are the benefits of doing this study? Think about agency and client benefits.

DATA COLLECTION:

Type of data to be collected:		• Plan questions around an outline (but be flexible in order) • Make questions short and to the point • Use nondirective probes • Follow-up questions can be tailored to answers • Tape recorders are a good idea as they are routinely ignored by interviewees; however, some respondents will give away good information when the tape recorder gets turned off • Constant note-taking is a distraction • Write immediately after observation period or as soon as possible • Takes up to three times as long as observation period • Distinguish direct quotes from paraphrased quotes • Surrounding context should be detailed • Record own thoughts and feelings in the field • Supplement notes with visual material as appropriate
Timeline for data collection:		Think about what you need to do to accomplish this project, what are your steps and when will you accomplish them?

Data verification process:		How do you know that you interpreted the data correctly? How will you ascertain the validity of the interview or focus group findings?
ANALYSIS:		
Steps needed to prepare for analysis:		How will you prepare the data for analysis? Do you have to transcribe information?
Thematizing:		How will you analyze results? Decide on the purpose, the topic, the nature, and methods of analysis that are appropriate.
WRITING UP AND PRESENTING RESULTS:		
Presenting results:		To whom will you present results? How will you present results? How will you communicate findings of the study based on scientific criteria?

WEBSITES

University of Colorado at Denver School of Education Qualitative Research Page
http://carbon.ucdenver.edu/~mryder/itc/pract_res.html
The Qualitative Report: an online bimonthly qualitative research journal
http://www.nova.edu/ssss/QR/practice.html
List of Qualitative Research Journals
http://www.slu.edu/organizations/qrc/QRjournals.html
Qualitative Research page from the University of Plymouth
http://www.edu.plymouth.ac.uk/resined/qualitative%20methods%202/qualrshm.htm
Association for Qualitative Research
http://www.aqr.org.au/
Qualitative Resource Page at the Qualitative Report
http://www.nova.edu/ssss/QR/web.html

PROGRAM AND PRACTICE EVALUATIVE

11

This chapter focuses on program and practice evaluation. It is a bit different from some of the other workbook chapters that are associated with one particular step in the research process as was presented in Chapter One. For example, Chapter Seven on sampling discusses "who" is being studied, whereas Chapter Eight on measurement is concerned with "what" is being studied. Evaluation research is not a specific activity that you can point to or associate with any particular step of the research process. Rather, it encompasses all aspects of research processes and methods. In other words, a major comprehensive program evaluation can include experimental and nonexperimental research designs, use both qualitative and quantitative approaches, collect data from secondary data sources, interview participants, use standardized or nonstandardized measurement instruments, include both probability and nonprobability samples, and must adhere to the standard research ethics.

Program evaluation is distinguished from other types of social science research not by the design, method, or the approach but the underlying intent, the assumptions that guide the evaluation process (Holosko, Thyer, & Danner, 2009), and the context within which the program evaluation is developed and implemented. As do other social work research authors (Engel & Schutt, 2009; Rubin & Babbie, 2011), we devote an entire chapter to evaluation research because it is the research that you are most likely to encounter in practice and often the type of research that many field agencies are most interested in having social work students do. If you reflect back on earlier chapters, you will realize that we have already provided many examples of evaluation research.

DEFINING EVALUATION

The best way to distinguish program evaluation research from basic social science research is to realize that evaluation research is program, policy, or intervention specific. A dictionary definition of "evaluation" is an assessment or determination of merit or worth. In social work research, evaluation is the use of any and all types of research methods to investigate, assess, or determine the merit or worth of a particular social program or policy or intervention. Agencies are often interested in who their services help or what aspects of service delivery are more or less useful for clients.

One way to answer such questions is through evaluation research. In evaluation research, we examine the independent variables which are most often the characteristics of the sample, the program, or the people delivering services in relation to the dependent variable which is the desired outcome of the service. One example is the Work Empowerment Program for individuals looking for employment after they have been incarcerated. The administrators wanted to understand whether greater program involvement (contact with caseworkers and employment workshops attended) was related to the person's ability to become employed. Another example involves a treatment foster care agency. A research team sought to understand whether characteristics of teens (such as the type of maltreatment for which they had originally entered foster care and the DSM diagnosis assigned to them) and program variables (such as the number and types of assignments of different caseworkers) was related to positive long-term outcomes of the teens, which included graduating from high school and being employed or going to college.

It is important for you to understand the differences between program evaluations which and social science research. Program evaluations are focused on identifying benefits to clients or client systems, whereas social science research aims to generate knowledge about and generalize findings to social phenomena that extend beyond a specific agency or program (Holosko, Thyer, & Danner, 2009). Example 11.1 compares evaluation research studies to social science studies that are not considered to be evaluative. Pay close attention to the underlined phrases. They will help you differentiate the nuanced purpose of each of the studies.

Example 11.1.

COMPARISON BETWEEN EVALUATION AND SOCIAL SCIENCE RESEARCH

EVALUATION RESEARCH	SIMILAR SOCIAL SCIENCE RESEARCH
This study *assessed the effect* of a dating violence sensitivity group intervention. The participants were 190 high school students, ages 13 to 19 years, with just more than half being boys (53%) and the remainder being girls (47%). Data about the knowledge, values, and skills needed to avoid dating violence were collected from the participants before the 12-week group training and at the end of the training sessions.	This study *assessed the relationship* between adolescents' dating violence victimization and their psychological well-being. The participants were 190 high school students, ages 13 to 19 years, with just more than half being boys (53%) and the remainder being girls (47%). Data were collected at one point in time during first period homeroom class during the first week of the school year.
This study *evaluated the effectiveness* of cognitive-behavioral interventions in the treatment of persons with schizophrenia who experienced significant residual symptoms and impaired functioning despite their adherence to medication. Standardized measures of psychosocial functioning and severity of symptoms were administered individually to 5 clients in an adult residential setting weekly for 6 weeks to establish a baseline. Each client received outpatient CBT for 18 months in sessions lasting up to 1 hour. Psychosocial functioning and severity of symptoms during the 18 months were plotted on a graph to determine the effectiveness of the intervention for each individual.	This study *investigated the awareness* of social workers about the merits of cognitive-behavioral interventions in the treatment of persons with schizophrenia. An e-mail list of random sample of practicing social workers was obtained from the National Association of Social Workers (NASW). The social workers were asked to complete an electronic survey that asked about their experiences working with persons with schizophrenia and their knowledge of cognitive-behavioral interventions.

EVALUATION RESEARCH	SIMILAR SOCIAL SCIENCE RESEARCH
This study *investigated the effectiveness* of a parenting intervention for mothers living in a residential domestic violence facility. Mothers participated in a 4-week on-site intensive parenting group. Each 2-hour session was taught by a domestic violence counselor and included 1 hour where women were taught parenting techniques and 1 hour where women demonstrated parenting skills.	This article *explored challenges* to understanding mothering under difficult and unusual circumstances—that is, in the context of a shelter for battered women and their children. Drawing on participant observation and interviews with staff at a local battered woman's shelter, the authors used data collected on field notes that were derived from unobtrusive participant observation and semi-structured interviews with the staff between 2002 and 2004.
This *study examined whether the services provided as part of the Family Independence Agency's TANF Program helped women experiencing domestic violence become financially self-sufficient* 1 year after participating in TANF services. Before receiving TANF services, 250 women were asked to complete the Job Assessment Inventory (JAI) and the Financial Self-Sufficiency Scale (FSSS). The JAI assessed current job skills and current and past employment. The FSSS assessed participants' level of self-sufficiency. Women then participated in TANF-sponsored job training activities (e.g., resume writing, computer skills classes, etc.) and domestic violence services (e.g., counseling, safety planning, etc.). Counselors tracked women and used the JAI and FSSS to assess participants' job skills and financial self-sufficiency at 6 and 9 months from the start.	Using data from a random sample of women from the welfare caseload in an urban county, the authors *investigated the prevalence of domestic violence and its association with mental health, health, and economic well-being.* Face-to-face interviews were conducted with a random sample of 753 women who were welfare recipients in February, 2002. The Family Independence Agency, which administers the state's TANF program, provided names and addresses of all single-parent cases.
A statewide evaluation of the Education Now and Babies Later (ENABL) program was conducted to assess its ability to increase adolescents' knowledge and beliefs about pregnancy prevention. ENABL is aimed at preventing teenage pregnancy through abstinence. Middle school students in one school district comprised a treatment group ($n = 974$), and students in another school district comprised a comparison group. Subjects completed a pretest and posttest reflecting knowledge and beliefs about teenage pregnancy before and after the ENABL program.	Researchers used data from a national probability sample of middle school youth to *determine whether there was a relationship between a child's religious/spiritual activity participation and positive beliefs about teen pregnancy* among lower income middle school students. Researchers used items from two scales, the Attitudes toward Teen Pregnancy Scale and the Religious/Spiritual Activity Participation Scale, to evaluate the research question.
A research team *examined whether participation in a 4-week prison employment program helped inmates secure employment upon being released from prison.* Inmates in a Midwestern prison were asked to participate in a 4-week employment preparation program. Inmates were given a work attitudes assessment to assess their beliefs about work and a job skills assessment. Inmates met 1 hour a week for 4 weeks. The employment status for participants was evaluated at 3, 6, and 12 months post-release. Results were compared to a comparable group of inmates who did not participate in the employment preparation program.	The study used a unique data set constructed from administrative *records to examine the relationship between incarceration and employment rates* for former female state prisoners from Illinois. The analysis indicated that although prison is associated with declining employment rates during the quarters leading up to women's incarcerations, it does not appear to harm their employment prospects later on.

PROGRAM-SPECIFIC QUESTIONS ANSWERED BY EVALUATION RESEARCH

As you can see from the examples above, evaluation research questions are specific to program services. Evaluation questions are grouped into four basic categories (Engel & Schutt, 2009; Rubin & Babbie, 2011) that seek to provide information about service needs, delivery, outcomes, and costs. Summary Content 11.1 identifies and summarizes these categories—needs assessment, formative or process evaluation about service deliver, summative evaluation about service outcomes, and cost-benefit analysis about program costs.

Summary Content 11.1.

QUESTIONS ANSWERED BY EVALUATION RESEARCH

PROGRAM-SPECIFIC QUESTION(S)	CATEGORY OF PROGRAM EVALUATION	COMMONLY USED RESEARCH METHODS
Is the program needed? *Is a new program needed?* *Who is our program currently serving?*	Needs assessment	• *Key informant interviews*—use individual interviews in-person, or by phone, structured or unstructured • *Community forum*—use a focus group • *Rates under treatment*—use secondary data from existing agencies (who uses existing services) • *Social indicators*—use secondary data from census or other well-being indicators(infant mortality rates, suicide rates) • *Surveys of community or target groups*—consideration has to be given to sampling unit
How does the program operate? *How do clients receive services?* *Is the program operating the way it was intended to operate?* *Is our program serving the clients that it was intended to serve?*	Formative evaluation also called Process Evaluation	Quantitative data and methods are useful but qualitative data and methods often are used to elucidate and explain internal program dynamics, unanticipated outcomes, and interaction among program participants • Must measure the independent variable, which is the delivery of the program • Use of agency records to assess staffing patterns and distribution • Have staff record use of time • Collect data on number of applications, number of clients, and length of service • Client satisfaction surveys

PROGRAM-SPECIFIC QUESTION(S)	CATEGORY OF PROGRAM EVALUATION	COMMONLY USED RESEARCH METHODS
What is the program's impact? *Does the program meet its intended goals and objectives?*	Summative evaluation	Experimental design is preferred method for maximizing internal validity • Program is independent variable (treatment) • Outcomes are dependent variables • Random assignment allows evaluation of program's impact independent of the types of people in different groups *Selection bias in nonexperimental designs is a common problem because people self-select to participate in programs.*
How efficient is the program? *Is the program cost-effective?* *Is the cost of the program justified by the outcomes?*	Cost-benefit or a cost-effectiveness analysis	Must measure the independent variable, which is the delivery of the program, and then compare to service units (outputs) or outcomes • Use of agency records to assess staffing patterns and distribution • Have staff record use of time • Collect data on number of applications, number of clients, and length of service

The examples presented in Example 11.2 will help you understand what is involved in these different categories of evaluation research.

Example 11.2.

QUESTIONS RAISED WITH DIFFERENT TYPES OF PROGRAM EVALUATION

Needs assessment

You are a social work student at a local YMCA and have been asked to do a needs assessment to determine if fathers in the community need support/services to help them be better parents.

• What is your research question?
• Who will you interview for key informant interviews?
• What will you ask them? (Remember, this is connected to the variable(s) that you will measure)
• Who would you invite to a community forum/focus group? What questions would you ask?
• What "rates under treatment" are important—What agency organizations would you go to for information? What information (i.e., variables) do you identify?
• What social indicators are important? Where would you go to collect them?
• Who would be your sample for a community survey? What would you ask?

Formative evaluation

You are a social work student at in-home counseling agency. The agency employs persons from multiple disciplines (e.g., counseling, social work, psychology, etc.) to deliver counseling services. Counselors are trained and they learn the agency's philosophy and service delivery model. Recently, the executive director has wondered whether the services are being delivered consistently and as planned. In summary, the director wants to know if counselors are following the agency's services delivery model.

- What is your research question?
- Who will you interview for key informant interviews? How will you approach them?
- What will you ask key informants? (Remember, this is connected to the variable(s) that you will measure)?
- What agency materials do you need to review?
- What is the time-frame for your study?

Summative evaluation

You are a social worker in a program that works with parents. Social workers have used the same parenting group curriculum for the past 3 years. This curriculum is evidence-based, but your boss wants to know whether this curriculum has the same or similar impact when compared to another curriculum that was developed last year. Both of the curricula are designed to increase parenting *knowledge* and the use of appropriate parenting *behaviors*. Propose an evaluation research study.

- What is the research question?
- In evaluation research language, how would you categorize this study?
- What is the dependent variable? What is the independent variable?
- Develop a null hypothesis for this study. Develop a research hypothesis for this study.
- Describe the threats to internal validity in this study.

Cost–Benefit:

Your agency received a $400,000 grant to provide an early intervention program to children whose parents are cognitively impaired. Your agency implements the program and serves 50 children within a 9-month period. At the end of the grant period, the agency's director was contacted by the grant administrator. It seems that the grant funders did not understand why only 50 children were served. They want to know how much a unit of service cost them and if the benefits of the program outweighed the costs. Propose an evaluation research study.

- What is the research question?
- In evaluation research language, how would you categorize this study?
- How will you define "one unit of service?"
- How will you define program benefits?
- What agency records, if any, will you need to use?

EVALUATION RESEARCH IN AGENCY SETTINGS

The climate, goals, procedures, and other factors unique to that agency will affect any agency evaluation. Often, a student gathering data for evaluation research must collect information about how individual employees function in their respective roles. Rather than welcoming the evaluation process and seeing it as an opportunity to strengthen services, staff persons may feel threatened by this process if they anticipate that it will reflect poorly on their performance and jeopardize their job or position in the agency. Such apprehension can sabotage even the most well-developed and methodologically sound evaluation; however, there are several strategies to increase the chances of staff cooperation with the evaluation activities. These strategies derive from the practice-research principles discussed in Chapter Two and are especially important when conducting a program evaluation. Use Test Your Skills Exercise 11.1 to consider how these specific practice-research principles might apply to your evaluation research project.

Test Your Skills Exercise 11.1.

STRATEGIES FOR EVALUATION IMPLEMENTATION

PRINCIPLE	STRATEGIES
Shared leadership Understanding, valuing, and balancing theoretical knowledge with practical knowledge.	It is up to you to understand research methodology and develop your project; however, it is important to invoke shared leadership by asking direct service practitioners for feedback before, after, and sometimes during the implementation of your project. For example, before you implement, ask them whether your variable definitions require any modifications. If you are collecting data from clients, ask practitioners what they believe is the best way to collect data. Ask if they see any pitfalls in your process. After the evaluation, ask the practitioners how they felt while it was being conducted. It is also important clear that the evaluation findings are intended for program improvement and to help everyone in the agency better serve the client population.
Feasibility Understanding that you must have knowledge of the service delivery process so that you can ensure that your evaluation methods are relevant and appropriate for the agency and its clients.	Make sure that you have an understanding of what your agency does (the activities), who provides the service (the direct practice workers), what they hope to accomplish (outcomes), what your agency collects (the data available to you), who your agency sees (the clients), and who has a vested interest in your agency's operations (stakeholders). For example, if you are conducting an evaluation of a teen pregnancy program, you must understand what they "claim to do" if you are to measure whether they are "doing that they claim to do." Many agencies will provide an orientation where each of these areas is discussed.
Program and client first Making sure that your actions reflect a respect for the client and the program; understanding that the primary role of the agency is to provide services to its targeted population.	Think about your methods for data collection and ensure that your methods do not put an undue burden on the program, the staff, or its clients. For example, asking a client to complete a five-page survey during the time when they are supposed to be receiving individual counseling means that your process has reduced that client's individual counseling time. However, asking a client to complete a two-page survey while waiting for services or after a service is more appropriate. Devising an evaluation that fits into the program's normal service delivery process and uses tools that workers are familiar with and currently use is advantageous to the client and program or agency.

LOGIC MODELS

To design an evaluation, there are many pieces of information that you must organize and then interpret. A logic model is one way in which this information can be organized. It is a schematic representation of the various components that make up a social service program and should describe:

- Theory and its link to change such that attention is on the "how and why" a program works (sometimes referred to as the "mechanism of change")
- Activities that are carried out by program staff and the resources used by the agency; this is similar to the formative evaluation focus.
- Expected client or agency outcomes; this is similar to the summative evaluation focus.

Logic models are increasingly required by many federal organizations and foundations that not only fund program evaluation research but also provide financial support for service delivery. These organizations want to ensure that their money is being spent on programs that can demonstrate a reasonable and rigorous and well-thought-out plan to achieve successful program outcomes.

For research to be useful in the real-world setting, it must derive from and be rooted in an understanding of the complexities of the lives of the people with whom we work and the complexities of the systems within which we deliver services (Proctor, 2003, as cited in Secret, Rompf, & Ford, 2003). In other words, good research questions that inform practice should be based in theoretical explanations that help you understand *why* a particular intervention is expected to work. Logic models help make these connections.

Although program evaluation can be understood and implemented using basic research methods and approaches, as you can guess from the introduction to logic models, evaluation research comes with its own language; this is another reason why it is important to present evaluation research in its own chapter. Summary Content 11.2 provides some of the terms and definitions most commonly associated with evaluation research and which you will see discussed in logic models.

Summary Content 11.2.

EVALUATION TERMS

EVALUATION TERM	DEFINITION
Outcomes—both short-and long-term	the impact of the program process on the cases processed
Outputs	the services delivered or new products produced by the program process
Target population	population for whom the program is designed
Feedback	information about service delivery system outputs, outcomes, or operations from the program stakeholders
Stakeholders	individuals and groups who have some basis of concern with the program, often setting the research agenda and controlling research findings
Program process	the treatment or services delivered by the program
Activity(ies)	specific actions/services (e.g., counseling group, self-esteem group, etc.) that programs conduct to reach outcomes
Inputs	resources, raw materials, clients, and staff that go into a program
Key informant	persons who have the first-hand knowledge about the program, services, or situations that you wish to know about
Rates under treatment	an approach to quantify the need for services by examining the rate of persons currently receiving treatment for a condition
Causal mechanism	the mechanism that provides an understanding of "why" something does "what it does"

In summary, a logic model lays out the key components of a human service program in an easy-to-read visual format. Example 11.3 is an example of a logic model of a federally funded evaluation done by one of the authors. As you review it, think about the evaluation terminology above.

Example 11.3.

DETERMINING KEY PIECES IN A LOGIC MODEL

Resources	Program procedures—interventions delivered by the program staff or volunteers	Psychological and social process undergone by the incarcerated fathers	Interim outcomes—program goals	Long-Term Outcomes
Direct service time (paid and volunteer) Managerial and administrative support time Equipment (VCR, monitors, overhead, tape recorders) Supplies (handouts, newsprint, markers, videotapes, audiotapes, workbooks, postage, newsletters, children's books, etc.) ⇑	12-week *parent education classes*, with specified goals and objectives for each class, delivered by paid and volunteer professionals, that provide content, materials, experiential learning activities on pre-specified topics relating to the increase of protective factors/decrease of risk factors regarding child abuse, and interactive discussions about how the fathers were parented as children and philosophies that emphasize the importance of fathers in the lives of children. ⇑	Understanding children's behavior; identification of situations which trigger anger and stress. Knowledge of child development and discipline. Support and insight from other fathers about parenting techniques. Increased parenting communication skills. Awareness of impact of family conflict on parent-child relationships. Awareness of feelings of sadness, anger, self-esteem. Awareness of effects of parental substance abuse on children. Awareness of how parenting skills are passed down from one generation to the next. Exposure to "Long Distance Dads" workbooks. ⇑	Decrease child abuse potential Increased knowledge and use of parenting skill Decrease in feelings of isolation Increased empathy with children Increased recognition of importance of role of fathers Increase understanding of how life experiences effect parenting Increased recognition of correct parenting ⇑	Decreased Recidivism Decreased Child Abuse ⇑

EVALUABILITY ASSESSMENT

If you are struggling to find the information to develop a logic model for a specific program, it may be that the program you have in mind is not ready for a summative program evaluation. Logic models are most useful for programs that have sufficient resources and program structures in place to produce measurable outcomes. Many new programs that are not fully operational are not ready for, and indeed can be tarnished by, a summative evaluation geared to assessing program outcomes. Before you begin to think about a summative program evaluation for your agency, review the criteria in Summary Content 11.3 to determine the program's "evaluability." If you cannot say "yes" to each of these following criteria, you might consider doing a formation evaluation at this time.

Summary Content 11.3.

EVALUABILITY ASSESSMENT

To implement a summative program evaluation, an ESTABLISHED PROGRAM should have
- measurable outcomes
- defined service components
- an established recruiting, enrollment, and participation process
- good understanding of the characteristics of the target population, program participants and program environment
- ability to collect and maintain information
- adequate program size

Success of the evaluation effort also depends on the RESEARCH SAVVY SERVICE DELIVERY STAFF regarding:
- problem-solving values and skills
- prior experience with evaluation and confidence in program
- commitment to "new knowledge"
- openness to change

Source: Kaufman-Levy & Poulin (2003).

Without question, there are many new terms to grasp when learning evaluation research. It is important to remember that many of these terms share meanings with what you have already learned about basic research methods. Even more importantly, logic models are especially useful for social work practitioners because they provide a common framework and language to discuss and compare many different types of services. We added evaluation terms to Example 11.3 to illustrate how the pieces of the logic model can be matched with the evaluation terms that you reviewed above.

As you can see from Figure 11.1, (1) measuring program activities provides information critical to formative or process evaluation; (2) measuring short- and long-term outcomes answers summative evaluation questions; and (3) measuring resources related to program inputs provides data for cost–benefit or cost-effectiveness studies.

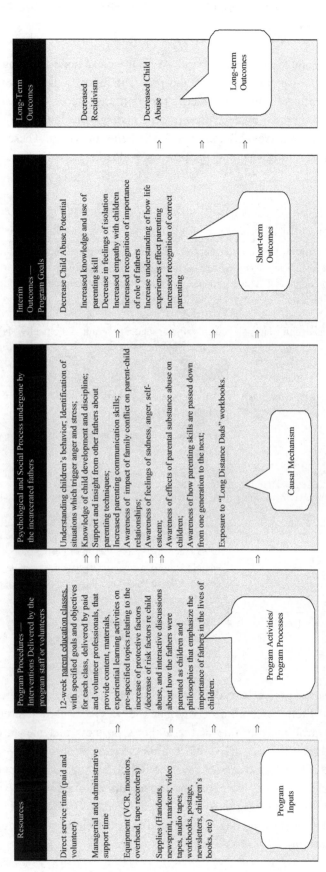

FIGURE 11.1 **Measuring Program Activities**

APPLYING RESEARCH METHODS TO FORMATIVE OR PROCESS EVALUATIONS

For a process evaluation, it is important to have a clear understanding of the program, the program components and the program functioning. For example, if a student is evaluating a domestic violence program, then he or she must understand "what" service is being provided, "how much" is being provided, "who" is providing the service, "who receives it," and "why" it is being provided. These components are directly linked to developing the process evaluation. See Example 11.4 for an illustration.

Example 11.4.	
UNDERSTANDING THE PROGRAM TO BE EVALUATED	

Kimberly's field supervisor has asked her to work on an evaluation project with three other social work students. They must evaluate the domestic violence program's short-term community counseling component. This component provides short-term counseling to people who have current experience or history with domestic violence.

Kimberly begins by familiarizing herself with the shelter program. Specifically, she begins by answering the who, what, when, where, and why questions.

QUESTION	ANSWER
What is provided and how much?	A maximum of 4 months of counseling for a minimum of 1 hour a week
Who receives it?	Those with a current experience with or history of domestic violence
Who provides it?	MSW level counselors and MSW- and BSW-level interns
When and where is it provided?	At the main office or in one of five confidential community satellite locations
Why is it provided?	Research has shown that counseling can reduce the cycle of violence (either as a victim or perpetrator). Counseling can also improve a person's self-esteem, understanding of domestic violence "red flags," and knowledge about healthy relationships.
How do clients receive it?	Clients can access services in two ways. They can walk in to the main or satellite office or they can call the 24-hour hotline.

To measure how services are delivered, you may ask clients and recipients of services about their perception of whether the service was delivered. Example 11.5 is an illustration from one of the author's projects that measured whether a required curriculum was delivered to a parent education class as intended. A report for each of the class sessions was completed by each of the parents at the end of every class session. Note that the statements were associated with the specific stated objectives of the particular class. Asking about these items allowed the researcher to assess the degree to which the curriculum was being delivered (process evaluation).

Example 11.5.

AN EXAMPLE OF A PROCESS EVALUATION MEASUREMENT TOOL

Class Session Two

Directions: Think about the class that you just took. Circle the words that express how much you understand each of the items after participating in each class. Please select only one choice per item

	1	2	3	4
AFTER THIS CLASS I UNDERSTAND . . .				
The basic needs of my children	Much better	Some better	No Better	Was not talked about in class
Why my kids do what they do at different ages	Much better	Some better	No Better	Was not talked about in class
Why my parenting is important to my children	Much better	Some better	No Better	Was not talked about in class
The difference between "SELF-CONCEPT" and "SELF-ESTEEM"	Much better	Some better	No Better	Was not talked about in class

1. What was the one most important thing you learned in today's session?

_____

_____

2. Tell how this information will help you as a father.

_____

_____

3. What feelings do you have about yourself as a parent after today's session?

_____

_____

APPLYING RESEARCH METHODS TO COST–BENEFIT OR COST-EFFECTIVENESS EVALUATIONS

In a cost–benefit evaluation, you can measure items to help you quantify the cost of services and compare those costs to the benefits that the program produces. For example, you may ask staff to record the amount of time spent in various agency and program activities. Example 11.6 is a data collection instrument used in a cost analysis. Notice how the instrument allows the researcher to collect multiple types of information and use it to compute a total cost for the program.

Example 11.6.
COST ANALYSIS FORM

Name _____   Date _____

Cost Analysis Data Form

Cost is defined as the value of each resource that is consumed when the program implements a service procedure.

Component = Classroom Session, Story book Activity, PLT activity or Parent/Child Saturday Visitation

Resource = Your Time, Volunteer Time, Space Used, Supplies Used, etc.

The Conversion and Total Cost columns will be computed at UK so you only need to complete the first three columns.

FACT Component	Resource	Amount Used	Conversion	Total Cost

APPLYING RESEARCH METHODS TO SUMMATIVE PROGRAM EVALUATION EFFORTS

Now that you have the framework such as logic model to approach your evaluation research project, it is important to consider the broad sweep of research methodologies available to you as you go about implementing your evaluation. As noted in the introductory paragraph to this chapter, evaluation research encompasses most all types of research designs and methods, and it is important that you can translate basic research methodologies to evaluation projects. Test Your Skills Exercise 11.2 involves figuring out the sampling approach, the research design, and the data collection methods in each of the evaluation studies presented in Example 11.1. Although there may not be enough information provided about some of the studies to make an informed choice in each category, do the best that you can. You should refer back to different chapters in the workbook for detailed information about these aspects of research methodology. The first row of the table provides a summary of some the choices available for each aspect of the research; the second row offers an example of how to approach this exercise.

Test Your Skills Exercise 11.2.

IDENTIFYING SAMPLING, DESIGN, DATA COLLECTING, AND MEASUREMENT FOR EVALUATION RESEARCH

	SAMPLING APPROACH	RESEARCH DESIGN	DATA COLLECTION	MEASUREMENT

	• Probability
	• Nonprobability
		• Nonexperimental
		• Experimental
		  Single-subject designs
		  Pre-experimental designs
		  True experimental designs
		  Quasi-experimental
		• Meta-analysis of intervention
			• Face to face or phone interview
			• Self-administered questionnaire
			• Survey and Self-Report
			• Observation
			• Secondary data
				• Standardized instruments
				• Nonstandardized instruments

Sample research study: This study assessed the impact of a dating violence sensitivity group intervention. The participants were 190 high school students, ages 13 to 19 years, with just more than half being boys (53%) and the remainder being girls (47%). Questionnaire data about the knowledge and values and skills needed to avoid dating violence were collected from the participants before the 12-week group training and at the end of the training sessions.	<u>Sample</u> Nonprobability	<u>Sample</u> Pre-experimental pretest posttest	<u>Sample</u> Self-administered questionnaire	<u>Sample</u> Not enough info to determine
This study *evaluated the effectiveness* of cognitive-behavioral interventions in the treatment of persons with schizophrenia who experienced significant residual symptoms and impaired functioning despite their adherence to medication. Standardized measures of psychosocial functioning and severity of symptoms were administered individually to five clients in an adult residential setting weekly for 6 weeks to establish a baseline. Each client received outpatient CBT for 18 months in sessions lasting up to 1 hour. Psychosocial functioning and severity of symptoms during the 18 months were plotted on a graph to determine the effectiveness of the intervention for each individual.				

This study *investigated the effectiveness* of a parenting intervention for mothers living in a residential domestic violence facility. Mothers participated in a 4-week onsite intensive parenting group. Each 2-hour session was taught by a domestic violence counselor and included 1 hour where women were taught parenting techniques and 1 hour where women demonstrated parenting skills.			
This study examined whether the services provided as part of the Family Independence Agency's TANF Program helped women experiencing domestic violence become financially self-sufficient 1 year after participating in TANF services. Before receiving TANF services, 250 women were asked to complete the JAI and the FSSS. The JAI assessed current job skills and current and past employment. The FSSS assessed participants' level of self-sufficiency. Women then participated in TANF-sponsored job training activities (e.g., resume writing, computer skills classes, etc.) and domestic violence services (e.g., counseling, safety planning, etc.). Counselors tracked women and use the JAI and FSSS to assess participants' job skills and financial self-sufficiency at 6 and 9 months after the program's start.			
A statewide evaluation of the ENABL program was conducted to assess its ability to increase adolescents' knowledge and beliefs about pregnancy prevention. ENABL is aimed at preventing teenage pregnancy through abstinence. Middle school students in one school district comprised a treatment group ($n = 974$), and students in another school district comprised a comparison group. Subjects completed a pretest and posttest reflecting knowledge and beliefs about teenage pregnancy before and after the ENABL program.			

A research team examined whether participation in a 4-week prison employment program helped inmates secure employment upon being released from prison. Inmates in a Midwestern prison were asked to participate in a 4-week employment preparation program. Inmates were given a work attitudes assessment to assess their beliefs about work and a job skills assessment. Inmates met 1 hour a week for 4 weeks. The employment status for participants was evaluated at 3, 6, and 12 months post-release. Results were compared to a comparable group of inmates who did not participate in the employment preparation program.				

EVALUATION RESEARCH: FOCUS OF RESEARCH DESIGN

Real versus Ideal. In previous chapters, we discussed research designs and how to determine whether an independent variable "caused" something to happen to a dependent variable. As you may recall, a true experimental design is needed if we are trying to determine "cause and effect." You may be thinking that evaluation research seeks to answer questions regarding the impact of independent variables on dependent variables. If you are thinking about evaluation in this manner, it seems only reasonable that you would expect evaluations to use true experimental designs. However, you should have noticed that most of the examples in this chapter have been non-experimental or quasi-experimental designs.

It is important to reiterate that we are discussing how to conduct evaluation research in "real-world" community agencies. Often, these agencies have policies and/or values that are contradictory to one of the hallmarks of a true experimental design, random assignment to group. For example, in your agency, randomly choosing those who will get an intervention may not be appropriate, especially if those coming in for services are in immediate need. Also, depending on the number of clients that your agency serves, you may not have enough clients to have more than one group. Succinctly put, a true experimental design may be desired but not practical.

To compensate for this, we can use quasi-experimental designs. These designs approximate true experimental designs while accounting for agency limitations. These designs are discussed in detail in Chapter Six (Quantitative: Research Designs).

The following summary content, examples, and exercises provide additional information regarding evaluation designs and provide opportunities for you to practice. Example 11.7 provides brief examples of nonexperimental and quasi-experimental evaluation designs. Exercise 11.3 asks you to diagram evaluation research and then make suggestions that you believe may improve the design. When you make the suggestions, please consider the feasibility issues inherent with agency-based evaluations. Test Your Skills Exercise 11.3 will give you the opportunity to practice using research design notations. Finally, Test Your Skills Exercise 11.4 will assess your knowledge about research design.

Summary Content 11.4.

RESEARCH DESIGN NOTATIONS

R—Random assignment
O—Observation
X—Intervention or treatment
A, B, etc.—Group A, Group B, etc.

Source: Engel & Shutt (2009).

Example 11.7.

EVALUATION DESIGNS

DESCRIPTION OF THE STUDY	TYPE OF DESIGN	NOTATION FOR DESIGN			
This study assessed the impact of a dating violence sensitivity group intervention. The participants were 190 high school students, ages 13 to 19 years. Questionnaire data about the knowledge and values and skills needed to avoid dating violence were collected from the participants before the 12-week group training and at the end of the training sessions.	Pretest/Posttest design	Group A	O **Pretest**	X 12-week training program	O **Posttest**
A statewide evaluation of the ENABL program was conducted to assess its ability to increase adolescents' knowledge and beliefs about pregnancy prevention. ENABL is a 4-week program aimed at preventing teenage pregnancy through abstinence. Middle school students in one school district comprised a treatment group ($n = 974$), and students in another school district comprised a comparison group. Subjects completed a pretest and posttest reflecting knowledge and beliefs about teenage pregnancy before and after the ENABL program.	Quasi-experimental design	Group A Group B	O **Pretest** O **Pretest**	X 4-week ENABL program X	O **Posttest** O **Posttest**
A local drug treatment program wanted to assess the effectiveness of adding an 8-week yoga class to their current counseling and medication treatment. A social worker selected 30 clients who had been in treatment for less than 2 weeks. She had all 30 clients complete an assessment packet that examined their substance abuse history and their social and emotional functioning. She picked 15 clients to participate in yoga. The other 15 participated in the regular treatment activities. After 8 weeks, she evaluated the participants' substance use and their social and emotional functioning.	Quasi-experimental design	Group A Group A	O **Pretest** O **Pretest**	X_1 8-week Yoga class medication and counseling X_2 8-week Medication and counseling	O **Posttest** O **Posttest**

Test Your Skills Exercise 11.3.

EVALUATION DESIGNS

Directions: Read each study and then use the notations found on Summary Content 11.4 to describe each design. Then, think about suggestions that you would offer to make each design more rigorous.

DESCRIPTION OF THE STUDY	NOTATION FOR DESIGN	SUGGESTIONS TO MAKE DESIGN MORE RIGOROUS
Marley sought to determine whether students participating in an after-school art program increased positive social behaviors. She administered the Children's Hope Scale to 25 children and then had them participate in the 16-week program. Marley had the children complete the Children's Hope Scale at the end of class during the 16th week.		
Lindsey coordinates violence prevention programs for a large state agency. Currently, most communities use one of three evidence-based programs. Lindsey's supervisor asks her to determine which program is more successful at reducing children's acceptance of violence. All of the programs are currently operating. Lindsay selects 15 programs, three using intervention A, three using intervention B, and three using intervention C. Each program is 8 weeks. She waits until week 8 and administers the Violence Acceptance Scale to all children.		
Geneen evaluated a therapeutic riding program for children with ADHD. She selected two groups. First, she selected 25 children who were about to start the program. Then, she selected a group of 25 children who were on the waiting list for the riding program. She gave both groups three pretest instruments to measure their social behaviors. One group participated in the program for 12 weeks. After the 12-week period, all children were evaluated again.		

Use the following exercise to test your knowledge about evaluation research.

Test Your Skills Exercise 11.4.

TEST YOUR KNOWLEDGE ABOUT EVALUATION RESEARCH

1. Mix and Match
   A. Needs assessment
   B. Logic model
   C. Formative/process evaluation
   D. Summative evaluation
   E. Evaluability assessment
   F. Efficiency analysis

   1) _____ evaluates how services are delivered
   2) _____ evaluates whether a new program is needed or an existing program should continue
   3) _____ evaluates costs versus benefits and cost-effectiveness of program
   4) _____ evaluates uses to help shape and refine the program
   5) _____ evaluates outcomes in terms of program effectiveness

---

2. Evaluation research is unlike traditional social work research because:
   a. It is designed to test the implications of a social theory.
   b. Program stakeholders have influence in how the study is designed.
   c. Evaluation research cannot ethically use randomization.
   d. Evaluation research rarely uses quantitative methods.
   e. There is no dependent variable to be measured.

Questions 3 through 7 are based on the following community-policing program scenario:

Eastern City proposes developing a community-policing program to reduce crime in one neighborhood. The police department, in conjunction with the mayor's office, held several meetings in which they discussed this proposal with neighborhood residents, business owners, and social organizations.

3. In this example, the police department, the mayor's office, and neighborhood residents are all:
   a. Program participants
   b. Key informants
   c. Research subjects
   d. Stakeholders
   e. Evaluators

4. In the Eastern City Scenario above, what is the independent variable? _____

5. The group gathered criminal justice statistics to indicate the crime rate in the community. This approach to documenting needs is known as:
   a. Rates under treatment
   b. Focus group data
   c. Social Indicators
   d. Community survey data

6. As a consultant to the police department, you have been asked to draw up a schematic diagram to show the resources needed by the proposed program, the proposed services that will be provided, the people who will be served, and what the program hopes to achieve. This diagram is referred to as:
   a. evaluability assessment
   b. measurement validity
   c. logic model
   d. sampling strategy
   e. none of the above

7. Before a summative evaluation of the community-policing program could be conducted, which of following conditions would the program need to have in place?
   a. measurable outcomes
   b. defined service components
   c. ability to collect and maintain information
   d. none of these conditions need to be considered
   e. all conditions need to be considered

8. When evaluating their program, researchers concluded that it didn't really matter how the community policing worked, just so long as it worked. This is an example of:
   a. Black box theory
   b. Program theory
   c. Utilization theory
   d. Theory-driven evaluation
   e. Process theory

CONCLUSION

This chapter has discussed an area of research that is especially important for good social work practice. Evaluation research is critical and allows practitioners to determine the answers to important questions, such as are social work interventions (a) successful, (b) cost-effective, (c) implemented as planned, (d) needed, or (e) reaching the targeted population? These are all questions that agencies should understand if they are to provide the highest quality of service to clients.

Students can participate in producing program evaluations that can have long-term impacts on agencies. Results can help agencies identify gaps in services and determine needed modifications. These changes may not have been identified without the evaluation. Thus, a student's presence may be felt long after the student's internship obligation ends. The following project development worksheet summarizes much of the material in this chapter and provides an opportunity for you to apply the material to your own project.

This workbook has helped you to formulate a good research question, identify and organize literature on your topic, and develop and implement a research design. Hopefully, all of the preceding chapters have helped to reduce your anxiety and have enhanced your research experience. Chapter Twelve will discuss a final and important task: the dissemination of results.

You may have questions regarding how you should organize your results and which method of dissemination you should use. Additionally, you may be asked to present results to different stakeholder groups (e.g., clients, administrators, classmates, etc.). The tools in Chapter Twelve will help you to identify your audience and provide guidance on distributing results. Before you read Chapter Twelve you may want to review Chapter Four. This chapter reviewed the ethics of social work research, and reviewing it can help you make decisions regarding what you can disseminate and to whom. For example, if you did not go through the Institutional Review Board, you will be limited in how you can disseminate results.

In summary, the chapter on data dissemination will help you translate your project into language that your audience(s) can understand. Sharing your findings with agency personnel is another way that you can make an impact on your agency and its functioning.

Project Development Worksheet 11.1.

WORKSHEET FOR DEVELOPING AN EVALUATION RESEARCH PROJECT

		IMPORTANT CONSIDERATIONS AND QUESTIONS
OVERVIEW OF PROJECT:		
Research question:		What is your question? Remember, the type of question that you want to answer will drive the type of evaluation that you conduct.
Type of evaluation:	____ Impact(Summative Evaluation) ____ Needs Assessment ____ Cost–Benefit/Cost-Effectiveness Analysis ____ Process Evaluation	What is the type of evaluation? Is it a combination of types?
Research design:	____ Nonexperimental ____ Quasi-Experimental ____ Experimental ____ Survey ____ Single Subject	What is the design? Is it a combination of types?
Target population for the program:		Who is your program trying to assist?
Concept(s)/ Interventions that need to be defined for this study:		What variables do you need to define for this study? For example, for an impact evaluation you need to define the intervention. For a cost–benefit/ effectiveness analysis, you need to define the service unit.
Barriers:		What are potential barriers that you may face? Have you thought about strategies to help you overcome these challenges?
Estimated time of project:		How much time do you anticipate this study will take? Think about what data you must collect and what you need to do with data to analyze and determine results.
AGENCY CONSIDERATIONS		
Resources needed from the agency (e.g., access to data, space for interviews, etc.):		Is your agency supportive of this project? What types of resources are available to you from the agency? What type do you need?
Permission secured from the following person/people:		From whom do you need to secure permission? Do you need written permission? Think about your data collection method(s)—Does the agency need to do anything to support your data collection method(s)?

Benefits to the agency and or clients:		What are the benefits of doing this evaluation? Think about agency and client benefits.

DATA COLLECTION

Type of data to be collected and from whom:	*Type of data* *Collected From* 1. _____ _____ 2. _____ _____ 3. _____ _____ 4. _____ _____	Think about all of the types of data that you need to collect and from whom. What you collecting from clients? What are you collecting from community stakeholders? What are you collecting from staff?
Timeline for data collection:	*Action Needed* *Task Completed By (Date).* 1. _____ _____ 2. _____ _____ 3. _____ _____ 4. _____ _____ 5. _____ _____	Think about what you need to do to accomplish this project, what are your steps and when will you accomplish them?

ANALYSIS

Steps needed to prepare for analysis:	Step 1. _____ 2. _____ 3. _____ 4. _____ 5. _____	How will you prepare for data analysis? Do you have to transcribe information?
Data analysis:		How will you analyze results?

WRITING-UP AND PRESENTING RESULTS

Presenting results:		To whom will you present results? How will you present results? How will you communicate findings of the study based on scientific criteria?

WEBSITES

Evaluation Strategies for Human Services Programs: A Guide for Policymakers and Providers
http://www.ojp.usdoj.gov/BJA/evaluation/guide/documents/evaluation_strategies.html
Issue Topic: Evaluating Community-Based Initiatives
http://www.hfrp.org/evaluation/the-evaluation-exchange/issue-archive/evaluating-community-based-initiatives
American Evaluation Association
http://www.eval.org/
CDC Program Evaluation Manual
http://www.cdc.gov/getsmart/specific-groups/program-planner.html
Program Development and Evaluation—University of Wisconsin
http://www.uwex.edu/ces/pdande/evaluation/evaldocs.html

WRITE-UP, PRESENTATION, AND DISSEMINATION OF RESULTS

12

In the last several chapters, we have been considering various aspects of research methods and data analysis piecemeal, but here we will concentrate on the full report. As well as writing up your research project, in this chapter, we discuss how to disseminate the findings of your project to your agencies and possibility more broadly.

THE RESEARCH PROJECT FINAL REPORT

For the proposal and the final write-up, your instructor may have a particular outline for you to follow, but we also offer a sample outline here in Summary Content 12.1. Roman numerals I–V and VIII of the outline involve the sections that comprise the proposal, which will have to be approved by your instructor before starting data collection. We also refer you back in these roman numeral sections to the chapters in which we covered this material. Roman numerals VI and VII are the part of the project that is written after you have collected and analyzed your data. Because we have covered the rest of the outline in other chapters, we move on from here to discuss how to report the results of your project and write up the discussion section.

Summary Content 12.1.
RESEARCH REPORT OUTLINE

I. Introduction (1 page)
See Chapter Three (Review of the Literature) for more detail on this section.

II. Literature Review (3–5 pages)
See Chapter Three (Review of the LIterature) for more detail on this section.

III. Research Questions and Hypotheses (1/2 page)
See Chapter Two (Research Fundamentals) for more detail on this section.

IV. Methods (3–5 pages)
    a. Design and Data Collection
See Chapter Six (Research Designs) for more detail on this section.
    b. Sample
* See Chapter Seven (Sampling) for more information on this section*
      1. Identify your target population (the group to whom the study's results are expected to apply).
      2. Explain how you will draw your sample from this population.
      3. What is your projected sample size and its justification?

---

c. **Instrumentation**
* See Chapter Eight (Measurement)

  1. Define the measures that you will use to collect data by operationalizing pertinent independent and dependent variables.
  2. If your research uses an existing instrument, describe what it should accomplish and justify your use of the instrument. Discuss how the scale is to be scored, what scores mean, and any clinical cut-offs. Discuss reliability and validity. Include the instrument as an appendix.
  3. If you develop your own instrument, describe its purpose and relevance. Provide a copy of the instrument. Justify your use of the instrument and ascertain how you will assess reliability and validity.

d. **Data Analysis**
* See Chapter Nine (Quantitative Data Analysis)

V. **Ethical Issues**
* See Chapter Five (Ethics and Values Related to Research)

  a. Risk/Benefit ratio: What are the risks to participants? What are the potential benefits to participants, the agency, and the field? What steps will you take to reduce risks?
  b. Informed consent: Where and when will consent be completed? How have you attended to the special needs of clients? (language, literacy, mobility, etc.)
  c. Attach your informed consent.

VI. **Research Findings (will be elaborated on below in its own section).**
Descriptives: Detailing of the demographic information of participants in the study (frequencies and percentages, often summarized in text and presented in tables, along with appropriate measures of central tendency).

If intervention or program research, then include fidelity (i.e., was the intervention implemented as planned, how was this assessed, how many sessions did each participant attend on average).

Bivariate and Multivariate: Statistical analysis procedures and the results of significance testing for each question/hypothesis guiding the research.

VII. **Discussion (will be elaborated on below in its own section)**
A narrative (not statistical) summary of the main findings. (Minimum 1/2 page)
Relate the findings back to your literature review. (1 page)
Indicate the limitations and strengths of the study. (1 page)
Discuss implications for social work research (1/2 page), policy (1/2 page), and direct practice (1/2 page).

VII. **References**—alphabetical order in APA style.

The Results Section

The results (or findings) section involves "just the facts," with no place for commentary or interpretation. Hence, it is very straightforward, involving the presentation of univariate, then bivariate, then any multivariate statistics.

Univariate Statistics. The presentation of univariate (or descriptive) statistics can be summarized in text and then shown graphically. Graphic depictions of findings are appealing both to students and to practitioners because of their simplicity and clarity (Secret, Abell, & Berlin, 2011). Some guidelines for tables and other graphics are as follows:

- Tables and figures should be able to stand alone.
- Table/figures must be introduced. Reader should also be told what to see.

- Don't replicate in tables what you've already presented in text; typically descriptive information is summarized and then tables detail the information as below.

In text, summarize the descriptive information and then detail the information in tables. For example, the student group doing the meta-synthesis on elderly depression summarized the information on their study sample in text as follows: "Inclusion criteria produced a total of 13 studies with 356 participants. A majority of these participants were women and either Caucasian or African-American. Most studies were from the United States; however, studies from Sweden and Australia were also included. Studies tended to report on participants who were in their 70s. The majority were recruited from either primary care physicians or inpatient treatment at hospitals." Example 12.1 presents a table showing more detailed demographic information of another study. Note how frequencies of nominal-level variables are shown with their accompanying percentages.

Example 12.1.

DEMOGRAPHICS OF THOSE COMMITTING VIOLENT INCIDENTS AT AN INPATIENT SETTING FOR MENTAL ILLNESS ($N = 24$)

CHARACTERISTIC	FREQUENCIES (PERCENTAGES)
Gender	
Male	15 (63%)
Female	9 (37%)
Legal Status	
Voluntary	13 (54%)
Involuntary	4 (17%)
Not Guilty by Reason of Insanity	7 (29%)
Length of Stay	
0–90 Days	6 (25%)
91–180 Days	7 (29%)
181+ Days	11 (46%)
Diagnosis	
Axis I Only	12 (50%)
Axis I & Axis II	12 (50%)

Bar charts and histograms, two of the more common graphic presentations, plot the number of times a particular value or category occurs in a data set. The height of the bar representing the number of observations with that score or are in that category. The y-axis could represent any measurement unit: relative frequency, raw count, percent, or whatever else is appropriate for the situation. The bar chart is used for ordinal or nominal data, and the bars are not touching. The histogram is used for interval data and the bars are contiguous. Test Your Skills Exercise 12.1 provides some sample graphics so that you can apply this information.

Test Your Skills Exercise 12.1.

IDENTIFYING CHARTS

Identify the type of chart presented below:

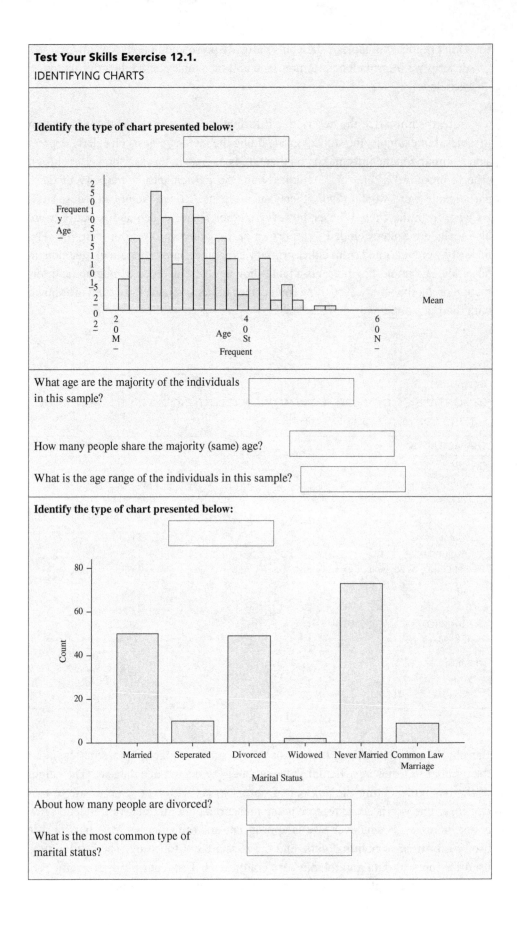

What age are the majority of the individuals in this sample?

How many people share the majority (same) age?

What is the age range of the individuals in this sample?

Identify the type of chart presented below:

About how many people are divorced?

What is the most common type of marital status?

BIVARIATE AND BI-BIVARIATE AND MULTIVARIATE STATISTICS

In the results section, bivariate and then multivariate statistics are provided. When giving the results of statistical tests, present the following:

- The results of the test itself
- Statistical significance of the test
- Data so that people can understand the pattern of results. For example, for dependent t-tests, you will have to give the means and standard deviations of the pretest scores and the posttest scores. For independent t-tests, the means and standard deviations of the scores for the two samples should be provided (*see* Chapter Nine).

A results section can be enhanced if each of the hypotheses are written out and then results of the statistical test for each hypothesis follows as Example 12.2 illustrates.

Example 12.2.

PRESENTATION OF RESULTS: PARENT NURTURING PROGRAM

Hypothesis #1: Scores on the Adult-Adolescent Parenting Inventory-2 will improve from pretest to posttest after participants attend the Parent Nurturing Program. Performance of a dependent t-test indicated that scores improved on all subscales: expectations ($t = -12.27$, $p = 0.000$); empathy ($t = -18.29$, $p = 0.000$); corporal punishment ($t = -17.58$, $p = 0.000$); role reversal ($t = -15.97$, $p = 0.000$); and power and independence ($t = -11.48$, $p = 0.000$).

Graphs can also be applied to bivariate analysis as Figure 12.1 illustrates. This graphic was developed to show the change in six outcome measures in a study conducted by one of the authors for an evaluation of a women's re-entry program from incarceration. Data were collected at the beginning of a group support program and 12 weeks post. The arrows in the chart indicate the change and the direction of change in scores from the pretest to the posttest. Visual interpretation of this chart suggests that although all outcome areas measured showed improvement, the greatest gains were made by in the increase in emotion focused coping outcome and in the decrease in depression outcome. The chart, used by the community-based agency

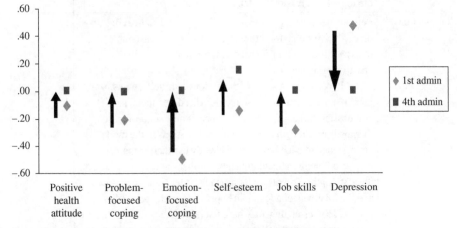

Figure 12.1 **Example graphic: pre-and posttest results for re-entry program**

at an onsite evaluation by the federal funding source, provided a clear and succinct representation of program impact.

Discussion Section

The discussion of the paper is where you bring together your study's findings and comment on their significance to the accumulated body of knowledge in your area and for social work practice. More specifically, you can begin by summarizing your findings in general and narrative (rather than statistical) terms. You can explain these findings and place them in the context of the existing literature. One tip is to stick to the studies that you brought up in your literature review and then circle around to them again here, as relevant. A subsection on limitations of the study is important so that you recognize some of the problems with the research. One of the authors of this book finds that a nice segue is to discuss the study's limitations one by one and then offer the implications for future research that emerge from these limitations. Other implications to write about in the discussion involve those for social work practice. Test Your Skills Exercise 12.2 is an example of these components of the discussion and space for you to write your own sections.

Test Your Skills Exercise 12.2.		
DISCUSSION SECTION EXAMPLES AND APPLICATION		
SECTION OF DISCUSSION	EXAMPLE	YOUR PROJECT
Summarize findings	The main objective of this study was to examine the differences between solution-focused therapy and "treatment-as-usual" for child behavior problems over time. The hypothesis was not supported: solution-focused therapy did not surpass the "treatment-as-usual" condition on outcome measures, although both groups made improvements over time. . . . However, it must be noted that these findings only apply to those that completed treatment, and dropout for both conditions was high. In the solution-focused therapy condition, only 42% of families completed both pre- and posttest measures. However, the treatment-as-usual comparison condition displayed an even higher rate of dropout: 73%. The difference between dropout rates for the two conditions proved to be statistically significant at the 0.05 level. Indeed, treatment condition was the only factor significant in the logistic regression model.	
Comment on findings	Perhaps because the comparison group relied so heavily on cognitive-behavioral therapy. . . it was not reasonable to expect the solution-focused condition to outperform "treatment-as-usual." . . .In considering some of the reasons families seemed to more readily engage in the solution-focused treatment, several possibilities exist. First, the emphasis on solution-focused therapy is on strengths and resources. Questions in the model are designed to elicit how people already use their resources to resolve problems, and children and families are complimented on these strengths. Parents might have felt better about themselves and the treatment and felt more hopeful about the possibility of change; as a result, they may have felt more inclined to continue when compared to the treatment-as-usual comparison group.	

	Another possible reason for increased retention in solution-focused therapy is that when children are referred for behavior problems, parents tend to expect that treatment will address their child's behavior. In both conditions, student therapist interns reported that some parents questioned why the majority of the counseling time was not spent with the child alone. Solution-focused therapy, however, was more directly focused on the child's behavior, whereas the treatment-as-usual comparison condition usually concentrated on helping parents with their skills via parent training to influence their child's behavior. The focus of solution-focused therapy on goals that people bring into treatment (child behavior problems) may have more relevance and face validity for parents. In addition, the source of the referral must be considered in explaining the difference in dropout between the solution-focused and treatment-as-usual conditions. Children were referred from the school system, usually because problems with their conduct were evident in the classroom. Often similar issues were present with the child's behavior at home, but sometimes problems were limited to the school setting. In these cases, focusing on parenting skills and family issues may have had reduced validity for parents. In contrast, the solution-focused emphasis was on how parents and children could work together, or how parents could help their children change their behavior to "prove" to the school system that treatment was no longer necessary.
Relate back to literature	cognitive-behavioral therapy. . . has shown to be empirically validated for child behavior problems (Bennett & Gibbons, 2000; Serketich & Dumas, 1996). . . Other factors associated with dropout in the parent training literature did not seem particularly predictive of dropout with this sample.
Limitations and suggestions for future research	A number of limitations might possibly influence the results of this study. First, a limited number of measures were used, and these included only self-report inventories. However, these choices were made to reduce burden on family members and to interfere as little as possible with services they were seeking. Although teacher reports could have also been taken, given the nature of the referrals (school referrals for behavior problems), and these would have provided triangulation of data, confidentiality issues posed an obstacle. Counselors from schools were the primary source of referrals. They might have received information about a particular child from a teacher, but sometimes school counselors handled students' problems outside teacher involvement. To survey teacher perceptions of child classroom behaviors would have violated the children's and their families' right to confidentiality of treatment. However, another option would have been to gain access to school-level data on attendance, academic achievement, and conduct problems. Future work could include this type of data in the research.

	Internal validity problems might also pose some methodological problems to the study. Perhaps the most salient problem involves history in that comparison treatment conditions occurred subsequent in time. It could be that different types of clients, not reflected in the demographic characteristics studied, accounted for differences between groups that had little to do with the intervention method. Or, for example, different types of student interns involved in the two different treatment conditions were attracted to the clinic for their field placement, which might have accounted for findings of the study. Although interns tended to be similar in terms of educational level (second-year Masters student), level of experience (minimal clinical experience), race (majority White), and gender (female), characteristics of student-practitioners were not tracked systematically. Future research on solution-focused therapy should strive toward tracking characteristics of practitioners. Engagement and outcome may have more to do with the process of therapy and the interaction patterns between practitioner and client (Beyebach & Carranza, 1997; Beyebach, Morejon, Palenuela, & Rodriques-Arias, 1996), rather than particular client characteristics. Toward this end, the videotaped interviews of first sessions of the solution-focused therapy study have been transcribed and certain attributional processes are being explored (*see* Corcoran, 2003).	
	As discussed, it might have been unreasonable to expect solution-focused therapy to outperform the comparison group when "treatment-as-usual" was already loaded with cognitive-behavioral components. Despite the challenges of comparing treatment against a no-treatment control, future work should strive toward control groups with randomization to groups.	
	An additional weakness of the study was that treatment fidelity was not examined in a systematic way. It could be that student interns deviated from certain techniques in a way that made either the solution-focused therapy less effective, or they were unable to follow through certain interventions the way they were developed for the "treatment-as-usual" condition. Future studies should ensure that treatment is carried out in a way that is standardized in fashion.	
	Another limitation of the study involves the lack of follow-up, which precludes knowledge about the progress on child behavior problems after treatment was terminated. Despite the difficulties of obtaining information after treatment has been terminated, future researchers are urged to consider tracking behavior over time beyond the posttest period. Such contact could also perhaps seek to determine the reasons for families not returning for scheduled appointments, if applicable.	
Implications for social work practice	Families who come to counseling for behavior problems in children generally benefit, and there may be little difference between solution-focused therapy and treatment as usual.	

AGENCY PRESENTATIONS

Students have mentioned their reluctance to present their findings to their agency because they are afraid that administrators won't like the results and the research may not cast the agency in a positive light. But research involves too much effort and time to act only as a classroom exercise. You selected a project because it had value to your agency and to social work practice, so now the results deserve to be shared. Of course, such sharing of results should also be tempered by the limitations and weaknesses of the research.

To whom should you present at your agency? Different venues are often appropriate. Often, staff meetings provide a natural setting so that people involved in providing services can hear about the project and its results. Sometimes, only administrators choose to be the audience for your presentation. For example, in a project on permanency planning in foster care, regional supervisors of various Child Protective Services branches attended the presentation.

Usually, students find it necessary to use Powerpoint to present their findings so that audience members can follow along. Research information is too complex to understand without some visual material. Poster presentations can also help you to distill and present large amounts of information in a visually appealing and succinct manner. Sumarry Content 12.2 provides some pointers for poster presentations (Hess, Tosney, & Liegel, 2010).

Summary Content 12.2.

POSTER PRESENTATION POINTS

- The title of your poster should be 2 inches tall.
- Use headings and subheadings to call attention to the main sections of your poster.
- Use images and graphics and a small amount of text to communicate your key points.
- Text for each of the points should be less than 50 words, either bulleted or in phrases.
- All major elements of the poster should be large enough to be read from 4 feet away.
- Recommended text size should be at least 36 point for headings and 24 point for text.

- Balance the placement of text and graphics so that the flow from graphics to text is clear; remember that reading flow is from top to bottom and left to right.

- Use white space creatively to define flow of information and color to emphasize important points.

- Column format makes poster easier to read in a crowd.

PRACTICE-RESEARCH PANEL DISCUSSIONS

The increasing investment of universities, funding sources, and community agencies in translational and community-based research initiatives creates new demands for dialogues about practice-research partnerships. Your experience in learning how to do research in practice settings captures valuable information that extends beyond the findings of specific studies to include insights about the processes and challenges of doing research in real-world settings. We have found that a culminating experience for social work research classes is to offer a panel discussion to social work community groups such as National Association of Social Workers (NASW) chapters or social work clinical societies that are interested in establishing and maintaining successful practice-research collaborations.

Below is an example of how a small group of social work research students shared their class research experiences with a local professional social work organization. The panel discussion developed around a practice-research model that identified guiding principles for various stages of the research process (Secret, Abell, & Berlin, 2011). The goals of the panel discussion were to explore the types of research questions relevant to clinical practice issues; to introduce new social work graduates to the social work professional organization; and to identify and discuss small-scale research studies relevant to clinical practice in social work agencies and settings.

The social work students were asked to reflect on how their projects embodied each of the principles as they carried out various research activities. Example 12.3 presents the stages of the research process and the accompanying questions are presented.

Example 12.3.

PANEL DISCUSSION FORMAT FOR RESEARCH PROJECT EXPERIENCES

RESEARCH STAGE	GUIDING PRINCIPLE	DESCRIPTION OF STAGE	REFLECTIVE QUESTIONS
Building relationships and getting started	Respect shared leadership Engage in the spirit of discovery	Appreciation of practice wisdom by the researcher; appreciation of science by the practitioner Openness to new ways of thinking about and defining the problems; reflection on and bringing new insights to practitioner and researcher roles	What insights and strengths come from the practice side of the profession? What insights and strengths come from the research side of the profession? What about the field placement or practice setting sparks your curiosity? Could you do a better job if you had a better understanding of what kinds of issues in your practice?
Framing the research question/identifying program evaluation goals	Consider the theoretical basis	Explanation of why the program or intervention should bring about desired change Articulation of measurable program outcomes	Why did you think that this particular therapeutic intervention should be effective? What is it about a particular therapeutic process or activity that is expected to produce client change in behavior, values, attitude, relationships, etc.?

Planning the research project	Be aware of the feasibility factor Begin where the client is	Selection of a research design appropriate for the program's experience and expertise and adaptable to service setting; data collection methods and instruments that resonate with the practitioner and that match the skill set and expertise of the researcher	**What** data are important to collect to answer the question... what are the variables in the study? **Who** are the study participants. . . who can best answer the research question? **How** will you collect data? What is best and most feasible option to collect data to answer the question?
Implementing the research/collecting the data	Put the client and the program first	Minimal disruption of the program; primacy of service delivery concerns Adherence to standards of ethical behavior and protection of research subjects	What kinds of problem-solving efforts might be necessary as you collect data? Where are possible barriers to completing the project? What should you do if clients don't want to participate? What if your response rate is low?
Analyzing the data	Look for patterns in the data	Description of the sample in terms of the demographic and other important characteristics of the sample Recognize difference between practical significance and statistical significance Examine the similarities and differences in outcome measurement findings	Who do these findings NOT apply? Is your sample large enough to provide statistical significance? In general, what is your data describing about the sample you are studying?
Reporting on the Study	Present findings visually Think about Practice Implications	Use of line or bar graphs rather than statistical tables; customize graphics Discuss the findings in terms of the original practice related question and other practice-research studies	Can anyone and everyone understand what you are trying to communicate about your findings? What do your findings suggest about your therapeutic practice and other related interventions? What are the unanswered questions?

PRESENTATIONS REQUIRING INSTITUTIONAL REVIEW BOARD APPROVAL

As noted in the Chapter Five, IRB approval is required for any research that is intended to generate and disseminate knowledge beyond the agency setting. Examples of broader applications include the agency wanting to post positive information on the organization's website, your presenting at a national conference, or submitting the research to an academic journal. In all these situations, IRB approval is required. We will discuss further here the possibility of disseminating the results through journals.

Publishing in Academic Journals

If you have gone through the IRB process and your research project was implemented as planned with findings that meaningful, then you may consider submitting your write-up for possible publication in a peer-reviewed academic journal. Your instructor can act as a consultant in such a situation, advising you on whether this is an appropriate path and how to prepare your manuscript, but we can offer some guidelines here.

1. The outline for a journal article is briefer than (but similar to) your project outline and follows a fairly standardized format: the literature review, research questions and hypotheses, methods (including data collection, research design, sampling, measurement, and data analysis), results, and discussion. Generally, manuscripts submitted for publication should not be longer than 20 pages, including references, a title page, and abstract. That's usually a lot shorter than the research paper final report.

2. As a general point, the order of the authors in a publication reflects the amount of work each person put into it. If one person emerged in your research team as a clear leader or is the most invested in doing the work required to turn it into a manuscript for submission, then consider listing that person as first author. If no one emerges particularly, alphabetical ordering of authors is used with a note that authors have contributed equally. If your instructor joins you on the project (becomes involved in the revision process), then he or she would usually be placed as last author, because he or she is coming in after the hard work of data collection is over.

3. There are a number of social work journals to which you can submit. To find an appropriate journal, a first step may be to look at the list of articles in your reference list. Are there particular social work journals that pop up time and time again? If so, they may provide a logical venue for submission of your manuscript.

We list a sampling of some of the social work journals here that may be amenable to well-conducted and well-written student research projects:

Families in Society: Originally started as *The Family* in 1920, this journal has served as a long-time resource for social workers. Although research articles are provided, there are plenty of practice applications, as well as articles of relevance to direct practitioners in different fields of practice.

Health & Social Work: Publishes a variety of practice-related articles on health, broadly defined as both physical and mental health.

Gerontological Social Work: A broad range of articles—theoretical and research-based that involve working with elderly clients.

Children in Schools: Formerly *Social Work in Education,* this practice-based journal contributes knowledge relevant for school social work. An international and interdisciplinary journal focused on research-based articles of relevance to practice and policy for the problem of child maltreatment.

After you submit a manuscript to a journal with a business cover letter, including your contact information, it is usually sent out for what's called "blind review." This means that your manuscript is de-identified and sent to people unknown to you to review. There may be as few as two people or as many as five. These reviewers give their recommendations to the editor, who then makes a decision.

A decision usually falls into one of these possibilities:

- Acceptance: This occurs very rarely, so if it happens to you, congratulations! If not, realize that this is a common occurrence.

- Revise and resubmit: This is still good news. The journal is interested in your manuscript, but the reviewers made some suggestions that the editor would now like you to incorporate. When you make revisions, you also have to write a letter accompanying your revised manuscript, detailing the changes that were made. If you decided not to make changes, then you have to discuss your rationale.

- Rejection. Sometimes, a manuscript is rejected based on the opinions of the reviewers and editor. This means that you can send it to another journal. You will find in your review letters that sometimes opinions can be very idiosyncratic to the people writing them, and some reviewers will hone in on certain aspects of your manuscript and others will have different opinions about other parts. Therefore, it is important to attend to *consistent* feedback that you get before deciding to revise and not just a one-off comment that makes no sense to you.

- Students are often surprised to hear that the time between submission and publication in a journal can span years, as there is a timely quality to research. However, you can keep tabs on the process and prevent it from becoming unnecessarily long by writing a polite letter after 3 months inquiring about the status of the review process. Otherwise, reviews may extend into a lengthy period of time.

- If you do get rejected, then you can submit to another journal. Unfortunately, we are unable to do simultaneous submissions, meaning that we can only submit a manuscript to one journal at a time.

Students should also be encouraged to know there are a variety of student journals in social work and related fields, which may offer possible venues for publication.

ADVOCATE'S FORUM

http://ssa.uchicago.edu/advocates-forum-student-journal
The New Social Worker
http://www.socialworker.com/home/index.php

Praxis
   http://www.luc.edu/socialwork/praxis/
Comm-org
   http://comm-org.wisc.edu/co/?q=node/4

CONCLUSION

This chapter has concerned itself with the write-up and presentation of the findings of your research project. Fairly standard outlines exist for the preparation of research reports. Options for presentations of your research certainly include in-class presentations to fellow research students and your instructor but also should extend beyond the classroom into the agency setting. In this vein, ways to present findings so that they are clear and visually appealing to your audience has also been a focus of this chapter. Other venues for disseminating the findings of your project require IRB approval, as these involve national forums, such as national presentations and academic journals. Student journals have also developed and may represent an excellent place to highlight your completed study.

WEBSITES

Designing posters
http://w http://colinpurrington.com/tips/academic/posterdesign

REFERENCES

Abu-Bader, S. H. (2006). *Using Statistical Methods in Social Work Practice: A Complete SPSS Guide*. Chicago, IL: Lyceum Books.

Arditti, J., Smock, S., & Parkman, T. (2005) It's been hard to be a father: a qualitative exploration of incarcerated fatherhood. *Fathering, 3*, 267–288.

Bayer, E. R. (2007). Impact of family and social interaction on depressive symptoms among older adults in a rural environment. *Dissertation Abstracts International, 68*, 08B, (UMI No. 3277077).

Beck, A. T., Ward, C. H., Mendelson, M., Mock, J., & Erbaugh, J. (1961). An inventory for measuring depression. *Archives of General Psychiatry, 4*, 561–571.

Bennett, D. S., & Gibbons, T. (2000). Efficacy of child cognitive-behavioral interventions for antisocial behavior: A meta-analysis. *Child & Family Behavior Therapy, 22*, 1–15.

Berkowitz, S., (1997). Analyzing qualitative data. In J. Frechtling & L. Sharp (Eds.), *User- Friendly Handbook for Mixed Method Evaluations* (Chapter 4). Retrieved March 4, 2012 from The National Science Foundation, Directorate of Education and Human Resources Web site: http://www.nsf.gov/pubs/1997/nsf97153/chap_4.htm

Beyebach, M., & Carranza, V. E. (1997). Therapeutic interaction and dropout: Measuring relational communication in solution-focused therapy. *Journal of Family Therapy, 19*(2), 173–212.

Beyebach, M., Morejon, A. R., Palenzuela, D. L., & Rodriguez-Arias, J. L. (1996). Research on the process of solution-focused therapy. In S. D. Miller, M. A. Hubble, & B. L. Duncan (Eds.), *Handbook of solution-focused brief therapy* (pp. 299–334). San Francisco, CA: Jossey-Bass.

Black, H. K., White, T., & Hannum, S. M. (2007). The lived experience of depression in elderly African American women. *The Journals of Gerontology, Series B, 62*(6), S392–S398.

Borrayo, E. A., & Jenkins, S. R. (2001). Feeling healthy: So why should women of Mexican descent screen for breast cancer? *Qualitative Health Research, 11*(6), 812–823.

Borrayo, E. A., Buki, L. P., & Feigal, B. M. (2005). Breast Cancer Detection Among Older Latinas: Is It Worth the Risk? *Qualitative Health Research, 15*(9), 1244–1263.

Brady, M. J., Cella, D. F., Mo, E., Bonomi, A. E., Tulsky, D. S., & Lloyd, S. R., et al. (1997). Reliability and validity of the Functional Assessment of Cancer Therapy-Breast (FACTB) quality of life instrument. *Journal of Clinical Oncology, 15*, 974–986.

Brink, P., & Wood, M. (1998). *Advanced Design in Nursing Research* (2nd ed.). Thousand Oaks, CA: Sage Publications.

Bronfenbrenner, U. (1979). *The Ecology of Human Development: Experiments by Nature and Design*. Cambridge, MA: Harvard University Press.

Brown, T. E. (2001). *Brown Attention-Deficit Disorder Scales for Children and Adolescents Manual*. San Antonio, TX: The Psychological Corporation.

Busch, C., De Maret, P. S., Flynn, T., Kellum, R., Le, S., Meyers, B., Saunders, M., et al. (2005). *Content Analysis*. Retrieved March 4, 2012 from Colorado State University Department of English website: http://writing.colostate.edu/guides/research/content/.

Code of Federal Regulation, Public Welfare, Protection of Human Subjects, 45 U.S.C. § 46 *et seq.* (2009).

Cohen, J. (1969). *Statistical power analysis for the behavioral sciences*. New York: Academic Press.

Cohen, J. (1988). *Statistical power analysis for behavioral sciences* (2nd ed.). Hillsdale, NY: Lawrence Earlbaum Associates.

Corcoran, J. (1995). Child abuse victim services: An exploratory study of the Austin, Texas Police Department. *Family Violence and Sexual Assault Bulletin, 11*, 19–23.

Corcoran, J. (2006). A comparison group study of solution-focused therapy versus "treatment-as-usual" for behavior problems in children. *Journal of Social Service Research, 33*, 69–82.

Corcoran, J., & Pillai, V. (2008). A meta-analysis of parent-involved treatment for child sexual abuse. *Research in Social Work Practice, 18*, 453–464.

Corcoran, K., & Hozack, N. (2010). Locating Assessment Instruments. In B.A. Thyer (Ed.) *The handbook of social work research methods* (2nd ed.) (pp. 65–74). Thousand Oaks, CA: Sage Publications.

Crawford, M. J., Thomas, O., Khan, N., & Kulinskaya, E. (2007). Psychosocial interventions following self-harm: systematic review of their efficacy in preventing suicide. *British Journal of Psychiatry, 190*, 11–17.

Daniel, S. S. & Goldston, D. B. (2009). Interventions for suicidal youth: a review of the literature and developmental considerations. *Suicide and Life Threatening Behavior, 39*(3), 252–268.

Davidson, J. R. T. (1996). Davidson Trauma Scale. Toronto: Mental Health Systems.

Dekker, R. L., Peden, A. R., Lennie, T. A., Schooler, M. P., & Moser, D. K. (2009). Living with depressive symptoms: patients with heart failure. *American Journal of Critical Care, 18*(4), 310–318. doi: 10.4037/ajcc2009672

Derluyn, I. & Broekaert, E. (2007). Different perspectives on emotional and behavioural problems in unaccompanied refugee children and adolescents. *Ethnicity & Health, 12*, 141–162.

Derluyn, I. & Broekaer, E. (2008). Unaccompanied refugee children and adolescents: the glaring contrast between a legal and a psychological perspective. *International Journal of Law and Psychiatry, 31*(4), 319–330.

Dillman, D. A. (2000). *Mail and internet surveys: the tailored design method* (2nd ed.). New York: John Wiley Company.

Drake, B., & Jonson-Reid, M. (2008). *Social Work Research Methods: From Conceptualization to Dissemination.* Boston, MA: Pearson Education.

Dunford, F. W., & Elliott, D. S. (1984). Identifying career offenders using self-report data. *Journal of Research in Crime and Delinquency, 21*, 57–86.

Early, T., & Newsome, W. S. (2004). Measures for assessment and accountability in practice with families from a strengths perspective. In J. Corcoran (Ed.) *Building strengths and skills: A collaborative approach to working with clients* (pp. 359–393). New York: Oxford University Press.

Elliot, D., Huizinga, D., & Ageton, S. (1985). *Explaining Delinquency and Drug Use.* Beverly Hills, CA: Sage Publications.

Ellis, B. H., MacDonald, H. Z., Lincoln, A. K., & Cabral, H. J. (2008). Mental health of Somali adolescent refugees: the role of trauma, stress, and perceived discrimination. *Journal of Consulting and Clinical Psychology, 76,* 184–193.

Engel, R. J., & Schutt, R. K. (2009). *The Practice of Research in Social Work* (2nd ed.). Thousand Oaks, CA: Sage Publications.

Engle, C. C., Reilly, N. P., & Levine, H. B. (2003). A case study of an academic retention program. *Journal of College Student Retention, 5*, 365–383.

Fawcett, J. (1999). *The Relationship of theory and Research* (3rd ed.). Philadelphia, PA: F. A. Davis Company.

Feder, L., Austin, S., & Wilson, D. (2008). Court-mandated interventions for individuals convicted of domestic violence. *Campbell Systematic Reviews*, 2008 (12). doi:10.4073/csr.2008.12

Finfgeld, D. L. (2003). Metasynthesis: the state of the art—so far. *Qualitative Health Research, 13*(7),893–904.

Foa, E., Riggs, D., Dancu, C., & Rothbaum, B. (1993). Reliability and validity of a brief instrument for assessing post-traumatic stress disorder. *Journal of Traumatic Stress, 6*, 459–474.

Fisher, J., & Corcoran, K. (2007a). *Measures for clinical practice and research: A sourcebook, Vol. 1: Couples, families and children*, (4th ed.). New York: Oxford University Press.

Fisher, J., & Corcoran, K. (2007b). *Measures for clinical practice and research: A sourcebook, Vol. 2 Adults*, (4th ed.). New York: Oxford University Press.

Gamst, G., Dana, R. H., Der-Karabetian, A., Aragon, M., Arellano, L., Morrow, G., & Martenson, L. (2004). Cultural competency revised: The California brief multicultural competence scale. *Measurement and Evaluation in Counseling and Development, 37*(3), 163–183.

Gibbs, G. R. (2009). *Introduction to Qualitative Data Analysis*. Retrieved March 4, 2012 from School of Human and Health Services, University of Huddersfield website: http://onlineqda.hud.ac.uk/Intro_QDA/index.php

Gibbs, G. R., & Taylor, C. (2010). *How and What to Code*. Retrieved March 4, 2012 from http://onlineqda.hud.ac.uk/Intro_QDA/how_what_to_code.php

Givens, J. L., Datto, C. J., Ruckdeschel, K., Knott, K., Zubritsky, C., Oslin, D. W., Nyshadham, S., et al. (2006). Older Patients' Aversion to Antidepressants. *Journal of General Internal Medicine, 21*, 146–151. doi: 10.1111/j.1525-1497.2005.00296.x

Grant-Vallone, E., Reid, K., Umali, C., & Pohlert, E. (2004). An analysis of the effects of self esteem, social support, and participation in the student support services on students' adjustment and commitment to college. *Journal of College Student Retention, 5*, 255–274.

Hawton, K. K., Townsend, E., Arensman, E., Gunnell, D., & Hazell, P. (1999) Psychosocial and pharmacological treatments for deliberate self harm. *Cochrane Database of Systematic Reviews, 3*.

Hedelin, B., & Strandmark, M. (2001). The Meaning of Mental Health from Elderly Women's Perspectives: A Basis for Health Promotion. *Perspectives in Psychiatric Care, 37*, 7–14. doi: 10.1111/j.1744-6163.2001.tb00611.x

Heptinstall, E., Sethna, V., & Taylor, E. (2004). PTSD and depression in refugee children. *European Child & Adolescent Psychiatry, 13*, 373–380.

Hess, G. R., Tosney, K., & Liegel, L. (2010). *Creating Effective Poster Presentations: An Effective Poster*. Retrieved March 4, 2012 from http://www.ncsu.edu/project/posters.

Hill, P. C. & Pargament, K. I. (2003). Advances in the conceptualization and measurement of religion and spirituality: Implications of physical and mental health research. *American Psychologist, 58*, 64–74.

Hinton, D. E., Pham, T., Tran, M., Safren, S. A., Otto, M. W., & Pollack, H. (2004). CBT for vietnamese refugees with treatment-resistant PTSD and panic attacks: A pilot study. *Journal of Traumatic Stress, 17*, 429–433.

Holosko, M. J. (2009). Enhancing practitioner knowledge through a unique abstracting format in Research on Social Work Practice journal articles. *Research on Social Work Practice, 19*, 234–238.

Holosko, M. J. (2006). Primer for Critiquing Social Research: A Student Guide. Belmont, CA: Thompson Brooks/Cole.

Holosko, M. J. (2010). What types of designs are we using in social work research and evaluation? *Research on Social Work Practice, 20*, 665–673.

Holosko, M. J., Thyer, B., & Danner, E. J. (2009): Ethical guidelines for designing and conducting evaluations of social work practice. *Journal of Evidence-Based Social Work, 6*(4), 348–360.

Hostetter, C. M. (2003). *Subthreshold depressive symptoms in elders: phenomenological exploration*. UMI Dissertation Services, ProQuest Information and Learning, Ann Arbor, MI. (UMI 3086769).

Inkelas, K. K., Daver, Z. E., Vogt, K. E. & Leonard, J. B. (2007). Living/learning programs and first generation college students' academic and social transition to college. *Research in Higher Education, 48*, 403–434.

Kaufman-Levy, D., & Poulin, M. (2003). *Evaluability Assessment: Examining the Readiness of a Program for Evaluation*. Retrieved March 4, 2012 from Justice Research and Statistics Association website at http://www.jrsa.org/pubs/juv-justice/evaluability-assessment.pdf.

Khamis, V. (2005). Posttraumatic stress disorder among school-age Palestinian children. *Child Abuse & Neglect, 29*, 81–95.

King, I. M. (1997). Knowledge development for nursing: A process. In I.M. King & J. Fawcett (Eds.), *The language of nursing theory and metatheory* (pp. 27–36). Indianapolis, IN: Sigma Theta Tau International Center Nursing Press.

Lipsey, M. W., & Wilson, D. B. (2001). *Practical meta-analysis*. Thousand Oaks, CA: Sage Publications.

Marshall, M., Gray, A., Lockwood, A., & Green, R. (1998). Case management for people with severe mental disorders. *Cochrane Database of Systematic Reviews*, 1998(2), Article CD000050. doi:10.1002/14651858.CD000050.

Marshall, M., & Lockwood, A. (1998). Assertive community treatment for people with severe mental disorders. *Cochrane Database of Systematic Reviews*, 1998(2), Article CD001089. doi:10.1002/14651858.CD001089.

McCarney, S. B. (1995). *Early Childhood Attention Deficit Disorder Evaluation Scales (ECADDES)*. Columbia, MO: Hawthorne Educational Services.

Mead, G. E., Morley, W., Campbell, P., Greig, C. A., McMurdo, M., & Lawlor, D. A. (2009). Exercise for depression. *Cochrane Database of Systematic Reviews*, 2009(3), Article CD004366. doi:10.1002/14651858.CD004366.pub4.

Mitchell, O., Wilson, D. B., & MacKenzie, D. L. (2006). The Effectiveness of Incarceration-Based Drug Treatment on Criminal Behavior [Campbell Collaboration Systematic Review]. Available at The Campbell Collaboration Library: http://www.campbellcollaboration.org/doc-pdf/ Incarceration-BasedDrugTxSept06final.pdf.

Monette, D. R., Sullivan, T. J., & DeJong, C. R. (2011). *Applied Social Research: A Tool for the Human Services* (8th ed.). Belmont, CA: Brooks/Cole, Cengage Learning.

National Association of Social Workers. (2008). *Code of ethics of the National Association of Social Workers*. Washington, DC: Author.

Neill, J. (2006). *Analysis of Professional Literature—Class 6: Qualitative Research I.* Retrieved March 4, 2012, from http://wilderdom.com/OEcourses/PROFLIT/Class6Qualitative1.htm.

Nelson, A. M. (2002). A metasynthesis: mothering other-than-normal children. *Qualitative Health Research, 12*, 515–530.

New York State Teacher Centers (2008). *Focus Groups*. Retrieved March 4, 2012, from http://www. programevaluation.org/focusgroups.htm.

Nye, C., Turner, H., & Schwartz, J. (2006). Approaches to parent involvement for improving the academic performance of elementary school age children. *Campbell Systematic Reviews*, 2006(4). doi:10.4073/csr.2006.

Oka, T. & Shaw, I. (n.d.). *Characteristics of Qualitative Research*. Retrieved November 16, 2008, from http://www.t-oka.net/.

Orr, A., & O'Connor, D. (2005). Dimensions of power: older women's experiences with electroconvulsive therapy (ECT). *Journal of Women & Aging, 17*(1–2), 19–36.

Oseguera, L., Denson, N., & Hurtado, S. (2009). Hispanic students and the Gates Millennium Scholarship program: Promising results extending to the third college year. *Journal of College Student Retention, 10*, 307–338. Oxford University Press. (2011). Problem. In *Advanced Learner's Dictionary*. Retrieved from http://www.oxfordadvancedlearnersdictionary.com/ dictionary/problem

Pan, M. L. (2008). *Preparing Literature Reviews: Qualitative and Quantitative Approaches* (2nd ed.). Glendale, CA: Pryczak Publishing.

Paterson, B. L., Thorne, S. E., Canam, C., & Jillings, J. (2001). *Meta-study of qualitative health research: A practical guide to meta-analysis and meta-synthesis.* California: Sage Publications.

Paunovic, N. & Ost, L.G. (2001). Cognitive-behavior therapy vs exposure therapy in the treatment of PTSD in refugees. *Behaviour Research and Therapy*, 39, 1183–1197.

Polit, D. F., & Hungler, B. P. (1995). *Nursing research: Principles and methods* (5th ed.). Philadelphia, PA: Lippincott.

Pollitt, P. A., & O'Connor, D. W. (2008). What was good about admission to an aged psychiatry ward? The subjective experiences of patients with depression. *International Psychogeriatrics, 20*, 628–640. doi: 10.1017/S104161020700600x.

roctor, E. K., Hasche, L., Morrow-Howell, N., Shumway, M., & Snell, G. (2008). Perceptions about competing psychosocial problems and treatment priorities among older adults with depression. *Psychiatric Services, 59*, 670–675. doi:10.1176/appi.ps.59.6.670

Radloff, L. (1977). The CES-D Scale: A self-report depression scale for research in the general population. *Applied Psychological Measurement, 1*, 385–401.

Ridley, D. (2008). *The Literature Review: A Step-by-Step Guide for Students*. Thousand Oaks, CA: Sage Publications.

Rodwell, M. K. (1998). *Social Work Constructivist Research*. New York: Garland Publishing.

Rubin, A. (2010). *Statistics for Evidence-Based Practice and Evaluation* (2nd ed.). Belmont, CA: Brooks/Cole, Cengage Learning.

Rubin, A., & Babbie, E. (2011). *Research Methods for Social Work* (7th ed.). Belmont, CA: Brooks/ Cole, Cengage Learning.

Sandelowski, M. & Barroso, J. (2006). *Handbook for Synthesizing Qualitative Research*. New York: Springer Publishing Company.

Scher, L. S., Maynard, R. A., & Stagner, M. (2006). *Interventions Intended to Reduce Pregnancy-Related Outcomes Among Teenagers* [Campbell Collaboration Systematic Review]. Available at The Campbell Collaboration Library: http://www.campbellcollaboration.org/doc-pdf/ teenpregreview__dec2006.pdf.

Secret, M. (2006). Integrating paid work and family work: A qualitative study of parenting in the workplace child care experiences. *Community, Work & Family.* 9(4), 407–427.

Secret, M. & Swanberg, J. (2008). Work-family experiences and insights of municipal government employees: A case study. *Public Personnel Management 37,* 199–221.

Secret, M., Abell, M., & Berlin, T. (2011). The promise and challenge of practice-research collaborations: Guiding principles and strategies for initiating, designing and implementing evaluation research. *Social Work, 56*(1), 9–20.

Secret, M., Berlin, T., Huebner, R., & Werner, M. (2007). Fathers and Children Together: An Evaluation of the Resources, Services, and Outcomes of a Prison-based Parenting Program. Final Report submitted to U.S. Children's Bureau. Grant Award # 90CW1107.

Secret, M., Rompf, E. L., & Ford, J. (2003). Undergraduate research courses: A closer look reveals complex social work student attitudes. *Journal of Social Work Education, 39*(3), 411–424.

Serketich, W. J., & Dumas, J. E. (1996). The effectiveness of behavioral parent training to modify antisocial behavior in children: A meta-analysis. *Behavior Therapy, 27*(2), 171–186. doi: 10.1016/S0005-7894(96)80013-X

Silove, D., Steel, Z., Bauman, A., Chey, T., & McFarlane, A. (2007). Trauma, PTSD and the longer-term mental health burden amongst Vietnamese refugees: A comparison with the Australian-born population. *Social Psychiatry and Psychiatric Epidemiology, 42,* 467–476.

Smedslund, G., Hagen, K. B., Steiro, A., Johme, T., Dalsbø, T. K., & Rud, M. G. (2006). *Work programmes for welfare recipients* [Campbell Collaboration Systematic Review]. Available at The Campbell Collaboration Library: http://www.campbellcollaboration.org/doc-pdf/Smedslund_Workprog_Review.pdf

Snyder, C. R., Hoza, B., Pelham, W. E., Rapoff, M., Ware, L., Danovsky, M., Highberger, L., et al. (1997). The development and validation of the Children's Hope Scale. *Journal of Pediatric Psychology, 22*(3), 399–421. doi: 10.1093/jpepsy/22.3.399

Standard, R. P., Sandhu, D. S., & Painter, L. C. (2000). Assessment of spirituality in counseling. *Journal of Counseling and Development, 78,* 204–210.

Stiffman, A. R., Orme, J., Evans, D., Feldman, R. A., & Keeney, P. (1984). A brief measure of children's behavior problems: The Behavior Rating Index for Children (BRIC). *Measurement and Evaluation in Counseling and Development, 17*(2), 83–90.

Strauss, A., & Corbin, J. (1990). *Basics of Qualitative Research: Grounded Theory Procedures and Techniques.* Newbury Park, CA: Sage Publications.

Strauss, A. L. & Corbin, J. M. (1998). *Basics of qualitative research: techniques and procedures for developing grounded theory.* London: Sage.

Sutton, A. J., Abrams, K. R., Jones, D. R., Sheldon, T. A., & Song, F. (1998). Systematic reviews of trials and other studies. *Health Technology Assessment, 2*(19).

Tarrier, N., Taylor, K., & Gooding, P. (2008). Cognitive-behavioural interventions to reduce suicide behaviour: a systematic review and meta-analysis. *Behavior Modification, 32,* 77–108.

Tripodi, S. J., & Bender, K. (2010). Descriptive studies. In B.A. Thyer (Ed.), *The handbook of social work research methods* (2nd ed.) (pp. 120–130). Thousand Oaks, CA: Sage Publications.

Trochim, W. M. K. (2006). *Interviews.* Retrieved from http://www.socialresearchmethods.net/kb/intrview.php

Tutty, L. M., & Rothery, M. A. (2010). Needs assessment. In B. Thyer (Ed.), *The handbook of social work research methods* (2nd ed.) (pp. 149–162). Thousand Oaks, CA: Sage Publications.

Tutty, L. M., Rothery, M. L., & Grinnell, R. M., Jr. (1996). *Qualitative Research for Social Workers: Phases, Steps, and Tasks.* Needham Heights, MA: Allyn & Bacon.

Ugarriza, D. N. (2002). Postpartum depressed women's explanation of depression. *Journal of Nursing Scholarship, 34,* 227–233. doi: 10.1111/j.1547-5069.2002.00227.x

Valenzuela, P., & Shrivastava, P. (2002). *Interview as a Method for Qualitative Research.* Retrieved March 12, 2012, from http://www.public.asu.edu/~kroel/www500/Interview%20Fri.pdf

Ward, M. F., Wender, P. H., & Reimherr, F. W. (1993). An aid in the retrospective diagnosis of childhood attention deficit hyperactivity disorder. *American Journal of Psychiatry, 150,* 885–890.

Weinbach, R. W. & Grinnell, R. M. (2010). *Statistics for social workers* (8th ed.), Boston MA: Pearson Education.

Weisz, J. R., McCarty, C. A., & Valeri, S. M. (2006). Effects of psychotherapy for depression in children and adolescents: a meta-analysis. *Psychological Bulletin, 132*, 132–149.

Wilby, F. E. (2008). *Coping and depression in community dwelling elders* (Doctoral Dissertation, University of Utah). Retrieved from: http://gradworks.umi.com/33/02/3302496.html\

Wilson, S. J., & Lipsey, M. W. (2006b). *The Effects of School-based Social Information Processing Interventions on Aggressive Behavior: Part II: Selected/Indicated Pull-out Programs* [Campbell Collaboration Systematic Review]. Available at The Campbell Collaboration Library: http://www.campbellcollaboration.org/doc-pdf/wilson_socinfoprocpull_review.pdf.

Wilson, S. J., Lipsey, M. W., & Soydan, H. (2003). Are mainstream programs for juvenile delinquency less effective with minority youth than majority youth? A meta-analysis of outcomes research. *Research on Social Work Practice, 13*(1), 3–26. doi:10.1177/1049731502238754

Wilson, D. B., MacKenzie, D. L., & Mitchell, F. N. (2005). *Effects of correctional boot camps on offending* [Campbell Collaboration Systematic Review]. Available at The Campbell Collaboration Library: http://www.campbellcollaboration.org/doc-pdf/Wilson_bootcamps_rev.pdf.

Winokur, M., Holtan, A., & Valentine, D. (2009). Kinship care for the safety, permanency, and well-being of children removed from the home for maltreatment. *Cochrane Database of Systematic Reviews*, 2009(1), Article CD006546. doi: 10.1002/14651858.CD006546.pub2

Wittink, M. N., Barg, F. K., & Gallo, J. J. (2006). Unwritten rules of talking to doctors about depression: integrating qualitative and quantitative methods. *Analysis of Family Medicine, 4*(4), 302–309.

Woods, P. (1999). *Successful writing for qualitative research*. New York, NY: Routledge.

Yick, A.G. (2008). A metasynthesis of qualitative findings on the role of spirituality and religiosity among culturally diverse domestic violence survivors. *Qualitative Health Research, 18*, 1289–1306.

Zung, W. W. (1965). A self-rating depression scale. *Archives of General Psychiatry, 12*, 63–70.

INDEX

A

academic journals
publishing in, 210
agency
data collection instruments, 124–25
evaluation research design, 283–285, 191–94
human subjects, 80
involvement in research, 26–28
presentation of research project, 206–7
Project Development Worksheet, 27
qualitative research project, 172–74
alpha level, *See* statistical significance, p value
statistics, 143
Analysis of Variance (ANOVA)
data analysis, 151–52
availability sample, *See* convenience sample, 107

B

bias
selection, 101, 105, 179
systematic vs. literature reviews, 51, 52
bivariate statistics
chi-square, 143, 147–149
correlations, 144–47
data analysis, 142–52
one-way ANOVA, 151–152
overview, 143
research project, 202–4
t-tests, 149–151
Boolean operators
database, 34–35

C

Campbell Collaboration, 53–57
causal mechanism
logic model, 184
Centers for Disease Control (CDC), 33
chi-square, 147–149
Cochrane Collaboration, 53–57, 56–57
Code of Ethics, 68–69,116
coding
in qualitative analysis, 166–167
term, 166
Collaborative Institutional Training
Initiative (CITI)
training program, 78
computer software
qualitative data analysis, 166–67
Statistical Package for the Social Sciences (SPSS),
24–25
confidentiality
informed consent letter, 87
ethics in qualitative research, 169–70
consent forms
sample forms, 70, 86, 88–92
sample waiver, 75
construct validity
measurement, 121–22
content analysis
guidelines for, 167
term, 166
convenience sample
intervention research, 113
term, 107
correlations
scatter diagram, 145, 146
statistics, 144–47
student research projects, 144, 147
understanding, 145
cost analysis; cost benefit
evaluation research, 282, 187–88

criterion
validity, 121–22

D

data analysis. *See* quantitative data analysis
bivariate, 142–52
chi-square, 147–49
multivariate statistics, 152–53
qualitative, 65, 166–168
as part of research process, 25–26
p value, 143
statistical testing, 143–44
t-tests, 149–51
univariate statistics, 141–42
data collection
cost benefit analysis, 187–88
evaluation research, 189–91
from agency records, 124–25
numbers trail, 138
qualitative, 160–163
research design, 20–21
as part of research process, 21–23
worksheet for qualitative research, 172–74
data management
software programs, 24
data processing
research process, 24–25
SPSS (Statistical Package for the Social Sciences), 24–25
data recording
qualitative research, 165–66
databases
application of key terms to, 35–38
using library, 34–35
demographics, 26, 40–43, 76, 89, 126, 139–141, 200–201, 206
dependent *t*-test, 239
dependent variables
in evaluation research, 179, 191
hypotheses, 16
outcome, 117, 179
statistics, 142, 153–155
student research projects, 3–4, 152
treatment fidelity, 133
design
experimental and quasi-experimental, 101–102
pre-experimental, 99–101
quantitative, 94–106
research process, 20–21
single-system, 97–99
surveys, 94–97
term, 4
directional hypothesis, 17
discussion section
as part of research, 26
research project, 204–6

E

effect size (ES)
meta-analysis, 51–53
electronic databases. *See also* databases
library, 34–35
E-mail surveying, Survey Monkey, 96
ethics
assent form sample, 89–90
consent form, 90–91
human subjects research, 81
informed consent worksheet, 73–74
NASW *Code of Ethics*, 69
Project Development Worksheet, 79–80
qualitative research, 169–70
sample consent forms, 86–88

ethics (*cont.*)
  sample cover letters, 85
  sample letter of consent, 70
  social work research, 68, 80
  Test Your Skills Exercise, 170
evaluation research
  agency settings, 180–81
  applying research methods, 184–87
  comparison to social science research, 177
  cost-benefit analysis, 187–88
  defining, 175–77
  design types, 192
  evaluability assessment, 183–84
  focus of research designs, 191–94
  logic models, 181–83
  NASW *Code of Ethics*, 69
  Project Development Worksheet, 196–97
  questions answered by, 178–79
  research process, 175
  rights of human subjects, 69–70
  sample letter of consent, 70
  summative program evaluation, 188–91
  terms and definitions, 182
  test your knowledge, 194
  Test Your Skills Exercise, 181, 189–91, 298–99
experimental designs
  evaluation research, 191–94
  research, 101–2
  treatment fidelity, 133
explanatory
  research, 19
exploratory
  research, 19
external validity
  intervention, 97

F
feasibility
  evaluation research, 181
  research question, 12
federal regulation
  research definition, 78–79
FedStats.gov
  federal resource, 33
field agency. *See* agencyfocus group study
  consent form, 88
  in program evaluation, 174, 178–180
  in qualitative research, 158, 159–160, 161, 162, 166–167
formative evaluation
  applications, 178, 181–183
  questions raised by, 179–80
frequencies
  data analysis, 112
  variables, 141
group behavior
  instrument for measuring, 123–24

G
Guttmacher Institute, 33

H
human subjects. *See* Institutional Review Board
  protecting rights of, 69–70
  review policy, 78
  testing knowledge of ethics, 81
hypotheses
  research process, 16–17
  types of, 17

I
identity disclosure
  confidentiality, 87
  ethics in qualitative research, 169–70

implementation
  program evaluation, 175, 188–191
  research process, 21–23, 28, 29
independent *t*-tests, 149–151
independent variables
  evaluation research, 176, 191, 200
  hypotheses, 16
  prediction research, 115
  statistics 142, 153–155
  student research projects, 3–4
  treatment fidelity, 132–36
informed consent, 70, 75, 86, 88–92
  IRB.*See* Institutional Review Board
  questionnaire, 76
  research subject information, 86–88
  sample form, 70
  social work research, 74–75
  worksheet, 73–74
Institutional Review Boards (IRBs)
  application review, 78
  exempt review, 76, 77, 83, 84
  expedited review, 76, 77, 83, 84
  determining the type of review, 77
  federal government, 68
  federal regulations regarding, 78–79
  full review, 76
  presentations requiring approval, 209–11
  product development worksheet, 77
  review levels, 76
  student research and agencies, 79
instruments
  adapting and creating, 122–24
  data collection, from agency records, 124–25
  levels of measurement, 125–29
  measuring positive group behavior, 123–24
  Project Development Worksheet, 122
interim outcomes
  logic model, 183
internal consistency
  reliability, 119–21
internal validity
  threats to, 103–6
inter-rater
  reliability, 119–21
interval
  measurement, 125–29
intervention research. *See* research designs
  designs, 97–106
  experimental and quasi-experimental designs, 101–2
  posttest-only design, 99–100
  pre-experimental designs, 98–99
  pretest-posttest designs, 100–101
  sample size, 114–15
  single-system designs, 97–98
  treatment fidelity, 132–36
interviewing
  qualitative, 162–172

K
key terms
  applying to databases, 35–38
  formulating, 34

L
letters of consent
  protecting human subjects, 69–70
  sample, 70
listserves
  survey access to, 96
literature review
  checklist for preparing, 49–50
  conducting, 29
  definition and purpose, 31
  determining value of study, 32

downloading articles, 35–38
formulating key terms, 34
instruments for measures, 119
justification for study, 32–33
learning, 32
nature of problem, 34
organizing framework, 38–39
paragraphs, 48
paraphrasing, 48
Project Development Worksheet, 40–42
reading literature, 38–42
reasons to conduct, 31–33
referencing, 36, 49–50
reviewing and integrating research, 46–48, 76–79
searching literature, 33–38
steps, 33
structuring, 44–45
systematic review vs., 51
transitions, 48–49
using library databases, 34–35
using outline to guide writing, 44–45
using systematic reviews for, 100–101
writing, 42–49
logic models
evaluability assessment, 183–84
evaluation research, 181–83
matching evaluation terms to, 184
components of, 183
logistic regression, 153

M
math
social work research, 5–6
measurement
adapting and creating instruments, 122–24
assigning values, 129–32
data collection instrument from agency records, 124–25
evaluation research, 189–91
independent variable, 132–36
levels of, 125–29
operationalization, 117–18
process evaluation tool, 187
Project Development Worksheet, 122, 129, 132
reliability and validity, 119–21
Test Your Skills Exercise, 124, 128
treatment fidelity, 132–36
types of validity, 121–22
using standardized, 118–22
measures of central tendency
statistics, 141
measures of dispersion or variability
statistics, 142
meta-analysis
systematic reviews, 51–53
meta-synthesis
sample, depression in older adults, 60–65
Project Development Worksheet, 58
steps in, 57–66
student projects, 101
systematic review, 51–53
method
term, 4
Multiple Analysis of Variance (MANOVA), 153
multivariate statistics
data analysis, 152–53
research project, 202–4

N
National Association of Social Workers (NASW)
Code of Ethics, 69
needs assessment
program evaluation, 179–80
surveying, 94
nominal

measurement, 125–29
non-directional hypotheses, 17
non-representative sampling
description, 108
method, 110–13
note-taking
qualitative research, 165–66
null hypothesis, 17

O
online surveys. *See* Survey Monkey
software, 96
operationalization, 117–18
ordinal
measurement, 125–29
outcomes
agency settings, 125
dependent variable, 55, 179
in program evaluation, 178
logic model, 183–86
outline
literature review, 44–45
research report, 199

P
p value. *See also* alpha level; statistical significance
statistics, 143
panel discussions
practice-research model, 207–9
participants
sampling, 107–8
percentages
variables, 141
plagiarism
ethics, 49
guarding against, 39
populations
hidden, and qualitative research, 171
sampling frames, 108–10
sampling underrepresented, 162
study, 107
positive group behavior
instrument development, 123–24
poster presentation, 207
posttest-only design
research design, 99–100
practice-research
guidelines, 58
panel discussions, 207–9
principles, 28–29
prediction research
sample size, 114–15
pre-experimental designs
intervention, 98–99
presentations
dissemination, 199–204
research project to agency, 206–7
pretest-posttest design
evaluation research, 192
research design, 100–101
principles
establishing, for research, 28–29
evaluation strategies, 181
feasibility principle, 29
program and client first, 29
shared leadership, 28–29
Principles for Research, 28–29
client first, 29
feasibility, 29
shared leadership, 29
probability sampling
term, 107
problem
definition, 11

process evaluation
   applying research methods, 184–87
   measurement tool, 187
program evaluation
   in agency settings, 180
   cost-benefit, cost-effective, 179, 184, 187–188
   different from social science research, 175
   definition, 175–176
   designs, 179, 188, 189, 191–193
   evaluability assessment, 184, 185
   formative, 187, 188
   logic models, 181–183
   needs assessment, 178, 179, 194
   questions raised by, 179–80
   summative, 188–191
   tools, 165–166
Project Development Worksheet, 12, 13
   data analysis plan, 153
   estimating time commitment, 171
   ethics summary, 79–80
   evaluation research project, 196–97
   field agency, 27
   identifying IRB review, 77
   informed consent, 73–74
   instruments, 122
   literature review, 40–42
   literature review checklist, 49–50
   locating systematic reviews, 54
   measurement table, 132
   paragraphs, 48
   population and sampling frame, 110
   research concepts, 129
   research design, 103
   sample size, 115
   sampling methods, 113
   summarizing systematic reviews, 56
   topic for meta-synthesis, 58
   transitions, 48–49
   treatment fidelity, 136
   variable and value, 130
publication
   academic journals, 210
   confidentiality, 87
   IRB, 78–79
   research, 88, 89
   systematic review, 57–59

Q

qualitative data analysis
   data collection, 157, 166–67
   evaluation research, 178
   meta-synthesis, 61, 65, 156
qualitative research
   content analysis, 167
   data analysis, 61, 65, 156, 157, 166–67, 178
   difference from quantitative research, 157–60
   ethics in, 169–70
   examples, 160
   hypothesis, 16
   meta-analysis, 51–53
   methods, 254–55, 171
   note-taking and recording, 165–66
   putting results together, 167–69
   real world settings, 162–64
   sample size, 114–15
   sampling underrepresented populations, 162
   semi-structured interviews, 162
   Test Your Skills Exercises, 251, 252–53, 164, 165
   Worksheet For Developing Qualitative Research Project, 172–74
qualitative studies
   data processing, 24
   description, 35
   design, 20–21

quantitative articles
   description, 35
quantitative data analysis. *See* data analysis
quantitative designs, 94–106
   data analysis, 25–26
   design, 20–21
   difference from qualitative research, 157–60
   experimental and quasi-experimental, 101–102
   measurement, 117–18
   meta-analysis, 51–53
   pre-experimental, 99–101
   research process, 20–21
   single-system, 97–99
   SPSS (Statistical Package for the Social Sciences), 24
   surveys, 94–97
   Test Your Skills Exercise, 159–60, 158
quasi-experimental design
   evaluation research, 192
   research design, 101–2
questionnaire
   data analysis, 138–41
   data collection, 16, 21–24, 27, 123, 124, 134, 157, 189
   informed consent, 76
   qualitative methods, 162
   sampling, 114
   surveys, 82, 95, 96
   testing, 104
   written consent, 75

R

ratio
   measurement, 125–29
real world settings
   evaluation research, 181–83, 191–94
   research findings vs., 6–7
   practice-research panel discussions, 207–9
references
   literature review, 49–50
reliability
   data collection instrument, 125
   measurement, 119–21
   systematic review, 59
   types of, 119–21
representative sample
   description, 108
   method, 111–113
   term, 107
research design
   differences between qualitative and quantitative, 157–60
   evaluation research, 189–91, 191–94
   experimental and quasi-experimental designs, 101–2
   intervention research, 97–106
   posttest-only, 99–100
   pre-experimental designs, 98–99
   pretest-posttest designs, 100–101
   Project Development Worksheet, 103
   qualitative, 160–65
   response rate and administration of surveys, 95–97
   sampling and, 113–14
   single-system, 97–98
   surveys, 94–95
   term, 12
   Test Your Skills Exercise, 102
   threats to internal validity, 103–6
research methods
   resources, 24
research process
   apprehension about, 2–3
   at a glance, 10–11
   data collection and study implementation, 21–23
   data processing and analysis, 23–26
   design, 20–21

developing research question, 11–19
establishing principles, 28–29
evaluation and interpretation, 26
field agency involvement, 26–28
hypotheses, 16–17
making decisions about methods, 19–21
measurement, 20
sampling, 20
theory, 13–16
vocabulary, 4–5
research project
agency presentations, 206–7
bivariate and multivariate statistics, 202–4
discussion section, 204–6
implementation worksheet, 28
panel discussion format, 208–9
poster presentation points, 207
practice-research panel discussions, 207–9
presentations requiring IRB approval, 209–11
project development worksheet, 27
publishing in academic journals, 210
report outline, 199
results section, 199–204
Test Your Skills Exercise, 204–6
univariate statistics, 200–201
write-up and dissemination, 199
research question
developing, 11–19
scientific relevance, 12
social importance, 12
student projects, 18–19
study answering, 26
theory, 13–16
research vocabulary, 4–5
response rate
surveys, 95–97
sampling
evaluation research, 189–91
illustrations of, terms, 110
methods, 110–13
populations and, frames, 108–10
Project Development Worksheet, 110, 113, 115
representative and non-representative, 108
research design and, 113–14
research process, 20
sample size, 114–15
terminology, 107–8
Test Your Skills Exercise, 114
underrepresented populations, 162

S
sampling frame
populations and, 108–10
term, 107
scatter diagram
correlations, 145, 146
schools
research involvement, 27
search terms
formulating, 34
semi-structured interviews, 162
simple random sampling, 113
single-system designs, 97–98
snowball sampling, 171
social importance
research question, 12
social work
practice vs. research, 6–7
social work
electronic databases, 34–35
ethics in qualitative research, 169–70
evaluation, 175
evaluation research, 195
federal regulations and IRB reviews, 78–79

importance of, 3–4
math anxiety, 5–6
measurement variables, 20
qualitative research findings, 167–69
workbook format, 1–2
software
SPSS (Statistical Package for the Social Sciences), 24–25
SurveyMonkey, 96
split-half
reliability, 119–21
SPSS (Statistical Package for the Social Sciences)
data processing, 24–25
standardized instrument
measurements, 118–22
standardized mean difference
meta-analysis, 51–53
statistics
correlations, 144–47
data analysis, 25–26, 138
data management, 24
sample size, 115
social work research, 5–6
sources of numbers, 138–41
statistical significance level, 143
testing, 143–44
stratified
sampling, 113
student research projects
analysis of variance (ANOVA), 151–52
chi-square results, 147, 149
correlations, 144, 147
data analysis, 25–26
dependent t-tests, 150
determining type of IRB review, 77
evolution of research questions, 18–19
Family Group Conferencing, 130–32
independent t-tests, 150
Independent and Dependent Variables in Student
    Research Projects, 3–4
integration of literature, 45–48
IRB review and federal regulation, 78–79
letter to prospective agencies, 79
posttest-only designs, 99–100
pretest-posttest designs, 100–101
quasi-experimental designs, 101–2
research question and agency, 12
sample letter, 30
sample student projects, 12–13
single-system designs, 97–98
surveys, 95
treatment fidelity, 135–36
Understanding "Real" Versus "Ideal" In Student
    Research Projects, 7
use of theory, 15–16
study implementation
data collection and, 21–23
overcoming barriers, 23
summative evaluation
questions raised by, 179–80
SurveyMonkey
online survey software, 96
surveys
creation of, 95–97
information gathering, 94–95
program evaluation, 178
response rate and administration, 95–97
student research projects, 95
SurveyMonkey software, 96
systematic reviews
description, 51
finding, 53–57
key information, 55
literature reviews vs., 51
Project Development Worksheet, 54, 56

systematic reviews (*cont.*)
  steps in, 57–66
  summary, 55
  writing for literature reviews, 56–57

T
telephone interviews
  surveys, 96
  program evaluation, 70
Terminology Worksheet, 16
  cheat sheet, 4–5
  design terms, 21
  measurement terms, 20
Test Your Skills Exercise
  chi-square for student projects, 149
  data analysis, 155
  defining variables, 118
  determining IRB review, 77
  discussion section, 204–6
  ethics in qualitative research, 170
  ethics of human subjects, 81
  evaluating results, 151
  evaluation designs, 193
  evaluation implementation, 181
  evaluation research, 189–91
  evaluation research knowledge, 194
  identifying charts, 202
  levels of measurement, 128
  literature review, 42
  measurement and validity, 124
  qualitative methods and study participants, 164
  quantitative and qualitative research, 158, 159–60
  research designs, 102
  sampling methods, 114
  threats to internal validity, 103–6
  treatment fidelity, 134, 135
  variable and value, 129
test-retest
  reliability, 119–21
theoretical articles
  description, 35
theory
  research question, 13–16
  student projects, 15–16
timeline
  Project Development Worksheet, 171
transparency
  systematic vs. literature reviews, 51
treatment drift
  intervention, 133
treatment fidelity

independent variable, 132–36
  Project Development Worksheet, 136
  program evaluation, 136
  protocol, 134–35
  student research projects, 135–36
  Test Your Skills Exercise, 134, 135
t-tests
  data analysis, 149–51
  dependent, 150
  independent, 150
Type I error
  statistics, 143
Type II error
  statistics, 143

U
U.S. Department of Health and Human Services Office of
    Human Research Protection (OHRP), 68
univariate statistics
  data analysis, 141–42
  research project, 200–201
universal population
  sampling, 108–10
unrepresentative sample
  description, 108

V
validity
  data collection instrument, 125
  measurement, 119–21
  Test Your Skills Exercise, 124
  types of, 121–22
variables. *See also* dependent variables; independent
    variables
  assigning values, 129–32
  correlations, 144–47
  data analysis, 138
  independent and dependent, 3–4
  Project Development Worksheet, 130
  research design, 20–21
  sampling, 20
  Test Your Skills Exercise, 129
vocabulary
  research, 4–5
voluntary participation
  ethics in qualitative research, 169–70

W
websites, 30, 50, 67, 91–93, 106, 116, 136–37, 156, 174,
    197–98, 211–12, 212

CPSIA information can be obtained
at www.ICGtesting.com
Printed in the USA
BVHW010118110121
597522BV00007B/88